New Casebooks

KING LEAR

WILLIAM SHAKESPEARE

EDITED BY KIERNAN RYAN

palgrave

Introduction, selection and editorial matter
© Kiernan Ryan 1993

Published by
PALGRAVE
Houndmills, Basingstoke, Hampshire RG21 6XS and
175 Fifth Avenue, New York, N. Y. 10010
Companies and representatives throughout the world

PALGRAVE is the new global academic imprint of
St. Martin's Press LLC Scholarly and Reference Division and
Palgrave Publishers Ltd (formerly Macmillan Press Ltd).

ISBN 0–333–55529–5 hardcover
ISBN 0–333–55530–9 paperback

This book is printed on paper suitable for recycling and
made from fully managed and sustained forest sources.

A catalogue record for this book is available
from the British Library.

12   11   10   9   8   7
07   06   05   04   03   02

Printed in China

PGHP

New Casebooks

POETRY

WILLIAM BLAKE Edited by David Punter
CHAUCER Edited by Valerie Allen and Aries Axiotis
COLERIDGE, KEATS AND SHELLEY Edited by Peter J. Kitson
JOHN DONNE Edited by Andrew Mousley
SEAMUS HEANEY Edited by Michael Allen
PHILIP LARKIN Edited by Stephen Regan
DYLAN THOMAS Edited by John Goodby and Chris Wigginton
VICTORIAN WOMEN POETS Edited by Joseph Bristow
WORDSWORTH Edited by John Williams
PARADISE LOST Edited by William Zunder

NOVELS AND PROSE

AUSTEN: *Emma* Edited by David Monaghan
AUSTEN: *Mansfield Park* and *Persuasion* Edited by Judy Simons
AUSTEN: *Sense and Sensibility* and *Pride and Prejudice* Edited by Robert Clark
CHARLOTTE BRONTË: *Jane Eyre* Edited by Heather Glen
CHARLOTTE BRONTË: *Villette* Edited by Pauline Nestor
EMILY BRONTË: *Wuthering Heights* Edited by Patsy Stoneman
ANGELA CARTER Edited by Alison Easton
WILKIE COLLINS Edited by Lyn Pykett
JOSEPH CONRAD Edited by Elaine Jordan
DICKENS: *Bleak House* Edited by Jeremy Tambling
DICKENS: *David Copperfield* and *Hard Times* Edited by John Peck
DICKENS: *Great Expectations* Edited by Roger Sell
ELIOT: *The Mill on the Floss* and *Silas Marner* Edited by Nahem Yousaf and Andrew Maunder
ELIOT: *Middlemarch* Edited by John Peck
E.M. FORSTER Edited by Jeremy Tambling
HARDY: *Jude the Obscure* Edited by Penny Boumelha
HARDY: *The Mayor of Casterbridge* Edited by Julian Wolfreys
HARDY: *Tess of the D'Urbervilles* Edited by Peter Widdowson
JAMES: *Turn of the Screw* and *What Maisie Knew* Edited by Neil Cornwell and Maggie Malone
LAWRENCE: *Sons and Lovers* Edited by Rick Rylance
TONI MORRISON Edited by Linden Peach
GEORGE ORWELL Edited by Byran Loughrey
SHELLEY: *Frankenstein* Edited by Fred Botting
STOKER: *Dracula* Edited by Glennis Byron
STERNE: *Tristram Shandy* Edited by Melvyn New
WOOLF: *Mrs Dalloway* and *To the Lighthouse* Edited by Su Reid

(continued overleaf)

DRAMA

BECKETT: *Waiting for Godot* and *Endgame* Edited by Steven Connor
APHRA BEHN Edited by Janet Todd
REVENGE TRAGEDY Edited by Stevie Simkin
SHAKESPEARE: *Antony and Cleopatra* Edited by John Drakakis
SHAKESPEARE: *Hamlet* Edited by Martin Coyle
SHAKESPEARE: *Julius Caesar* Edited by Richard Wilson
SHAKESPEARE: *King Lear* Edited by Kiernan Ryan
SHAKESPEARE: *Macbeth* Edited by Alan Sinfield
SHAKESPEARE: *The Merchant of Venice* Edited by Martin Coyle
SHAKESPEARE: *A Midsummer Night's Dream* Edited by Richard Dutton
SHAKESPEARE: *Much Ado About Nothing* and *The Taming of the Shrew*
   Edited by Marion Wynne-Davies
SHAKESPEARE: *Romeo and Juliet* Edited by R. S. White
SHAKESPEARE: *The Tempest* Edited by R. S. White
SHAKESPEARE: *Twelfth Night* Edited by R. S. White
SHAKESPEARE ON FILM Edited by Robert Shaughnessy
SHAKESPEARE IN PERFORMANCE Edited by Robert Shaughnessy
SHAKESPEARE'S HISTORY PLAYS Edited by Graham Holderness
SHAKESPEARE'S TRAGEDIES Edited by Susan Zimmerman
JOHN WEBSTER: *The Duchess of Malfi* Edited by Dympna Callaghan

GENERAL THEMES

FEMINIST THEATRE AND THEORY Edited by Helene Keyssar
POST-COLONIAL LITERATURES Edited by Michael Parker and Roger Starkey

---

New Casebooks Series
Series Standing Order
ISBN 0–333–71702–3 hardcover
ISBN 0–333–69345–0 paperback
(outside North America only)

You can receive future titles in this series as they are published by placing a standing
order. Please contact your bookseller or, in case of difficulty, write to us at the address
below with your name and address, the title of the series and the ISBN quoted above.

Customer Services Department, Macmillan Distribution Ltd
Houndmills, Basingstoke, Hampshire RG21 6XS, England

For
Rosemary Ryan

Contents

Acknowledgements

The editor and publishers wish to thank the following for permission to use copyright material:

Terry Eagleton, excerpt from *William Shakespeare* (1986) by permission of Basil Blackwell Ltd;

Howard Felperin, excerpt from *Shakespearean Representation: Mimesis and Modernity in Elizabethan Tragedy* (1977). Copyright © 1977 by Princeton University Press, by permission of Princeton University Press;

Stephen Greenblatt, 'The Cultivation of Anxiety: King Lear and his Heirs' in *Learning to Curse: Essays in Early Modern Culture* (1990), by permission of Routledge;

Jonathan Goldberg, excerpt from 'Perspectives: Dover Cliff and the Conditions of Representation' in *Shakespeare and Deconstruction*, ed. David M. Bergeron and G. Douglas Atkins (1988), by permission of Peter Lang Publishing, Inc.;

Coppélia Kahn, 'The Absent Mother in *King Lear*' in *Rewriting the Renaissance*, ed. Margaret Ferguson, Maureen Quilligan and Nancy Vickers (1986), by permission of University of Chicago Press;

Arnold Kettle, excerpt from *Literature and Liberation: Selected Essays* (1988), by permission of Manchester University Press;

Kathleen McLuskie, excerpt from 'The Patriarchal Bard: Feminist Criticism and Shakespeare: *King Lear* and *Measure for Measure*' in *Political Shakespeare: New Essays in Cultural Materialism*, ed. Jonathan Dollimore and Alan Sinfield (1985), by permission of

Manchester University Press;

Leah Marcus, 'Retrospective: *King Lear* on St Stephen's Night, 1606' in *Puzzling Shakespeare: Local Reading and its Discontents* (1988). Copyright © 1988 The Regents of the University of California, by permission of The University of California Press;

Annabel Patterson, excerpt from *Shakespeare and the Popular Voice* (1989), by permission of Basil Blackwell Ltd;

Kiernan Ryan, excerpts from *Shakespeare* (1989), by permission of Harvester-Wheatsheaf and Humanities Press International, Inc.;

Leonard Tennenhouse, excerpt from *Power on Display: The Politics of Shakespeare's Genres* (1986), Methuen & Co., by permission of Routledge.

Every effort has been made to trace all the copyright holders but if any have been inadvertently overlooked the publishers will be pleased to make the necessary arrangement at the first opportunity.

General Editors' Preface

The purpose of this new series of Casebooks is to reveal some of the ways in which contemporary criticism has changed our understanding of commonly studied texts and writers and, indeed, of the nature of criticism itself. Central to the series is a concern with modern critical theory and its effect on current approaches to the study of literature. Each New Casebook editor has been asked to select a sequence of essays which will introduce the reader to the new critical approaches to the text or texts being discussed in the volume and also illuminate the rich interchange between critical theory and critical practice that characterises so much current writing about literature.

The series itself, of course, grows out of the original Casebook series edited by A. E. Dyson. The original volumes provide readers with a range of critical opinions extending from the first reception of a work through to the criticism of the twentieth century. By contrast, the focus of the New Casebooks is on modern critical thinking and practice, with the volumes seeking to reflect both the controversy and the excitement of current criticism. Because much of this criticism is difficult and often employs an unfamiliar critical language, editors have been asked to give the reader as much help as they feel is appropriate, but without simplifying the essays or the issues they raise.

The project of the New Casebooks, then, is to bring together in an illuminating way those critics who best illustrate the ways in which contemporary criticism has established new methods of analysing texts and who have reinvigorated the important debate about how we 'read' literature. The hope is, of course, that New Casebooks will not only open up this debate to a wider audience, but will also encourage students to extend their own ideas, and think afresh about their responses to the texts they are studying.

John Peck and Martin Coyle
University of Wales, Cardiff

Introduction

KIERNAN RYAN

I

During the last decade the impact of developments in modern literary theory has transformed the landscape and climate of Shakespeare studies. Nowhere has the transformation been more striking than in the interpretation of what 'seems now to be virtually unchallenged as the greatest monument of our literature: the most admired play by the most admired writer in the English language'.[1] This book documents the decisive changes in the perception of *King Lear* in recent years and stages the key debates between and within the main critical movements currently disputing the significance of Shakespeare's supreme tragedy.

Until the 1960s, criticism of *King Lear* was dominated by overtly or implicitly Christian accounts. Despite the play's pagan setting and deliberate reduction of the Christian allusions overpopulating its chief dramatic source, a host of critics had laboured to turn the tragedy back into the kind of drama whose doctrinal clutch it was plainly anxious to escape.[2] Still more had followed the less blatant trail blazed by A. C. Bradley and G. Wilson Knight, who devised readings in which Christian patterns and concepts survived in figurative disguise with their moralising spirituality intact. Bradley thought 'nothing more noble and beautiful in literature than Shakespeare's exposition of the effect of suffering in reviving the greatness and eliciting the sweetness of Lear's nature';[3] for Wilson Knight *Lear* was Shakespeare's *Purgatorio* and *Book of Job* rolled into one.[4]

The idea of *King Lear* as a dramatised parable of sin, sacrifice and redemption took a nosedive, however, after Barbara Everett's sceptical attack in 1960,[5] and never regained height after the publication of W. R. Elton's *King Lear and the Gods*. From his exhaustive study of the whole question of religion in *King Lear* Elton concluded that the tragedy was not a drama of meaningful suffering and redemption within a just universe ruled by higher powers, but one whose last act 'shatters, more violently than an earlier apostasy might have done, the foundations of faith itself'.[6]

Such refutations helped foster the environment in which two new critical dynasties emerged to contest the throne from which the Christian interpretation of *King Lear* was being toppled. Conservative humanist critics redefined Lear's heroism as his capacity to absorb endless agonies and endure death itself without prospect of salvation, finding his life's purpose in this world rather than beyond the grave. Thus Maynard Mack's *Lear* compels us 'to seek the meaning of our human fate not in what becomes of us, but in what we become'.[7] Pitted against this view, though, was a far bleaker reading of the play as refusing altogether the consolation of significance, whether Christian or secular, and abandoning us at the close 'without any support from systems of moral or artistic belief at all'.[8] This existentialist angle on the tragedy took an influential turn for the Absurd in Jan Kott's essay '*King Lear*, or Endgame', which perceived in the monarch driven witless by a universe drained of providential intent a grotesque clown straight from the pen of Samuel Beckett.[9]

Most of the kingdom of *Lear* criticism remained divided between these antagonistic approaches well into the 1970s, notwithstanding sterling efforts to reconcile, or at least accommodate, the arguments for redemption and despair, nihilism and affirmation, within the bounds of a single interpretation.[10] Nor has the criticism of subsequent years ceased to involve conflicts between those who detect in the tragedy a coherent, positive statement, those whom *King Lear* pitches into the void, and those whose accounts mirror its imputed ambivalence. But the framework of assumptions and objectives within which these and other kinds of reading are now pursued has altered so dramatically over the last ten years as to justify our speaking of a new era in the study of *King Lear*.

The reasons for the shift in direction can be summed up in one word: politics. Hitherto, critical quarrels about the vision of *King Lear* had largely been conducted in blithe indifference to the play's social implications for the present or its past political function reconsidered from a modern point of view. But the 1980s spawned a whole series of theoretically informed, polemical studies of Shakespeare, which exposed the conservative consequences of established approaches to his drama and promoted instead a range of perspectives committed to re-reading the plays in the light of innovative work on gender, race, power, language and the function of criticism itself.[11] For this fresh generation of critics steeped in feminism, poststructuralism and new kinds of Marxist and historical analysis, the issue was no longer whether *King Lear* was Christian, absurdist or somewhere in between, but rather how far the play could be seen as sustaining or sabotaging oppressive structures of power and perception in his world and our own.

Apart from the first two essays, all the contributions to the present anthology date from this ground-breaking decade in Shakespeare criticism. The opening pieces by Arnold Kettle and Howard Felperin are offspring of the 1960s and 1970s respectively, but are included because, quite apart from their intrinsic merits, they bridge the gap between the old and the emerging dispensations. They should provide more familiar points of departure for readers unacquainted with recent developments in the field; but they also anticipate important currents within the subsequent criticism of *King Lear*.

What unites all eleven essays in this book, despite the arresting diversity of their aims and methods, is their dissent from the critical priorities in whose arthritic grip *Lear* had mouldered for too long. On the threshold of the 1980s Thomas P. Roche summed up the principal tenets of this already embattled orthodoxy in a vain bid to shore up the dyke dividing him from the rising tide of change. For Roche there was no doubt that *King Lear* guides us

> toward a providential view of history, toward a hierarchical view of society, toward a moral view of human action. In my view Shakespeare is not showing us the meaninglessness of history, nor the tyranny of society, nor the psychological needs of fathers, daughters or bastards, nor even the limitation and duplicity of language . . .[12]

The critics gathered in this volume would either profess precisely the opposite view of *Lear*'s endeavour, or concur only as a prelude to subjecting the play to critique from a historical or frankly modern perspective. However future commentators on the tragedy may judge the value of these readings, the age of apparent political innocence in which its previous critics thrived has vanished with their arrival. *King Lear* will never look quite the same again.

II

The essay by Arnold Kettle which opens this collection has obvious roots in the critical idiom and concerns of the period in which it was written. Kettle focuses on the evolution of the king's character as his chief guide to the play's import, which crystallises round the moral education Lear undergoes as a result of his afflictions and descent into madness. 'His story, put in its simplest terms, is the story of his progress from being a king to being a man.'[13] Kettle joins the 1960s battle against the retreating Christian colonists of *King Lear*, but what separates his interpretation from humanist accounts of a conservative bent is his Marxist stress on *Lear*'s value as a powerful indictment of the social conditions and ruling ideas of the age in which it was written. Lear's personal, purely human odyssey cannot be divorced from the seismic clash it dramatises between the ebbing values of the feudal era and an emergent epoch of competitive individualism, both of which are questioned by what the crazed monarch's ordeal reveals to him:

> The social emphases are not more or less casual sidethoughts but are absolutely basic to the whole conception of the play . . . The new humanity which Lear achieves is not simply a self-knowledge acquired by introspection or any kind of mystical or religious experience; it is an outlook gained through experience and action, through the necessity that has been forced upon him of exposing himself to feel what wretches feel.[14]

The 'new humanity' Lear discovers is directly linked by Kettle to egalitarian pressures in contemporary popular thought and the democratic challenge to absolutist power which would lead to the beheading of the real sovereign within a few decades of *King Lear*. But Kettle also discerns in the visionary humanism of the tragedy an even more far-sighted hint of 'utopian promise' which, 'without a removal of the play into the realms of abstraction and metaphysics', suggests that 'the experience and meaning of the play cannot be confined within the limits of seventeenth-century social thinking'.[15] In this respect Kettle's essay continues to pose a challenge to most previous and much subsequent historicist criticism, which has proved only too eager to restrict Shakespeare's imagination in *King Lear* to voicing the prevalent attitudes of his day.

This notion of *Lear*'s power to reach forward imaginatively to expose the limits of conventional understanding then and now is pushed further in my own contribution (essay 5). I start by spelling out the radical humanist objections to Christian, conservative humanist and traditional historicist ideas of Shakespearean tragedy. Whether by supposition or design, these approaches in effect regard the tragedies as compelling vindications of the permanence of the human condition and the inviolability of the status quo. My essay proposes instead a view of Shakespearean tragedy as subverting the status quo and betraying its repressed hunger for liberating transformation. Far from persuading us to acquiesce in the inevitability of human suffering, *King Lear* – like all the major tragedies of Shakespeare – refuses to accept

> the heartbreaking contradiction between what men and women want to be and could be, and what the particular social scenario into which they have been scripted by history cruelly condemns them to be, in spite of the superior selves and more satisfying lives struggling within them for realisation.[16]

Lear dramatises the cost in potential equality and mutual fulfilment of the humanly contrived structures of division and domination responsible for the tragedy. From this standpoint attempts to reduce *King Lear* to a mere tool of Christian or contemporary political doctrine are as blind to its prefigurative power to judge our modern world as the venture to enlist it in the theatre of futility.

III

If placed in the dock by Howard Felperin, however, both Kettle's essay and my own would stand accused of imposing upon *King Lear* a critical coherence which it is inherently disposed to refuse. In 'Plays Within Plays' Felperin charges upbeat Christian or humanist and downbeat existentialist readings alike with failing to confront the intractable enigma at the heart of the tragedy. The failure proceeds from their habitual misconception of the relation between the main plot devoted to Lear and the subplot centred on Gloucester. Felperin shows how time and again the predictable moralistic platitudes generated by the latter have been conscripted to contain the turbulence of the former. Whereas it would be apter to construe the subplot as included precisely to disqualify by contrast its oversimplified version of events, to break its judgemental hold on the response of the audience and so intensify our experience of 'Lear's descent into a more modern and secular perception of ironic discontinuity'[17] beyond moral categories altogether.

The temptation to privilege the 'new sense of existential indeterminacy'[18] which Lear's derangement affords him should nevertheless be resisted, Felperin warns. For that would be simply to invert the priority of the moralistic over the meaningless and fall into the same trap as those for whom the key words of *Lear* are 'nothing' and 'never'. Neither alternative does justice to *King Lear*'s own deconstruction of the polarising, hierarchical mentality that locks it into the opposition of madness and morality, and elevates one term of this binary double-bind over the other. As long as it continues to shuttle back and forth between the nihilistic and the affirmative poles of interpretation, criticism of *Lear* remains in thrall to the very categories of intelligibility the tragedy strives to problematise.

'In the end the play renounces its own mediations of morality and madness alike and redirects our attention to an undetermined reality that exists prior to and remains unavailable to both.'[19] *King Lear* abandons us in what deconstructionists like to call a 'state of aporia'[20] or radical uncertainty, which thwarts our craving for unity and resolution to make us query the validity of the beliefs underwriting our interpretive procedures. Shakespeare's text, concludes Felperin, 'remains a step ahead of its critics, even at the very moment we think we have caught up with it'.[21]

Terry Eagleton's dense, elliptical excursion into poststructuralist discourse (essay 6) creates a *Lear* equally intent on liberating its vision from the false dualities by which its characters are fatally enslaved. The tragedy tosses all and nothing, body and mind, sense and insanity into a vortex of reversals which confounds the complacent distinctions they suppose and discloses how fragile and arbitrary they are. But for Eagleton *King Lear* lures its antitheses into mutual negation not merely to release us from their crippling spell, but in the belief that 'only the coupling of two negatives can hope to produce a positive'.[22] Eagleton's Marxist commitment to social renewal puts a constructive spin on his deconstructive strategy. His *Lear* holds out the prospect of combating if not overcoming the hierarchical impulses and irreconcilable antagonisms which still rule our lives.

Eagleton too locates a fundamental aporia, an ultimate impasse, at the core of *King Lear*. It is entrenched in the fact that the natural creative drive of the human animal to exceed its own bounds, to flout its own norms, is also the mainspring of humanity's destructive belligerence. So that, although Eagleton feels fleetingly tempted to enshrine Cordelia as a symbolic resolution of the play's antinomies,

> It is not, after all, simply a matter of reconciling fixed opposites: it is a matter of regulating what would seem an ineradicable contradiction in the material structure of the human creature. *King Lear* is a tragedy because it stares that contradiction full in the face, aware that no poetic symbolism is adequate to resolve it.[23]

Whereas Felperin's aporia leaves off at baffling our stock responses, Eagleton's poses a more overt political challenge.

At the same time, both critics plainly share a confidence that the deconstructive process in *King Lear* has a stopping-point in a bedrock physical reality that validates its vision. Jonathan Goldberg, on the other hand, pursues the consequences of his deconstructive method to a more bewildering and uncompromising conclusion. What a radical deconstructionist might well call the residual humanist and empiricist delusions of Eagleton and Felperin stand blatantly exposed by comparison. For in 'Perspectives: Dover Cliff and the Limits of Representation' Goldberg's account of *Lear* plunges us headlong into a bottomless aporia in which no firm ground of perception or judgement is ever reached. The tragedy contrives the suicidal dissolution of the very premises upon which its possibility depends.

Goldberg's case pivots on the notorious 'Dover Cliff' scene of Act IV. He examines in close detail the passage in which the disguised Edgar marshals all the resources of verbal illusion to persuade his blind father that he stands indeed upon the precipitous edge of England, from which he yearns to hurl himself down. Goldberg contends that the very success of Edgar's illusionistic rhetoric in summoning a realistic impression of the downward prospect from the brink only underlines the dependance of the visual illusion on words and thus the actual impotence of the stage and of language to capture the reality evoked. The speech provokes reflection on the impossibility of bridging the gulf between the world and the word, experience and performance. In short, 'the limits that Dover represents in the text are the limits of representation themselves'.[24]

The cliff-scene becomes a kind of textual black hole into which vanishes both the play's and our faith in telling the real from the written. As a result: 'In *King Lear*, nothing comes of nothing, and the very language which would seem (to us) solidly to locate the world slides into an abyss, an uncreating, annihilative nothingness.'[25]

We have travelled a long way indeed from Bradley's tranquil conviction that the play might be more aptly retitled *The Redemption of King Lear*.[26]

IV

What cuts across the manifest divergences between the five essays discussed so far is their common supposition that *King Lear* radically questions the accepted version of things at the time Shakespeare wrote and even in the age in which we read him. Kathleen McLuskie's feminist critique of *Lear* springs from the diametrically opposed presumption that Shakespeare's vision of his world is flagrantly conventional and conservative. Indeed 'The Patriarchal Bard: Feminist Criticism and *King Lear*' proceeds from the assertion that tragedy as such is a reactionary genre designed to perpetuate the illusion that our destinies are governed by a universally binding, immutable human nature. This ideological distortion of reality is compounded by the fact that, as *King Lear* confirms, 'the human nature implied in the moral and aesthetic satisfactions of tragedy is most often explicitly male'.[27] McLuskie's blunt and bold polemical stance compels most previous criticism on the play, whether radically or traditionally inclined, to face the unsettling possibility that one of the most sacred texts in the canon of English Literature might be warped beyond repair by its misogynistic representation of women and consolidation of sexual injustice.

Lear is unmasked by McLuskie as a patriarchal morality play, whose female characters are demonised or sanctified stereotypes, and whose climactic scenes hijack the full emotional range of Shakespeare's eloquence to clinch even the female spectator's compassion for the tormented monarch, despite the violent loathing he expresses for the female sex. 'Any dispassionate analysis of the mystification of real socio-sexual relations in *King Lear* is the antithesis of our response to the tragedy in the theatre where the tragic power of the play endorses its ideological position at every stage.'[28]

Since dislodging this cornerstone of the curriculum seems an unlikely prospect, the one resource left to the feminist critic, McLuskie argues, is to undermine that ideological position by explaining it as the product of specific historical circumstances and social contradictions. In this way *King Lear*'s pretence to speak for all mankind in all times is exploded by a strategy which offers 'the pleasure of understanding in place of the pleasure of emotional identification'.[29] By returning the play to its historical context as a first step towards turning it to progressive political ends in the present, McLuskie is making a move characteristic of what has come to be known as cultural materialism.[30] The feminist application of this criticism advocated by McLuskie aims to help break the stranglehold of misogynistic attitudes on male and female readers and spectators by stimulating resistance rather than submission to the seductive wiles of the patriarchal Bard.

That the judgement reached by the feminist reappraisal of *King Lear* is far from undivided becomes clear if we compare McLuskie's account with Coppélia Kahn's essay, 'The Absent Mother in *King Lear*'. Kahn is no less committed to revising our view of Shakespeare in the light of modern feminist ideas and aims. But on balance she regards *King Lear* as an ally rather than an antagonist of emancipation. Kahn proves as keen as McLuskie to situate the tragedy in its precise seventeenth-century context of shifting power-relations between men and women. But Kahn's restoration of the particular social pressures to which *Lear* reacts reveals a drama anxious to corroborate the insights of feminist psychoanalytic theory rather than a devious double-agent of masculine oppression.

Kahn sets out 'like an archaeologist, to uncover the hidden mother in the hero's inner world'.[31] Her excavations unearth a tragedy which, far from reinforcing male domination, depicts instead 'the failure of a father's power to command love in a patriarchal world and the emotional price he pays for wielding power'.[32] Where McLuskie perceives a universalising apology for patriarchy, which conceals the masculine nature of the power at stake, Kahn identifies a quite explicit 'tragedy of masculinity',[33] which spells out the terrible personal and collective price paid by a culture dedicated to 'repressing the vulnerability, dependency and capacity for feeling which are called "feminine"'.[34] At the very historical moment when 'a masculine identity crisis'[35] was inciting an intensified effort to buttress patriarchal authority in reality, Shakespeare's tragic imagination was parading and aggravating that crisis on the stage in *King Lear*.

Kahn's historical and psychoanalytic perspective endorses in broad outline the radical humanist reading of *Lear*, while correcting its blindness to the whole question of gender and rephrasing its argument in feminist terms. It is another striking measure of how the criticism of *King Lear* has changed over the last thirty years that what Arnold Kettle had called Lear's 'progress from being a king to being a man'[36] resurfaces in Kahn as 'Lear's progress toward acceptance of the woman in himself'.[37]

V

Leonard Tennenhouse contributes the first of four new-historicist essays reprinted here, which together reflect not only the vitality of this form of criticism in Shakespeare studies, but also the fact that new historicism is a far broader church than is sometimes supposed.

In 'The Theatre of Punishment' Tennenhouse returns us to a conception of *King Lear* closer to that of Kathleen McLuskie, whom he joins in assuming Shakespeare's theatrical complicity in preserving the existing social order. The (mostly American) new historicists and the (largely British) cultural materialists are at one in their fascination with unpacking the original political implications of literary texts like *Lear*. But the cultural materialist tends to tie the text into a variety of domains and practices in the surrounding society, and is equally concerned with appropriations of the text in modern culture; while the attention of new historicists has concentrated more on recovering the past historical significance of a work at the point where literary forms and institutions intersect specifically with institutional expressions of the power of the state.[38]

Tennenhouse's reading of *Lear* is intricately argued. It rides on the distinctively new-historicist thesis that the theatre in Shakespeare's England served, like the more patently sinister scaffold, as a stage for the spectacular public display and legitimation of the ruling power. The pristine purpose of *Lear*, once dug out from under the centuries of interpretation obscuring it, turns out to have been an exemplary dramatisation of 'the terrible consequences of violating the patriarchal prerogative'[39] and the metaphysical taboos on which the authority and mystique of the presiding hierarchy depended. 'When the will of the king is to divest monarchy of power, the carnage that

ensues implies that it is a primal law of nature that has been violated.'[40] Hence what was enacted on the stage for the first audiences
of *King Lear* was the ritual punishment of the royal transgressor
himself, and the ritual purging of those characters who are guilty of
polluting the blood-codes deemed vital to the body politic in its
absolutist incarnation.

A still more exacting urge to trace *Lear* back to its historical roots
and free it from the rhetoric of universality leads Leah Marcus (essay
8) to focus on the possible impact of one particular performance of
the tragedy: the production known to have been mounted at Whitehall for King James on St Stephen's Night in 1606.

Gauging the contemporary significance of that production involves for Marcus sifting out and analysing suggestive differences
between the quarto version of *King Lear* which James is presumed to
have seen, and which was published in 1608, and the revised version
of the text published in the folio edition of 1623. (There has been
intense scholarly controversy about the nature and editorial consequences of these differences since the early 1980s.[41]) In Marcus's
judgement, the 1608 quarto is 'richer in particularised materials
which can easily be interpreted as criticism of King James I',[42] and
which the folio consistently filters out.

The quarto's 'intense Stuart topicality'[43] obviously raises the in-
triguing question of why the text of *Lear* likely to have been acted
before James himself should be the one with the most pointed allusions to controversial royal policies. Part of the answer might lie in
the licence conceivably accorded the play by the date of its court
performance. For 'in the liturgical lessons proper for the feast of St
Stephen, the idea of bending to succour the less fortunate, of shedding "pompe" to "take physicke" and "feele what wretches feele"
occurs again and again'.[44] Yet, as Marcus observes, the perspective
supplied by St Stephen's Day could also intimate praise of James's
capacity for Christian humility and a cloaked exhortation of a truc-
ulent Parliament to respond more generously to their sovereign's
demands.

The play's historical meaning proves, in a word, ambiguous.
Paradoxically, the more exclusive and definite the location of *Lear*
becomes, the more the prospect of nailing its initial intention and
effect recedes into the realms of uncertainty. Even if the political
orthodoxy of the St Stephen's Night performance were clear-cut, ' a
play which was orthodox in one setting could have been unorthodox
in another'.[45] This leaves the ideological allegiance of *King Lear*

intrinsically volatile, the protean creation of its always local and particular reception. In sharp contrast to the more definite diagnosis reached by Tennenhouse, Marcus's historical scholarship steers her to a recognition of the play's constitutive indeterminacy, to a kind of new-historicist aporia which even the most stubbornly unhistorical exponent of deconstruction could not fail to appreciate.

In 'The Popular Voice of *King Lear*' Annabel Patterson concurs with Leah Marcus's opinion that, as far as references to James I are concerned, the St Stephen's Night production of the quarto version could only have encouraged a 'flexible hermeneutics' over which 'undecidability reigns'.[46] But whereas Marcus extends undecidability to the play as a whole, Patterson finds it largely confined to the more narrowly topical first act, which gives way to an unambiguous and more important critique of the economic and social inequities of Jacobean England.

Nor need the impact of this indictment be limited to its Jacobean context, as Patterson demonstrates by showing how *King Lear* inspired James Agee's powerful documentary account of rural poverty during the American Depression in *Let Us Now Praise Famous Men*. Patterson's mode of new historicism differs decisively from the approaches of Tennenhouse and Marcus in the way it invites a dialogue between original and succeeding receptions of a work, and contemplation of the continuities as well as the disparities between them. 'Historicity, then, may itself encourage transhistoricity, even or especially when what is transferred to later cultures is the clash of human with economic values and structures.'[47] Patterson's standpoint opens up the possibility of uniting new-historicist reconstructions of the past with a radical humanist commitment to activating the subversive modern potential of Shakespeare's drama.

The coupling of *King Lear* with Agee's book does not merely reveal how the masterpiece from the seventeenth century enhances the resonance of its twentieth-century heir; the complexity of Agee's predicament as a radical critic of American society illuminates in turn the strategy of the man who penned the 'Poor naked wretches' speech (III.iv.28–36)[48] which Agee takes as his epigraph. Though three hundred years divide them, Patterson sees Shakespeare in *King Lear* adopting, just as Agee would later have to, the imaginative guise of 'the basest and most poorest shape / That ever penury, in contempt of man, / Brought near to beast' (II.iii.7–9) in order, 'as a playwright, to take up the case of society's victims, but by the grace of the dramatic metaphor, to do so "undisclosed"'.[49]

For Tennenhouse *King Lear* is the amplified voice of power itself on display. Marcus considers it impossible to decide from the textual and contextual evidence whether Shakespeare was a 'king's man' or not. Annabel Patterson, however, is in no doubt that the Shakespeare who made the king in this play 'his own most powerful social critic'[50] speaks with the voice of the people, using whatever resources of ambivalence and conventionality he must to throw the hounds of authority off his scent.

The closing contribution to this volume, Stephen Greenblatt's 'The Cultivation of Anxiety: King Lear and his Heirs', furnishes further and eloquent proof that contextualisation need not sentence *Lear* to incarceration in its moment of genesis, but can stimulate commerce between seemingly unrelated historical worlds. At the same time, Greenblatt's essay attracts a reservation provoked by much new-historicist criticism. For even when its practitioners make a forward leap from a Renaissance to a more recent text (as Greenblatt does here), and even when the aim is to recover evidence that the author's intention was progressive rather than orthodox, the meaning ascribed to the work by new-historicist scholarship remains purely retrospective, the past-bound revelation of a superseded reality. Consequently new historicism tends to rule out in advance both Felperin's belief that Shakespeare stays one step ahead of his modern critics and the radical humanist hunch that *King Lear* might be gazing as much into the future beyond our own horizon as back to its point of departure in the past.

Be that as it may, from the surprising affinities between *King Lear* and a nineteenth-century American Baptist's account of breaking his infant son's will Greenblatt weaves a spellbinding meditation on how power has sought to secure itself down the centuries by fostering in its subjects a compliant state of 'salutary anxiety'.[51] This spurs him to the further speculation that *King Lear* itself, as part of a theatrical institution intimately allied with the crown, may have aroused the same kind of gratified apprehension in its audience in order to reinforce their voluntary acquiescence in their own subjection to authority.

> The very practice of tragedy depends upon a communal conviction that anxiety may be profitably and even pleasurably cultivated. That is, tragedy goes beyond the usual philosophical and religious *consolations* for affliction, and both exemplifies and perfects techniques for the creation and intensification of affliction.[52]

This view of *King Lear* as a subtly bewitching instrument of oppression, echoed as it is by the arguments of Tennenhouse and McLuskie, is the exact antithesis of the case made for *Lear*'s imaginative dissidence in the opening essay of this volume and in the contributions of Kahn and Patterson among others. But Greenblatt's essay does not merely challenge us to dwell once more on the original social function of *King Lear*. It leaves us with the more disturbing question of how far this mighty drama's continued exaction of cultural worship in exchange for our enthralling ordeal confirms its success in cultivating our own appetite for subjection as we applaud and explore it today.

NOTES

1. Ann Thompson, *King Lear: The Critics Debate* (London, 1988), p. 59.

2. For a concise summary of the Christian criticism see ch. 1 of William R. Elton, *King Lear and the Gods* (San Marino, Calif., 1966).

3. A. C. Bradley, *Shakespearean Tragedy* (London, 1904), p. 284.

4. G. Wilson Knight, *The Wheel of Fire* (1930; revised edn, 1949), chs VIII and XIV.

5. Barbara Everett, 'The New *King Lear*', *Critical Quarterly*, 2 (1960), 325–39; reprinted in Frank Kermode (ed.), *Shakespeare: 'King Lear': A Casebook* (London, 1969), pp. 184–202.

6. William R. Elton, *King Lear and the Gods* (San Marino, Calif., 1966), p. 337.

7. Maynard Mack, *King Lear in Our Time* (Berkeley and Los Angeles, 1965), p. 117.

8. Nicholas Brooke, *Shakespeare: King Lear* (London, 1963), p. 60.

9. Jan Kott, *Shakespeare Our Contemporary* (London, 1965), pp. 100–33.

10. See, for example, John D. Rosenberg, 'King Lear and his Comforters', *Essays in Criticism*, 16 (1966), 135–46; S. L. Goldberg, *An Essay on King Lear* (Cambridge, 1974); Michael Long, *The Unnatural Scene* (London, 1976), ch. 7.

11. See Further Reading, pp. 181–3 below.

12. Thomas P. Roche, '"Nothing Almost Sees Miracles": Tragic Knowledge in *King Lear*', in Lawrence Danson (ed.), *On King Lear* (Princeton, 1981), p. 160.

13. See p. 21 below.

14. See pp. 25–6 below.

15. See p. 28 below.

16. See p. 75 below.

17. See p. 39 below.

18. See p. 39 below.

19. See p. 43 below.

20. See p. 43 below. For a concise account of what deconstruction involves, see Terry Eagleton, *Literary Theory: An Introduction* (Oxford, 1983), pp. 132–4; 145–7. For a fuller account see Christopher Norris, *Deconstruction: Theory and Practice* (London, 1982).

21. See p. 44 below.

22. See p. 86 below.

23. See p. 90 below.

24. See p. 147 below.

25. See p. 153 below.

26. A. C. Bradley, *Shakespearean Tragedy* (London, 1904), p. 285.

27. See p. 48 below.

28. See p. 50 below.

29. See p. 56 below.

30. The term was coined by Raymond Williams in *Marxism and Literature* (Oxford, 1977). On the scope and aims of cultural materialism, see Jonathan Dollimore and Alan Sinfield (eds), *Political Shakespeare* (Manchester, 1985), pp. vii–viii; 2–17.

31. See p. 94 below.

32. See p. 95 below.

33. See p. 95 below.

34. See p. 95 below.

35. See p. 107 below.

36. See p. 21 below.

37. See p. 105 below. For a lucid exposition of the theoretical issues at stake in the conflicting feminist perspectives of Kahn and McLuskie, see Toril Moi, *Sexual/Textual Politics: Feminist Literary Theory* (London, 1985)

and 'Feminist Literary Criticism', in Ann Jefferson and David Robey (eds), *Modern Literary Theory*, 2nd edn (London, 1986), pp. 204–21.

38. See Jean E. Howard, 'The New Historicism in Renaissance Studies', in Arthur F. Kinney and Dan S. Collins (eds), *Renaissance Historicism* (Amherst, Mass., 1987), pp. 3–33, and H. Aram Veeser (ed.), *The New Historicism* (New York and London, 1989). For a comparison of new historicism and cultural materialism, see K. M. Newton, *Interpreting the Text* (New York and London, 1990), pp. 119–29.

39. See p. 63 below.

40. See p. 63 below.

41. For a summary of this controversy and a list of the main studies spawned by it, see Further Reading, pp. 180–1 below.

42. See p. 115 below.

43. See p. 117 below.

44. See p. 121 below.

45. See pp. 124–5 below.

46. See pp. 131, 132 below.

47. See p. 133 below.

48. Textual references in this Introduction are to Kenneth Muir (ed.), *King Lear*, The Arden Shakespeare, revised edn (London, 1972).

49. See p. 141 below.

50. See p. 142 below.

51. See p. 170 below.

52. See p. 170 below.

1

The Humanity of 'King Lear'

ARNOLD KETTLE

Lear's story begins where most stories end. The old man seems to be at the finish of his reign and time. But in fact his journey has not yet begun. The opening scene is a statement – the statement of where we and Lear start from – and Shakespeare has neither the time nor the concern to make it naturalistically convincing in its every detail. Lear is there, every inch a king, disposing of his kingdom. Essentially one has to see him as a feudal king, but in saying this I refer less to the social and economic relations of feudalism than to its characteristic ideology. The point, and also its significance, becomes clear, when we remember that within Lear's kingdom there are, inside the ruling class, two tendencies or camps, which are not simply or primarily a matter of conflicting generations or social status. On the one hand are those who accept the old order (Lear, Gloucester, Kent, Albany) which has to be seen as, broadly speaking, the feudal order; on the other hand are the new people, the individualists (Goneril, Regan, Edmund, Cornwall) who have the characteristic outlook of the bourgeoisie.

These correspondences are underlined – as Professor Danby has very suggestively pointed out[1] – by the differing ways in which the people of the two camps use the word Nature, a key-word which crops up nearly fifty times in the course of the play. To Lear and those associated with him Nature is essentially a benignant traditional order, like the 'Natural Law' of the Middle Ages, in which human and divine society are at one. In Lear's language the 'offices of nature' are always linked with such concepts as

17

> bond of childhood,
> Effects of courtesy, dues of gratitude.
> (II.iv.177–8)

Goneril and Regan become, to him, 'unnatural hags', and Gloucester, from his side, talks of 'the King falling from the bias of Nature,
there's father against child'.

Such uses of the word are in direct contrast to Edmund's forthright

> Thou, Nature, art my Goddess; to thy law
> My services are bound. Wherefore should I
> Stand in the plague of custom . . .?
> (I.ii.1–3)

Here Nature is seen as the opposite of custom, tradition, hierarchy,
established order. And Professor Danby shrewdly points out that
Edmund's use of Nature is precisely the use which, within half a
century, the most remarkable and most consistently materialist of the
early bourgeois philosophers, Thomas Hobbes, was to give the word.
Hobbes, as is well known, saw the state of Nature as a state of war.
Man was to him not *naturally* a social animal but had to be made
one. The author of the *Leviathan* would not, of course, have ap-
proved of Edmund's worship of the Natural man; but he would have
understood it and, in a wry way, appreciated its 'realism'.

In *King Lear* Shakespeare reveals, from the very start, a society in
turmoil in which (in contrast to *Hamlet*) it is the representatives of
the old order who feel that everything is out of joint:

> . . . love cools, friendship falls off, brothers divide; in cities, mutinies;
> in countries discord; in palaces, treason; and the bond crack'd 'twixt
> son and father. . . . We have seen the best of our time: machinations,
> hollowness, treachery, and all ruinous disorders, follow us disquietly
> to our graves.
>
> (I.ii.110–20)

It is Gloucester speaking and the particular speech is not a deep one
(Gloucester himself being a conventional and – as he comes appallingly
to realise – blind old man); but it is, from his point of view and,
indeed, objectively, a quite true description of the state of affairs in
Lear's kingdom. And it cannot but remind us of such a poem as
Donne's *First Anniversarie*, written in 1611, in which the state of the
contemporary world is strikingly expressed.

'Tis all in peeces, all cohaerence gone;
All just supply, and all Relation:
Prince, Subject, Father, Sonne, are things forgot,
For every man alone thinkes he hath got
To be a Phoenix . . . .[2]

Gloucester, in the speech I have just quoted, superstitiously links the social crack-up with the eclipse of the sun and moon. It is all, he insists, thoroughly unnatural. And he wanders off, scratching his head, leaving his bastard son Edmund to pour scorn in a brilliant soliloquy on his superstitious unscientific outlook: 'An admirable evasion of whoremaster man, to lay his goatish disposition on the charge of a star.' Edmund has none of his father's amiable, conservative illusions. He is intelligent, active and ruthless. His immediate personal motive is simple – 'Legitimate Edgar, I must have your land.' No beating about the bush. Edmund is emancipated. The ancient sanctities of law (he is in every sense illegitimate) and order (kingship, the property rights of fathers, primogeniture, the identity of the man-made hierarchy with a God-made one), these mean nothing to him. He is the new man of the incipient bourgeois revolution, the private enterprise man, the man who thinks he has got to be a phoenix, the individualist go-getter, the machiavel, Marlowe's aspiring hero taken to his extreme conclusion: man with the lid off.

Edgar of course is Edmund's opposite. The brothers are contrasted at every point, and it is not the crude static moral contrast of the good and the bad, even though something of this – the structure of the old morality plays – remains in *Lear*. Edgar is the loyal son of the feudal father, pious, resourceful, kind, and above all legitimate, and when in the last act he steps forward at the third trump to defend the right, he carries on his shoulders all the glamour and the chivalry of a formalised feudal past.

Edgar defeats Edmund. Gloucester, though hideously punished for his moral laxity and political blindness, is avenged, even redeemed, gaining in his suffering, through his contact with Poor Tom, an insight which, seeing, he had lacked. His profoundest moment is when he gives Tom his purse:

Here, take this purse, thou whom the heavens' plagues
Have humbled to all strokes: that I am wretched
Makes thee the happier: Heavens, deal so still!
Let the superfluous and lust-dieted man,
That slaves your ordinance, that will not see

> Because he does not feel, feel your power quickly;
> So distribution should undo excess,
> And each man have enough.
>
> (IV.i.64–70)

It is a wonderful moment, the full significance of which lies in its echoing of some of Lear's own words which I will refer to in a moment. The power Gloucester has not seen because he has not felt it can only, in the context, be that of common humanity, embodied in Poor Tom. Yet in the Gloucester story, even though Tom does save Gloucester and help him onwards, this outburst, moving as it is, is not really developed. It is not developed because the relation between Tom and Edgar remains ill-defined or, rather, too well-defined. Edgar simply pretends to be Tom and then becomes Edgar again. Tom is a richer character than Edgar because he includes Edgar, whereas Edgar doesn't include Tom. Edgar is not really changed by being Tom, though the play is, through the experiences of Lear and Gloucester. But the Edgar of the last act is essentially St George, the feudal hero, and he has to be, for he will become king. Only in the four final lines of the play does a doubt creep in and we are allowed to wonder whether Edgar perhaps remembers Tom.

The Lear story is deeper, more complex and more variously moving than the Gloucester story, for Lear, unlike Gloucester, is a hero.

At the beginning of the play he is not a hero at all, but a king to whom the forms of kingship and hierarchy are the basis and reality of the world. It is Cordelia who, at this stage of the story, is the heroic one, for it is she who speaks the words of aspiring humanity. When she has to define her feelings about her father she can only say

> I love your Majesty
> According to my bond; no more nor less.
> (I.i.92–3)

The words bear close scrutiny. Obviously they are not the words of a twentieth-century daughter, royal or common. Their form is essentially feudal, as the word 'bond' emphasises. Yet it becomes clear that by 'according to my bond' Cordelia is not thinking in formal feudal terms but defining as realistically and truthfully as she can a human relationship between two people, of whom one happens to be her father and a king and therefore has special claims on her. I think Cordelia's view of love is very much akin to that expressed two hundred years later in another poem about an innocent child faced with angry authority. In Blake's 'A Little Boy Lost' the child says to the inquisitor Priest:

'And Father, how can I love you
Or any of my brothers more?
I love you like the little bird
That picks up crumbs around the door.'

Such heresy, the expression of a relationship honourable and *natural* in senses which neither party in the *Lear* world can accept, leads the child to the stake as it leads Cordelia to the gallows. And it is interesting that, near the end of the play, in a beautiful scene which shows us a Lear and a Cordelia who have come through to 'a better way', the old man uses the very Blakean image

We two alone will sing like birds i' th' cage.
(V.iii.9)

It is also interesting that Cordelia's phrase 'no more nor less' is echoed by Lear when, the great rage dead, he comes to describe himself in the terms of his new understanding:

I am a very foolish fond old man,
Fourscore and upward, not an hour more or less;
And, to deal plainly,
I fear I am not in my perfect mind.
(IV.vii.60–4)

He is now, like Cordelia, dealing plainly, describing the situation realistically. He has reached the view of Nature implicit in her first statement. I can find no better way of describing it than as the humanist view of Nature. And in the course of discovering it Lear has become a hero. His story, put in its simplest terms, is the story of his progress from being a king to being a man, neither more nor less. It is a story so fearful and yet so wonderful that all human society is shaken by the terrible beauty of it and at its supreme moments man and the universe are seen in relationships which it is scarcely possible for words other than Shakespeare's own to describe.

When I say that *Lear* is the story of how a king becomes a man I do not mean at all that it is an allegory or that we should use a word like 'symbolic' to describe it. For Shakespeare does not work in abstractions. He is a supremely realistic writer who presents us all the time with actual situations, actual relationships, and what general conclusions he offers are always based on particular observations and insights. He is not, of course, a *naturalistic* dramatist, attempting a 'slice of life' kind of realism, and he uses every resource of his teeming imagination to create means of penetrating, through words and fantasy, to the inner processes of the situations and people he presents. The storm in *Lear* 'works' artistically on a number of levels: the elemental storm, the social storm which shakes the divided kingdom, the inner storm that drives Lear mad, all are interconnected and reinforce one another to achieve what is, I suppose, the most extraordinary and harrowing representation of crisis in the whole of art. But every device of art is used to produce, not some effect above or beyond reality, but the deepest, most complex exploration of the actual nature of reality, its texture and its implications, its movement and its interconnectedness.

In the first three acts of *Lear* we have almost unrelieved horror and pessimism, broken only by isolated gleams of human decency and hope. It is one of Shakespeare's triumphs that, without compromising for a moment on their hideousness, he does not make the opponents of Lear crude villains. Edmund, with his gusto and energy, is in many respects a more vital creature than the rather colourless Edgar. Goneril and Regan have a terrible common-sense effectiveness, almost a normality, about them. Their very baiting of their father by the reduction of the numbers of his retainers is not mere insolence: they have a strong case and argue at least partly in the terms of a modern-sounding contempt for the hierarchical principle.[3] They are at once shrewd, able, shallow and morally impervious, and they are rivals because they are alike.

It is the new people with their heartless rationalisation – 'the younger rises, when the old doth fall' – who bring down Lear. And his friends, the ineffectual unseeing Gloucester and the loyal but too simple Kent, are unable to save him from the new ruthlessness. Kent's role in the play is interesting because he is of all the 'feudal' characters the most courageous and least corrupt. And he is able to shield Lear to some extent. But his ultimate failure to cope with the situation – he is unable to hold Lear within the bounds of sanity and is in fact of far less use to him than either the Fool or Poor Tom – is echoed by his own prognostications of his death in the final scene. The ultimate inadequacy of Kent despite his decent, old world virtues, is one of the expressions in the play of the impossibility of a return of the feudal past.

What we have, then, in the first three acts of *Lear* is a world in which the older order is decadent and the new people unprincipled and both, as the treatment of Cordelia shows, inhuman. Horror dominates. The terrible curse on Goneril – made by Lear in the name of Nature –

> Into her womb convey sterility!
> Dry up in her the organs of increase,
> And from her derogate body never spring
> A babe to honour her! If she must teem,
> Create her child of spleen, that it may live
> And be a thwart disnatur'd torment to her.
>   (I.iv.287–92)

– this curse, whose imagery overflows into the verse of scene after scene, is a measure of the depth of the horror; but not its ultimate expression. For the equal horror is Lear's own impotence. When Goneril rejects him he still can threaten vainly to 'resume the shape' of the past – to be king again. When Regan's cruelty is added to her sister's, and personal ingratitude is, so to speak, turned into a system, he is literally unable to express his emotion, though he still mutters of revenge.

> No, you unnatural hags,
> I will have such revenges on you both
> That all the world shall – I will do such things,
> What they are, yet I know not, but they shall be
> The terrors of the earth.
>   (II.iv.280–4)

Lear has, literally, no resources of action, language or even emotion to be able to cope, within the bounds of the consciousness he has so far achieved, with the situation which faces him. From here to madness is but a short step. And the very word madness needs our thought. It can no more be taken for granted in *Lear* than in *Hamlet*. The more one examines the play the more one comes to feel that Lear's madness is not so much a breakdown as a breakthrough. It is necessary.

In the storm scene comes the first hint of resolution, the first turning-point of the play, the first breakthrough of humanity, co-incident with the words 'My wits begin to turn'. For the phrase is followed by some words to the Fool:

> Come on, my boy. How dost, my boy? Art cold?
> I am cold myself. Where is this straw, my fellow?
> The art of our necessities is strange,
> That can make vile things precious. Come, your hovel.
> Poor fool and knave, I have one part in my heart
> That's sorry yet for thee.
>
> (III.ii.68–73)

The words represent a change in direction: away from self-pity, pride, revenge and kingliness, towards fellow-feeling and co-opera-tion, the minimum qualities of humanity. I do not want to present Shakespeare as some kind of 'unconscious' precursor of Engels; but I think it is very interesting that at this crisis of the play, when Lear is first beginning to feel his way towards a new freedom, Shakespeare should use the word 'necessities' and use it in a context which forbids any but a materialist significance.

It is through his madness – his incapacity to deal with reality any longer within the framework of his accepted standards of sanity – that Lear comes to a new outlook on life. The moving prayer just before his meeting with Tom is now fairly generally recognised as a crux of the whole play.

> Poor naked wretches, whereso'er you are,
> That bide the pelting of this pitiless storm,
> How shall your houseless heads and unfed sides,
> Your loop'd and window'd raggedness, defend you
> From seasons such as these? O! I have ta'en
> Too little care of this. Take physic, Pomp;
> Expose thyself to feel what wretches feel,
> That thou mayst shake the superflux to them,
> And show the Heavens more just.
>
> (III.iv.28–36)

This speech, echoed so soon by Gloucester's words to Tom, in which precisely the same ideas are expressed and the word 'superflux' returned to, is absolutely central to the structure and meaning of the play. Lear's incapacity to deal with the inhumanity of the new people is what drives him into a solidarity, and, later, an identification, with the poor. For in his powerlessness he is forced to recognise the pervasive helplessness of the poor in the face of the power of the rich, those who have property. Thus his direct personal contact with ruling-class inhumanity leads him to question the validity of property itself and the authority and exemption from elementary human moral values it confers. In this, Lear's development is not at all unlike that of later seventeenth-century radicals like Winstanley.

There is method, Polonius discovers, in Hamlet's madness; and Edgar, listening to Lear's mad wanderings, remarks to the audience 'Reason in madness!' The speech he is referring to contains some of the deepest and acutest social criticism in all Shakespeare, or indeed anywhere.

> . . . A man may see how this world goes with no eyes. Look with
> thine ears: see how yond justice rails upon yond simple thief. Hark,
> in thine ear: change places and, handy-dandy, which is the justice,
> which is the thief? Thou hast seen a farmer's dog bark at a beggar?
>
> **Gloucester** Ay, sir.
>
> **Lear** And the creature run from the cur? There thou mightst behold
> the great image of authority: a dog's obey'd in office.
> Thou rascal beadle, hold thy bloody hand!
> Why dost thou lash that whore? Strip thy own back;
> Thou hotly lusts to use her in that kind
> For which thou whip'st her. The usurer hangs the cozener.
> Through tatter'd clothes small vices do appear;
> Robes and furr'd gowns hide all. Plate sin with gold,
> And the strong lance of justice hurtless breaks;
> Arm it in rags, a pigmy's straw does pierce it.
> None does offend, none, I say none; I'll able 'em:
> Take that of me, my friend, who have the power
> To seal th' accuser's lips. Get thee glass eyes,
> And, like a scurvy politician, seem
> To see the things thou dost not. Now, now, now, now!
> Pull off my boots; harder, harder; so.
>
> (IV.vi.151–75)

When that speech has the currency of Polonius's advice to Laertes it will seem less strange to British readers to refer to the democratic content of the bourgeois–democratic revolution and to link Shakespeare's greatness with his humanism.

If we describe Lear's, or Gloucester's, experiences as 'spiritual', that is to say, involving a change not just in fortune and circumstance but in values and quality of being, it is essential to recognise that Shakespeare links this change at every step with actual actions and social attitudes. The social emphases are not more or less casual sidethoughts but are absolutely basic to the whole conception of the play. You cannot understand it without them. The new humanity which Lear achieves is not simply a self-knowledge acquired by introspection or any kind of mystical or religious experience; it is an

outlook gained through experience and action, through the necessity
that has been forced upon him of exposing himself to feel what
wretches feel, of facing reality in all its horror and splendour, of
judging men and women by their simplest, most essential actions,
and of learning who his friends are. The experience results in a
turning upside-down, handy-dandy, of accepted social assumptions.
The pulling off of the boots at the end of the speech I have just
quoted is, everyone realises, significant. Already in the hovel in the
storm Lear has insistently taken off his clothes, feeling them an
impediment, a mark of rank, preventing complete identification with
Poor Tom. 'Off, off you lendings' he cries. The phrase is almost a
summary of the play. Lear, the king, reduced by the new people of
the bourgeois world to the depth of human humiliation, falls only to
rise, and becomes a man. And the people who help him to achieve
humanity are by no means the wise or great or powerful, but a Fool
and a beggar who has gone mad.

The turning point of the play is Lear's losing of his wits to find
them; and it is followed by a decisive moment of action – the first
instant in the play when the evil characters are checked in their
deeds. Up to the moment of the blinding of Gloucester the decent
people have seemed impotent. And then of a sudden a blow is struck
– and again it is not by the great or the wise, but by the servant who,
his humanity outraged by the torturing of Gloucester, kills the Duke
of Cornwall. Regan's horrified comment is more eloquent than a
long speech:

> A peasant stand up thus?
> (III.vii.79)

And from now on a fight is put up.

I have said nothing so far of the role of the Fool. We should not
sentimentalise him or exaggerate his importance. He is less significant to Lear's progress than Poor Tom. But his comments – the
shrewd and cynical paradoxes, the irreverent thrusts at Lear's dignity
– form a kind of choric counterpoint of the main themes of the play
which not only adds a depth and complexity but helps define the
essential 'popular' element within this play of kings and nobles. It is
not easy to get a consistent pattern from the Fool's remarks. His
Blakean prophecy (at the end of Act III, scene ii) is puzzling and
apparently inconsistent, yet it expresses with an exciting vividness

the historical tensions 'and contradictions which lie behind the whole play. Perhaps it is the cynical realism of his comments which is most striking. He has been ground down too long to have much hope of salvation, so that his resilience is spasmodic, his pessimism deep-rooted. He reminds one a little of the old soldier whose hatred and contempt of the army has been fed on a lifetime of chastening experience and who cannot – for all his irreverence – shake off the habits of servitude he despises. One might describe him as the opposite of the eternal butler, an eternal batman, a sort of Elizabethan Schweik.[4]

When Lear awakes from his madness the Fool is no longer with him, but Cordelia is. The realm of Albion has indeed come to great confusion and Lear has come through to a new state of mind. He has not merely been purged of pride and learned a proper humility, as Christian critics point out, he has changed his whole attitude to people and society and there is, most significantly, no desire in him to get his throne back. On the contrary, the court is mentioned only with contempt, not at all unlike the contempt of Hamlet: Lear and Cordelia will

> hear poor rogues
> Talk of court news; and we'll talk with them too,
> Who loses and who wins; who's in, who's out,
> And take upon's the mystery of things
> As if we were God's spies: and we'll wear out,
> In a wall'd prison, packs and sects of great ones
> That ebb and flow by th' moon.
> (V.iii.13–19)

The whole emergent world of bourgeois politics is somehow evoked and placed in that single sentence and a modern reader can scarcely fail to hear in *Lear* constant pre-echoes of Swift and Blake.

Towards the end of the play Cordelia, with whom Lear now unequivocally associates himself, is seen explicitly as the alternative to the old order (which by her honesty she has exposed) and to the new people who hate and fear her.

> Patience and sorrow strove
> Who should express her goodliest. You have seen
> Sunshine and rain at once: her smiles and tears
> Were like a better way.
> (IV.iii.17–20)

'Sunshine and rain at once', the image of the rainbow, the pledge of future harmony arising out of contradiction, is associated with Cordelia. She seems to express in her very person the 'better way' to which Lear has come through. If there is a kind of utopian promise here – the sort of thing Shakespeare comes back to in his final plays – the suggestion is achieved without a removal of the play into the realms of abstraction or metaphysics. For it is because of what she does and thinks, not what in some safe way she 'is', that the new people cannot let Cordelia live. And Lear, too, in this ineffably beautiful yet most terrible play, must die. He cannot be set back – an even older but a wiser man – upon his throne. Shakespeare has revealed a struggle more desperate than such a resolution could encompass.

It is worth comparing the end of *Lear* with that of *Hamlet*. In both plays the protagonist has been defeated, not by his enemies or by his weaknesses but by history. Both plays end with the implied accession of a new king, a promise of continuity as opposed to death; but in neither case does the new king in any serious sense fill the bill. The point about Fortinbras is that he is incapable of understanding what Hamlet has understood; so that there is, despite the survival of Horatio, a distinctly hollow sound in the closing commonplaces of the play. The most that can be said for Edgar is that he is something to be going on with. But he is, nevertheless, a considerable advance on Fortinbras. The final words of *King Lear* are moving and curiously profound.

> The weight of this sad time we must obey;
> Speak what we feel, not what we ought to say.
> The oldest hath borne most; we that are young
> Shall never see so much nor live so long.
> (V.iii.323–6)

That the experience and meaning of the play cannot be confined within the limits of seventeenth-century social thinking is implicit in these lines. Conventional assessment (what we *ought* to say) is quite inadequate. What raises Edgar so far above Fortinbras is that he recognises his own inferiority; he has not seen what Lear has seen, but he has seen and felt enough to recognise the quality of Lear's experience, to know that he does not know. Perhaps, after all, he has not quite forgotten Poor Tom.

From Arnold Kettle, *Literature and Liberation: Selected Essays* (Manchester, 1988), pp. 70–82.

NOTES

[Kettle's account of *King Lear* is the second half of his essay 'From Hamlet to Lear', first published in 1964 in the centenary volume *Shakespeare in a Changing World*, a collection of Marxist and radical humanist essays edited by Kettle himself. The original essay begins with a reading of *Hamlet*, to which the discussion of *Lear* occasionally returns to make points of comparison, especially regarding the ends of the plays. What binds these two tragedies together for Kettle is the fact that both protagonists are 'heroes' in a special sense he explains in the paragraph preceding the extract. A hero is someone who 'bears on his shoulders, sometimes without realising it, something of the actual aspirations of humanity in its struggles to advance its condition'. As a theatrical instance of such a hero, Lear like Hamlet demands from us a response which is at once sympathetically involved in his individual fate and yet sufficiently detached to allow an objective grasp of its social grounds and wider significance. In this respect Kettle finds a strong resemblance between Shakespeare's dramatic practice and that of Bertolt Brecht, for whom (in Kettle's words) 'a revolutionary drama must at the same time be 'committed' (i.e. committed to the solving of actual problems, to the changing of the world) and, in his sense of the word, 'epic' (i.e. involving the conscious realisation by the spectator that he is watching actions that are outside himself, so that in one sense he must remain cool and uninvolved'.

Textual references are to Peter Alexander (ed.), *William Shakespeare: The Complete Works* (London, 1951). Ed.]

1. John F. Danby, *Shakespeare's Doctrine of Nature* (London, 1949).

2. Lines 213–17. I have drawn attention elsewhere (*Zeitschrift für Anglistik und Amerikanistik*, X [1962], 117–27) to the number of phrases in this poem which are directly reminiscent of some of the key phrases of *Hamlet*, e.g.:

> Then, as mankinde so is the worlds whole frame
> Quite out of joynt, almost created lame

and Donne's vision of

> Corruptions in our braines, or in our hearts,
> Poysoning the fountaines, whence our actions spring

3. When Goneril and Lear argue about the question of Lear's retainers they use the word 'need' in different senses. Goneril uses the word to mean something like 'efficiency'; Lear's use of the word is very different.

4. The most effective Fool I have seen on the stage was that of a German actor, Edwin Marian, in a production at the Deutsches Theater in East Berlin in 1957. This Fool was a plain, down-to-earth, somewhat Brechtian peasant, neither fey nor eccentric, like most British interpretations.

2

Plays Within Plays

HOWARD FELPERIN

The ways in which a play's central interpretive problem arises from specific changes Shakespeare has wrought on his traditional models are particularly clear and traceable in the case of *King Lear*. At least as early as Samuel Johnson's pained observations on the ending of the play, interpretation has concerned itself with what to make of Shakespeare's alteration of the traditional story of Lear and Cordelia away from poetic justice and toward unprecedented suffering. As everyone knows, all of Shakespeare's immediate sources – the old play *King Leir*, Holinshed's *Chronicles*, Spenser's *Faerie Queene*, and *A Mirror for Magistrates* – present Lear and Cordelia triumphant at last, with virtue rewarded and vice punished. Though some versions return Cordelia to prison, the victim of further rebellion and finally her own suicide, these events occur after Lear's vindication and peaceful death. Moreover, Shakespeare has made other changes which would seem to redouble the deliberate violence of this basic change. For one thing, he has omitted the wealth of consoling Christian and Biblical parallels that interlace the play of *Leir*, as well as most of the Christian atmosphere that permeates the other versions. Then too, he has included the parallel subplot of Gloucester and his sons, derived from Sidney's *Arcadia*, and apparently serving to universalise and underscore the cruelties of the Lear action. As if this were not enough, he adds the ordeal of madness to Lear's other afflictions. It is not difficult to see how these changes encourage the two basic possibilities of response I have termed pious and romantic, each of which informs a school of criticism on the play. A neo-romantic or modernist response oriented toward the result of Shakespeare's alterations of his Christian sources rather than the sources themselves has stressed the godless secularity of the play, the paganness of its world, and the unredeemed or 'absurd' nature of its suffering. To a more allegorising and archaeological school, however, it remains possible to see through or past Shakespeare's alterations of his Christian sources in order to reconcile the play with them. 'Only to earthbound intelligence', writes one critic, 'is Lear pathetically deceived in thinking Cordelia alive. Those familiar with the Morality plays will realise that Lear has found in her unselfish love the one companion who is willing to go with him through Death up to the throne of the Everlasting Judge.'[1]

These are of course the extreme possibilities of response to the play. But there is a third possibility, more problematic and interesting in that it combines elements of both the modernist and pious approaches to the play in uneasy suspension. This is the view most fully articulated by A. C. Bradley, who represents the culmination of the romantic approach and sees the implications of Shakespeare's changes in their full horror, yet who also cannot resist suggesting that the play might be piously retitled 'The Redemption of King Lear'. In his ambivalence Bradley anticipates what has perhaps become the dominant approach to the play, an approach that is not explicitly Christian but that displaces the older Christian meanings into the terms of a secular humanism, the Christian origin and structure of which are still clear. Lear changes, grows, gains wisdom, even a kind of redemption as the result of his suffering, madness, and death. Though Cordelia may not be the incarnate principle of Faith or Love, she is the human mediator of those virtues. Through strenuous exegesis along these lines, a critic such as Maynard Mack can argue for the modernity of the play and at the same time reassimilate it to the vision of redemption offered in its sources, Shakespeare's departures from them serving only to humanise and deepen that vision by making it harder-earned and by that token more valuable:

> If there is any 'remorseless process' in *King Lear*, it is one that begs us to seek the meaning of our human fate not in what becomes of us, but in what we become. Death, as we saw, is miscellaneous and commonplace; it is life whose quality may be made noble and distinctive. Suffering we all recoil from; but we know it is a greater thing to suffer than to lack the feelings and virtues that make it possible to suffer. Cordelia, we may choose to say, accomplished nothing, yet we know it is better to have been Cordelia than to have been her sisters. When

we come crying hither, we bring with us the badge of all our misery; but it is also the badge of the vulnerabilities that give us access to whatever grandeur we achieve.[2]

Quite apart from the statement itself, Mack's conclusion recalls in its rhetoric of contrast and compensation – 'Death ... life'; 'Suffering ... a greater thing'; 'nothing ... better'; 'misery ... vulnerabilities' – nothing in the play so much as Edgar's own summing-up: 'Speak what we feel, not what we ought to say. / The oldest hath borne most: we that are young. ...' Of course it also recalls the homiletic rhetorical mode of Shakespeare's own Christian sources, not only the old *Leir* and *A Mirror for Magistrates* but the medieval dramatic and visionary tradition that Mack himself discovers behind the play. In the effort to argue the play's modernity, its special relevance for 'our time', Mack draws our attention, stylistically and substantively, to its most conventional and Christian elements.

What is it, then, in the structure of *King Lear* that moves such critics as Bradley and Mack to reach conclusions manifestly at odds with their own critical premises, the one employing a romantic approach in the service of Christianising the play, and the other an archaeological approach in the name of its presumed modernism? Such paradoxes of critical response can be traced directly to one of the major changes Shakespeare has worked on his sources, the introduction of the story of Gloucester as a reflection of the story of Lear. Bradley was, in fact, among the first to explore the implications of this parallelism, and most commentators since have followed him in seeing its effect as one of mutual reinforcement. The Gloucester subplot, that is, works 'to enact and express a further aspect of the Lear experience'.[3] It now becomes clearer how the Christianity Shakespeare has apparently taken pains to remove from *King Lear* finds its way back into its interpretation. For the Gloucester action embodies an essentially Christian structure, or at least a concerted attempt on the part of its principal actors to discover or recreate such a structure:

> **Albany** If that the heavens do not their visible spirits
> Send quickly down to tame these vile offences,
> It will come,
> Humanity must perforce prey on itself,
> Like monsters of the deep.
> (IV.ii.45–9)

Albany This shows you are above,
You justicers, that these our nether crimes
So speedily can venge. But, O poor Gloucester!
Lost he his other eye?

(IV.ii.78–81)

Edgar It was some fiend; therefore, thou happy father,
Think that the clearest gods, who make them honors
Of men's impossibilities, have preserved thee.

(IV.vi.72–4)

Edgar The gods are just, and of our pleasant vices
Make instruments to plague us:
The dark and vicious place where thee he got
Cost him his eyes.

(V.iii.171–4)

Each of these expressions of belief in divine justice and providential purpose – the most explicit in the play – occurs at a major turning point in the plot, but in each instance it is the Gloucester plot that is involved. If the Gloucester plot is supposed to exist in a mirroring or parallel relation to the Lear plot, it becomes not only possible but inevitable that the Christian structure and sentiment expressed through the former will be transferred to the latter, whatever critical premise we start from.

Yet it is precisely the pervasive Christianising of the subplot that puts into question its supposed parallelism with the main plot. It is almost as if the older Christian structure deliberately dismantled in the story of Lear is just as deliberately reconstructed in the story of Gloucester, which had been only implicitly Christian in Sidney. With its black-and-white contrasts of good and bad, lawful and illegitimate, 'natural' and 'unnatural' sons, its clear symmetries of cause and effect, sin and retribution, moral blindness and physical blinding, the Gloucester action is basically as simple and homiletic in structure as any of the neat little 'tragedies' of *A Mirror for Magistrates* and the long medieval tradition of the falls of illustrious men that lies behind it. The Gloucester action, like the medieval and morality-derived models of the *Lear* action, is not 'tragic' at all in the sense we have been exploring. It offers none of the fatal discrepancies between form and experience, role and self, sign and significance that we have seen beset Hamlet and Othello, no heroic casting about for roles and forms to define present experience, and no ironic awareness of their inadequacy even as they are played out. In this respect, the Gloucester–Edgar–Edmund subplot in *Lear* resembles nothing in the earlier tragedies so much as the Polonius–Laertes–Ophelia sub-plot in *Hamlet*, with which it shares the common function of re-enacting a recognisably conventional 'tragedy' that throws the more intractable experience of Hamlet and Lear into stark relief. Just as the Polonius subplot turns out to be a simple revenge melodrama with the stock revenger Laertes as protagonist, as latter-day Nemesis, so the Gloucester subplot turns out to be a simple dramatic *exemplum* illustrating the educative abasement of the complacent sinner. Its essential Christian structure is foreshadowed as early as Kent's casual reply to Gloucester's tasteless jokes over Edmund's bastardising: 'I cannot wish the fault undone, the issue of it being so proper' (I.i.17–18). The action, that is, illustrates a fortunate fall and issues in redemptive suffering, a sadder but wiser man, and a happy death: 'his flawed heart . . . 'Twixt two extremes of passion, joy and grief, / Burst smilingly' (V.iii.198–201). The Gloucester action at no point puts into question its initial assumptions concerning the origin of evil or the meaning of suffering, for in its fulfilment of a conventional Christian design those questions are answered in advance and those answers only confirmed by its outcome. Something always comes of something, evil of illegitimacy and good of legitimacy. The universe of the Gloucester action operates by strict and transparent laws of cause and effect, which are at no point challenged, though of course they can be disobeyed: 'I stumbled when I saw.' The assumption here is that he now sees 'feelingly' and truly. Just as his 'pilgrimage' to Dover has an attainable goal, though it is not the one he intended, so experience has an ascertainable meaning, though it may not be ascertained until the end.

The Gloucester action is designed throughout to illustrate that meaning, negatively and positively, through the theatrical endeav-ours of Edmund and Edgar. For their histrionics, though morally contrasting, are always of a distinctly programmatic and emblematic kind. Their role-playing, that is, is only skin-deep. In Edgar's appear-ance as Poor Tom and later as unnamed challenger, there is nothing of the groping toward self-definition we associate with Shakespear-ean tragic role-playing. His roles are as easily and completely put on and off as the costume or visor they depend on: 'Edgar I nothing am' (II.ii.21). They are mere expedients contrived for the temporary purpose of preserving himself, bringing Gloucester through despair to repentance, and recovering his own legitimate rights, and once they have successfully achieved those purposes they are shed as the mere disguises they are. Edmund's role-playing is equally superficial.

There is none of the mystery behind his Vice-like plot of ambition and intrigue that there is in the case of Iago, with whom he is often misleadingly equated. Edmund's 'motivation' is only too clear from the patronising treatment we see him receive at Gloucester's hands and from his own soliloquy on his status as bastard. To be a bastard is, as Edmund makes clear, to be superfluous, to have no rightful or legal place within the social structure. He *therefore* attempts to legitimate himself in the name of an amoral nature that exists prior to social forms, to create a rival structure proceeding from and centred on the self. All this is perfectly logical, as Richard III's 'And *therefore*, since I cannot prove a lover. . . / I am determined to prove a villain' (*Richard III*, I.i.28–30) is logical. But in neither case is it psychological; it points to no hidden depths. Edmund has in fact more in common with such early and morality-derived Shakespearean villains as Aaron the Moor, Don John, and Richard III, who carry around with them an external sign or stigma that serves as badge and pretext for their villainy, than he does with Iago, whose alienation goes deeper and carries no badge, who is at some level a mystery to himself, and whose cultivation of a Vice-like evil can be neither fully explained nor fully demystified. For unlike that of Iago, Edmund's role can be put off as easily as it was put on: 'Yet Edmund was beloved . . . some good I mean to do / Despite of mine own nature' (V.iii.241–6). Of course the scene of Edmund's 'reformation' is no less naturalistic, no more openly homiletic in conception and derivation, than the scene of Gloucester's 'suicide' and 'salvation' stage-managed by Edgar. But then, these moments are not to be regarded as lapses on the part of a Shakespeare aiming at naturalistic consistency but here and there falling short of his mark. For it is within the Gloucester action that these 'lapses', which are part and parcel of its homiletic structure, moral emblematisation, and allegorical motivation, are largely confined.[4] The air of contrivance that hangs about the Gloucester action is pervasive, and it smells of morality.

Why, then, is the Gloucester action not more generally recognised to be deliberately archaic and artificial but is discussed instead as if it possessed or ought to possess a naturalistic coherence comparable to that of the Lear action? Here again the presupposition of a mutually reinforcing parallelism between the two plots is the source of potential misinterpretation. Just as the assumption of parallelism tempts us to expect from the Lear action a Christian allegorical coherence it does not have, so too it tempts us to expect from the

Gloucester action a naturalistic coherence and dimensionality it does not have. Edgar's rhyming conclusion to the play, for example, in which he enjoins all present to 'speak what we feel, not what we ought to say', is often cited and discussed as if it constituted a deep and authentic response to the play's tragic experience and confirmed Edgar's wisdom and humanity. This is particularly ironic and revealing in so far as the speech may well belong to Albany – only the folio assigns it to Edgar – and it would make little difference if it were spoken by Albany. For quite apart from its choric conventionality familiar from previous summings-up by the likes of Horatio and Fortinbras, Cassio and Lodovico, the speech actually indicts its own speaker and its own idiom for having consistently done just the opposite. Edgar and Albany, who serve within the play as interpreters of Gloucester's experience, have throughout traded in a consoling and instructive morality with an unself-questioning assurance and an easy credulity that puts into question what it is they feel and whether they feel at all. Albany's assertions, for example, of divine justice – 'This shows you are above / You justicers . . . But, O poor Gloucester! / Lost he his other eye?' – or his reassertion at the end of its secular counterpart – 'All friends shall taste / The wages of their virtue, and all foes / The cup of their deservings. O, see, see!' (V.ii.304–6) – are dramatically undermined by events that would seem blatantly to contradict them: the loss of Gloucester's other eye, the death-pangs of Lear. But when faced with the choice between revising their Christian vision in the face of adverse experience and simply reasserting that vision, such characters as Albany and Edgar invariably choose the latter course, persist in speaking what they 'ought to say' at the expense of what they 'feel'. Or perhaps for such determined moralists there is finally no consciousness of a gap between saying and feeling, since their action is shaped by them precisely to do away with all such discrepancies by containing, in the manner of medieval allegory, its own interpretation within it. The temptation to which many, if not most, commentators on the subplot have succumbed has been to follow their example and suppress their own sense of difference between the voice of convention and the voice of feeling – that is to say, between the subplot and the main plot.[5]

This is not finally to suggest, as up to now I may have seemed to be doing, that Shakespeare has indeed purged the Lear action of all remnants of older Christian dramatic convention. On the contrary, the main action often turns toward conventions of emblem and allegory not essentially different from those that govern the subplot, despite the fact that Shakespeare has in the end denied the poetic justice of his Christian sources. The very first scene of the division of the kingdom, for example, with its emblematic map and ritualistic speeches has struck many as archaic and anti-naturalistic, a scene out of fairy-tale. In fact it recalls, in its stylised presentation of kingly pride and folly, the opening scene of one of the oldest extant moralities, *The Pride of Life* (1425) or, closer to home, the opening scene of *Gorboduc* (1562). Like his prototypes, Lear persists, against the admonitions of his wise counsellors, in a course that proves disastrous, and, like them too, lives to repent of his actions. Given this initial and basic resemblance between the structure of the play and such models as these, a resemblance that has clearly survived Shakespeare's reworking of his immediate sources, it is little wonder that Bradley and others have glimpsed a vision of redemption in the play. Nor are these resemblances confined to the opening scene or the overarching structure of the Lear action. They reappear in many of its local details: in the banishment and stocking of the forthright Kent as the figure of Justice in several moralities had been banished and stocked; in Lear's homily on charity on the heath; in his mock trial of his daughters and indictments of earthly justice; in his madness itself, for which there are precedents in pictorial and morality tradition if not in the play's actual sources; in the vision of redemption Lear superimposes on Cordelia at his reunion and again even amid the shambles of the closing scene. And given this wealth of archaic reference within the Lear action, the question arises: why does all that has just been said of the gross conventionality of the Gloucester action not apply to it as well? What is it that makes the one modern, mimetic, and tragic and the other conventional and pseudo-tragic?

What distinguishes the main plot from the subplot is not the extent to which but the manner in which these older conventions are employed. In fact, the opening scene of the Lear action is much closer to the moralities in its ritual stylisation than is the more domesticated and fluent opening scene of the Gloucester action. For that opening scene, staged by Lear himself, proceeds from and reflects his absolute confidence in the sacred authority of his role of king and the perfect correspondence among the natural, moral, and linguistic orders that supports it. In the security of this traditional vision of the world, Lear cannot imagine any possible disjuncture between role and self, appearance and reality, 'sentence and power', *signum* and *res*. Hence

his surprise at Cordelia's unprogrammatic response of 'nothing' and
Kent's irreverent rejoinder to 'see better'. It is against this initial
morality vision of sacred unity that Lear's descent into a more
modern and secular perception of ironic discontinuity is defined. The
movement of the Lear action away from a morality vision thus
opposes and crosses that of the Gloucester action toward a morality
vision. Of course Lear does not abandon his original mode of vision
immediately or willingly. He clings to his former way of seeing
himself and his world, curses his daughters with a residual belief in
the magical efficacy of his word, and calls down 'plagues that in the
pendulous air / Hang fated o'er men's faults' (III.iv.65–6). But these
invocations of a morality scheme of divine justice inherent in the
natural order now ring increasingly hollow even to him and almost
as he utters them: 'What *is* the cause of thunder?' (III.iv.146); '*Is*
there any cause in nature that makes these hard hearts?' (III.vi.75–6).
The change that Lear undergoes in the course of his play is not a
change from one moral state to another, such as from pride to
charity, but a change away from self-definition in terms of moral
categories altogether and toward a new sense of existential indeterminacy, the very opposite of Gloucester's change. For whereas
Gloucester is increasingly allegorised within his action, Lear is increasingly humanised within his, though not in the sense of becoming
more humane – witness his cruel greeting of the blinded Gloucester
and his accusations of the reassembled court as 'murderers, traitors
all' (V.ii.271) – but in the sense of becoming more fully and merely
human.

This is not to suggest that he does not continue to fall back on
moral categories of self-definition, but that he recognises them to be
somehow inadequate even as he does so. His set speech on charity
toward the 'poor, naked wretches' (III.iv.28–36), for example, is
right out of morality tradition and often cited as the beginning of
Lear's moral re-education. But its imperative mood ('Take physic
pomp') gives way by the end of the homily to the subjunctive and
optative mood ('That thou may'st shake the superflux to them / And
show the heavens more just'). Man, by practising charity, can only
hope to *show* the heavens more just; he cannot make them so.
Similarly, his mad re-enactments of the forms of justice on the heath
work to undermine the morality vision they represent. In that older
drama, the satiric castigation of judicial corruption deals in such
negative *exempla* as Lear offers, but only on the way to establishing
a vision of true justice. Lear's recourse in his madness to this strain

of morality rhetoric and imagery, however, works to strip away these social and religious legitimations to the emptiness and arbitrariness of the idea of justice itself, its fundamental disjuncture from a human nature that exists beneath or beyond moral and legal categories. Vice and guilt do not exist – 'Die for adultery? No . . . None does offend' (IV.vi.165) – and neither does virtue and innocence: 'Behold yond simp'ring dame . . . / The fitchew nor the soiled horse goes to 't / With a more riotous appetite' (IV.vi.108–12). Lear's view of the discrepancy between social forms and the human nature to which they are supposed to correspond is not at this point very far from Edmund's. The difference between them is not in moral outlook but in mimetic realisation. Edmund holds his views lightly and complacently as a means of justifying himself and his actions; Lear comes to his reluctantly and painfully, after a lifetime of believing the opposite and against his present interests. Uniquely in the play, Lear's adoption of morality forms leads in each local instance and within his larger itinerary to a desperate fluctuation between his maddening perception of their inadequacy and a wishful retreat into the shelter they provide, however momentary.[6]

This breakdown of the morality forms by which the social order and the individual mind maintain their stability conditions not only Lear's madness in particular but Shakespearean madness in general. For the roles and forms of morality convention are employed by Shakespeare's characters as a protection against the confusion of raw experience, a screen that selectively permits only that which can be made sense of within a predetermined order to reach the perceiving mind. But it is an inflexible screen, whose very rigidity renders it breakable, exposing the self to that which it can no longer process. It is only Shakespeare's protagonists – Hamlet, Othello, Lear, and Lady Macbeth – as characters whose role-playing is precarious and whose naked humanity is therefore most vulnerable, who are capable of true madness. Their foils are immune to madness, precisely because they are too thoroughly engrossed in their protective roles for an underlying self ever to be exposed in its naked frailty. Lear in his madness thus stands in contrast to Gloucester, who naïvely wishes he could go mad like Lear, mistaking madness for a protection against pain when it is in fact an exposure to it:

> The King is mad: how stiff is my vile sense,
> That I stand up, and have ingenious feeling
> Of my huge sorrows! Better I were distract:

So should my thoughts be severed from my griefs,
And woes by wrong imaginations lose
The knowledge of themselves.

(IV.vi.284–9)

Like his nakedness – to which it is the psychological correlative – Lear's madness also stands in contrast to Edgar's stagey and conventional madtalk of 'sin' and 'foul fiends'. Edgar's 'madness', as a role based upon a wholly traditional and external view of madness as demonic possession, is actually the antithesis of the true madness of Lear, since the latter arises from the breakdown of roles whereas the former is itself a role and therefore a protection against a maddening overperception. Like Edgar's mock-beggary, also deriving from a long tradition of moral iconography, his mock-madness is thus a shadow or parody of 'the thing itself'. It has the status of a sign emptied of its significance and divorced from the realities of nakedness and madness to which it refers, the absent referent in both cases being supplied by Lear. Within the universe of Shakespearean tragedy, madness is thus the opposite pole to morality, a vision of undifferentiated anarchy as opposed to one of a wholly mapped-out order.

The temptation at this point is to grant this vision of madness and absurdity a privileged status and equate it with the meaning of the play. But this tendency is only the modernist counterpart of the archaeological tendency to do the same with the earlier vision of morality, and is no more valid. Because Lear's vision of madness is an inversion of his vision of morality, it remains dependent on it, derives its terms from it, and is capable of being turned back into it. This is exactly what happens, for neither morality nor madness constitutes a resting-point for Lear or Shakespeare, and both are left behind on the way to a truer, more austere mimesis. The fact is that Lear is able to maintain neither the complacent vision he shared with his society at the beginning nor the painful counter-vision he comes to in his alienation, though he tries desperately to maintain each in turn. For when he awakens from his ordeal in the presence of Cordelia, he would seem to have renounced his restless probing for a demystified and naturalistic explanation of his world. Cordelia seems to him 'a soul in bliss', his madness the infernal or purgatorial punishment of 'a wheel of fire', and his recovery nothing less than a resurrection wrought by this 'spirit' to whom he now kneels and prays for benediction. Not only has Lear renounced his maddening effort to explain the world, to find out its true causes, he has renounced the world itself. In a spirit of *contemptus mundi*, he resigns all interest in the vindication he had formerly tried to call down on his persecutors, leaving them to 'The good years' (V.iii.24) of plague and pestilence to be devoured in due course. He welcomes his life with Cordelia in prison with a religious joy, as if it were a posthumous or monastic existence removed from the mutability of earthly life. Indeed, Lear has awakened to find himself, like several converted morality protagonists before him, clothed in the fresh garments traditionally emblematic of an inner and spiritual reaccommodation.[7] Nowhere in the play is the return to an older morality vision so pure and complete, so strenuously and extra-vagantly re-enacted – for we are still in the realm of histrionic recreation – as it is by Lear himself at the start of the final act. The play has all but reunited with its prototype, the wheel of interpretation come full circle.

If *King Lear* had ended here, we should still have had to say that Shakespeare has altered his sources significantly and, in so doing, achieved a representation of human depth and complexity quite beyond them and very much of the order of displaced Christian vision ascribed to the play by Bradley and Mack. But the final stage in the process of mimetic realisation toward which the play moves consists in a still more radical putting into question of all prior visions – the vision of morality taken over from its sources and the counter-vision of madness introduced by Shakespeare alike – and that process has at this point only begun. For when Lear re-enters shortly afterward with Cordelia in his arms, he no longer speaks in the recovered language of morality but in his earlier language of madness: 'Howl, howl, howl, howl . . . / I know when one is dead and when one lives; / She's dead as earth' (V.iii.259–63). Yet by the end of this speech, he is calling for a looking-glass in the hope of life, which he then discovers in the very terms of Christian mystery: 'This feather stirs; she lives. If it be so, / It is a chance which does redeem all sorrows / That ever I have felt' (V.iii.267–9). Again, the play might well have ended here on this act of recuperation, however tentative, of the older vision. But it does not: 'A plague upon you, murderers, traitors all! / I might have saved her. . . .' Or it could have ended soon afterward with Albany's assertion, however muted, of a restored justice of rewards and punishments. But it does not:

And my poor fool is hanged: no, no, no life?
Why should a dog, a horse, a rat have life,
And thou no breath at all? Thou'lt come no more,
Never, never, never, never, never.
Pray you, undo this button. Thank you, sir.

(V.iii.307–11)

Lear's fluctuation between the visions of morality and madness, meaning and absurdity, accommodation and disaccommodation becomes dizzying in its intensity. But still it seems to go on: 'Do you see this? Look on her. Look, her lips, / Look there, look there.' These parting lines might well be interpreted as another and final access of faith or delusion, yet they are themselves remarkably free of the mythologisations of either morality or madness, which have been only preludes to this moment and are now left behind. Lear's language and gesture now proceed not out of a convention of vision but out of a depth and fullness of feeling that is unquestionably 'there' but unfathomable in its inwardness. His last lines merely point to a form that has also been 'there' all along, though repeatedly misconstrued and overlooked, with no longer any attempt to define it. In the end, the play renounces its own mediations of morality and madness alike and redirects our attention to an undetermined reality that exists prior to and remains unavailable to both.

In the play that has come to be regarded as the definitive achievement of Shakespearean tragedy, Shakespeare has certainly not made things easy for us. For he leaves us in the end with not a choice of *either* morality and meaning *or* madness and absurdity, but more like an ultimatum of *neither* morality and meaning *nor* madness and absurdity, an ultimatum that becomes inescapable as a result of Lear's own strenuous and futile effort to remain within the realm of choice. Lear enacts in advance our own dilemma as interpreters, alternating between antithetical visions of experience, only to abandon both in favour of a pure and simple pointing to the thing itself. Interpreters of the play, like Albany, Kent, and Edgar within it, have been understandably reluctant to follow him into this state of aporia, of being completely at a loss, so peremptory is the human need to make sense of things, to find unity, coherence, resolution in the world of the text and the text of the world. Yet the aporia toward which not only *Lear*, but Shakespeare's other great tragedies, move represents the very negation of the possibility of unity, coherence, and resolution, of the accommodation that all our systems of explanation provide, be they pious or modernist, consoling or painful, older or newer. In his dizzying fluctuation between contradictory meanings, Lear re-enacts the intense shifting between demystification and remystification of the self we see in Othello's closing speech, which also ends with an act of pointing. We see a similar movement in Hamlet's division between a last-gasp impulse to shape and tell his story – 'O, I could tell you!' – and his equal and opposite impulse to repudiate self-mythologisation altogether and return his play to the status of the most inexplicable dumb-show of all – 'The rest is silence.' Yet this very process of casting off inherited forms and imposed meanings to point to the thing itself only invites their reimposition. Like Horatio and Fortinbras, Cassio and Lodovico, Edgar and Albany, we feel we still can and must report Hamlet's story to the world and tell Othello and Lear who they are, even though they themselves, possessed of larger, tougher, and finer minds than we, have anticipated our attempt and thrown up their hands. The characters we *can* denote truly – Laertes, Cassio, Gloucester – do not ask to be told who they are, for such characters are content to remain within the defining forms that tradition provides and that society, with the wisdom of self-preservation, maintains as 'true'. Unlike his interpreters and his own choric commentators, however, Shakespeare never succumbs to the rhetorical pressure of the traditional forms he employs, to their built-in claim to have made sense of the world, but keeps them always in brackets and puts them ultimately into question. The Shakespearean text remains a step ahead of its critics, even at the very moment we think we have caught up with it.

From Howard Felperin, *Shakespearean Representation: Mimesis and Modernity in Elizabethan Tragedy* (Princeton, 1977), pp. 87–106.

NOTES

[The source of this essay was one of the first sustained attempts to apply poststructuralist thinking and the deconstructive method to Shakespeare. The book acknowledges a direct debt to leading figures of the so-called Yale school of deconstruction, in particular Paul de Man, Geoffrey Hartman and Harold Bloom. There is a lively, critical exposition of their position in Terry Eagleton, *Literary Theory* (Oxford, 1983), pp. 145–6, and a fuller but still concise introduction in chapter 6 of Christopher Norris, *Deconstruction:*

Theory and Practice (London, 1982). A distinctive assumption of the Yale school is that great literature like *Lear* has already anticipated any deconstruction of its concerns the modern critic might wish to inflict on it, and that this process of self-deconstruction ultimately becomes its own most profound theme. Hence Felperin's demonstration of how *King Lear* undermines the twin perspectives it constructs to make sense of reality concludes that at the close 'Lear enacts in advance our own dilemma as interpreters, alternating between antithetical visions of experience, only to abandon both in favour of a pure and simple pointing to the thing itself'. Felperin has since published a book entitled *Beyond Deconstruction* (Oxford, 1985).

Textual quotations are from Alfred Harbage (ed.), *The Complete Pelican Shakespeare* (Baltimore, 1969). Ed.]

1. O. J. Campbell, 'The Salvation of Lear', *English Literary History*, 15 (1948), 107. A useful review of Christian and existentialist, optimist and pessimist readings of the play is provided by William R. Elton in the opening chapter of his study of its renaissance theological content and context, *King Lear and the Gods* (San Marino, Calif., 1966).

2. *King Lear in Our Time* (Berkeley, 1965), p. 117.

3. L. C. Knights, 'The Question of Character in Shakespeare', in John Garrett (ed.), *More Talking of Shakespeare* (London, 1959). p. 66. The *locus classicus* of this view within Shakespearean criticism is to be found in A. C. Bradley: 'The secondary plot fills out a story which would by itself have been somewhat thin. . . . This repetition does not simply double the pain with which the tragedy is witnessed: it startles and terrifies by suggesting that the folly of Lear and the ingratitude of his daughters are no accidents or merely individual aberrations, but in that dark cold world some fateful malignant influence is abroad, turning the hearts of the fathers against their children and of the children against their fathers, smiting the earth with a curse, so that the brother gives the brother to death and the father the son, blinding the eyes, maddening the brain, freezing the springs of pity, numbing all powers except the nerves of anguish and the dull lust of life' (*Shakespearean Tragedy* [1904; reprinted New York, 1955], pp. 210–11). Like Mack and most others, Bradley transfers the superstitious or pious view of moral causality expressed by Gloucester onto the Lear action and proceeds to expound that view in the rhetoric of Christian homiletic.

4. Bradley, for example, lists a number of 'improbabilities' and 'inconsistencies' in the play: Edmund's ruse of writing a letter when he and Edgar live in the same house; Gloucester's journey to Dover to destroy himself when he might have done it closer to home; Edgar's unexplained decision not to reveal himself to his father; and so on. Bradley does state, however, that the improbabilities he lists are 'particularly noticeable in the secondary plot' (ibid., pp. 207–8).

5. Despite the pervasiveness of the critical tendency to assimilate the two
    actions to one another, a nagging sense of tonal and structural differ-
    ence is expressed by some critics. Bradley himself qualifies his assertion
    of a mutually reinforcing parallelism by stating that the subplot 'pro-
    vides a most effective contrast between its personages and those of the
    main plot, the tragic strength and stature of the latter being heightened
    by comparison with the slighter build of the former' (ibid., pp. 210–11).
    See, for example, Alvin B. Kernan, 'Formalism and Realism in Eliza-
    bethan Drama: The Miracles in *King Lear*', *Renaissance Drama*, 9
    (1966), 59–66; Sigurd Burckhardt, *Shakespearean Meanings* (Princeton,
    1968), pp. 237–59; and Richard Levin, *The Multiple Plot in English
    Renaissance Drama* (Chicago, 1971), pp. 12–13. The 'grotesque awk-
    wardness', 'mediacy', and 'externality' which these critics respectively
    find in the subplot are all a function of its deliberate archaism and
    conventionality in contrast to the main plot.

6. In contrast to the easy volubility and willing credulity with which the
    characters of the subplot express and accept a moral for all occasions,
    Lear repeatedly displays a problematic relation to language itself almost
    from the beginning:

    > Who is it that can tell me who I am?
    > (I.iv.236)

    > I can scarce speak to thee. Thou'lt not believe
    > With how depraved a quality – O Regan!
    > (II.iv.135–6)

    > I will have such revenges on you both
    > That all the world shall – I will do such things –
    > What they are, yet I know not; but they shall be
    > The terrors of the earth.
    > (II.iv.278–81)

    > Howl, howl, howl, howl! O you are men of stones:
    > Had I your tongues and eyes, I'd use them so
    > That heaven's vault should crack.
    > (V.iii.259–61)

    These failures of speech, stammerings, outcries have no counterpart
    among the characters of the subplot, who are never at a loss for words.
    They point to a larger frustration and failure on the part of the princi-
    pals – for Cordelia has foreseen the condition Lear discovers – to find
    an expressive form for feeling and action in the dramatic language of
    morality convention. By contrast, even Gloucester's 'despair' is cogently
    expressed, and his own wavering between despair and faith is more a
    parody than a parallel of Lear's fluctuations. The 'ill thoughts' he falls
    into after Edgar has indoctrinated him at Dover may correspond to

Lear's own relapses into incoherence after his recuperation in the presence of Cordelia, but whereas Gloucester's wavering "twixt joy and grief' is finally and happily resolved into joy as his heart bursts 'smilingly', Lear's desperate fluctuation between morality and madness, as we shall see, goes too deep to achieve resolution.

7.   In the early morality, *Wisdom, Who Is Christ* (1425), for example, the regeneration of the protagonist Anima is marked by the following stage direction. 'Here entrethe ANIMA, wyth the Fyve Wyttys goynge before, MYNDE on the on syde and WNDYRSTONDYNGE on the other syde and WYLL followyng, all in here fyrst clothynge . . .' (Mark Eccles [ed.], *The Macro Plays* [Oxford, 1969], p. 149.) On the significance of changes of costume in morality tradition, see T. W. Craik, *The Tudor Interlude: Stage, Costume and Acting* (Leicester, 1967), pp. 49–92. Shakespeare calls attention to the fresh garments worn by his protagonists in similar moments of reunion and restoration in *Pericles* and *The Tempest*.

3

The Patriarchal Bard: Feminist Criticism and 'King Lear'

KATHLEEN McLUSKIE

Tragedy assumes the existence of 'a permanent, universal and essentially unchanging human nature'[1] but the human nature implied in the moral and aesthetic satisfactions of tragedy is most often explicitly male. In *King Lear* for example, the narrative and its dramatisation present a connection between sexual insubordination and anarchy, and the connection is given an explicitly misogynist emphasis.

The action of the play, the organisation of its points of view and the theatrical dynamic of its central scenes all depend upon an audience accepting an equation between 'human nature' and male power. In order to experience the proper pleasures of pity and fear, they must accept that fathers are owed particular duties by their daughters and be appalled by the chaos which ensues when those primal links are broken. Such a point of view is not a matter of consciously-held opinion but it is a position required and determined by the text in order for it to make sense. It is also the product of a set of meanings produced in a specific way by the Shakespearean text and is different from that produced in other versions of the story.

The representation of patriarchal misogyny is most obvious in the treatment of Goneril and Regan. In the chronicle play *King Leir*, the sisters' villainy is much more evidently a function of the plot. Their mocking pleasure at Cordella's downfall takes the form of a comic double act and Regan's evil provides the narrative with the exciting twist of an attempt on Lear's life.[2] In the Shakespearean text by contrast, the narrative, language and dramatic organisation all define the sisters' resistance to their father in terms of their gender, sexuality and position within the family. Family relations in this play are seen as fixed and determined, and any movement within them is portrayed as a destructive reversal of rightful order (see I.iv). Goneril's and Regan's treatment of their father merely reverses existing patterns of rule and is seen not simply as cruel and selfish but as a fundamental violation of human nature – as is made powerfully explicit in the speeches which condemn them (III.vii.101–3; IV.ii. 32–50). Moreover when Lear in his madness fantasises about the collapse of law and the destruction of ordered social control, women's lust is vividly represented as the centre and source of the ensuing corruption (IV.vi.110–28). The generalised character of Lear's and Albany's vision of chaos, and the poetic force with which it is expressed, creates the appearance of truthful universality which is an important part of the play's claim to greatness. However, that generalised vision of chaos is present in gendered terms in which patriarchy, the institution of male power in the family and the State, is seen as the only form of social organisation strong enough to hold chaos at bay.

The close links between misogyny and patriarchy define the women in the play more precisely. Goneril and Regan are not presented as archetypes of womanhood for the presence of Cordelia 'redeems nature from the general curse' (IV.vi.209). However, Cordelia's saving love, so much admired by critics, works in the action less as a redemption for womankind than as an example of patriarchy restored. Hers, of course, is the first revolt against Lear's organising authority. The abruptness of her refusal to play her role in Lear's public drama dramatises the outrage of her denial of conformity and the fury of Lear's ensuing appeal to archetypal forces shows that a rupture of 'Propinquity and property of blood' is tantamount to the destruction of nature itself. Cordelia, however, is the central focus of emotion in the scene. Her resistance to her father gains audience assent through her two asides during her sisters' performances; moreover the limits of that resistance are clearly indicated. Her first defence is not a statement on her personal autonomy or the rights of her individual will: it is her right to retain a part of her love for 'that lord whose hand must take my plight'. Lear's rage thus seems unreasonable in that he recognises only his rights as a father; for the patriarchal family to continue, it must also recognise the rights of future fathers and accept the transfer of women from fathers to husbands. By the end of the scene, Cordelia is reabsorbed into the patriarchal family by marriage to which her resistance to Lear presents no barrier. As she reassures the king of France:

> It is no vicious blot, murder or foulness,
> No unchaste action or dishonoured step
> That hath deprived me of your grace and favour.
> (I.i.228–31)

Her right to be included in the ordered world of heterosexual relations depends upon her innocence of the ultimate human violation of murder which is paralleled with the ultimate sexual violation of unchastity.

However, any dispassionate analysis of the mystification of real socio-sexual relations in *King Lear* is the antithesis of our response to the tragedy in the theatre where the tragic power of the play endorses its ideological position at every stage. One of the most important and effective shifts in the action is the transfer of our sympathy back to Lear in the middle of the action. The long sequence of Act II, scene iv dramatises the process of Lear's decline from the angry autocrat of Act I to the appealing figure of pathetic insanity. The psychological realism of the dramatic writing and the manipulation of the point of view forge the bonds between Lear as a complex character and the sympathies of the audience.

The audience's sympathies are engaged by Lear's fury at the insult offered by Kent's imprisonment and by the pathos of Lear's belated attempt at self-control (II.iv.101–4). His view of the action is further emotionally secured by his sarcastic enactment of the humility which his daughters recommend.

> Do you but mark how this becomes the house:
> Dear daughter, I confess that I am old.
> Age is unnecessary. On my knees I beg
> That you'll vouchsafe me raiment, bed and food.
> (II.iv.53–6)

As Regan says, these are unsightly tricks. Their effect is to close off the dramatic scene by offering the only alternative to Lear's behaviour as we see it. The dramatic fact becomes the only fact and the audience is thus positioned to accept the tragic as inevitable, endorsing the terms of Lear's great poetic appeal:

> O reason not the need! Our basest beggars
> Are in the poorest things superfluous.
> Allow not nature more than nature needs,
> Man's life is cheap as beast's.
> (II.iv.263–6)

The ideological power of Lear's speech lies in his invocation of nature to support his demands on his daughters; its dramatic power lies in its movement from argument to desperate assertion of his crumbling humanity as the abyss of madness approaches. However, once again, that humanity is seen in gendered terms as Lear appeals to the gods to

> touch me with noble anger,
> And let not women's weapons, water drops
> Stain my man's cheeks.
> (II.iv.275–7)

The theatrical devices which secure Lear as the centre of the audience's emotional attention operate even more powerfully in the play's denouement. The figure of Cordelia is used as a channel for the response to her suffering father. Her part in establishing the terms of the conflict is over by Act I; when she reappears it is as an emblem of dutiful pity. Before she appears on stage, she is described by a 'gentleman' whose speech reconstructs her as a static, almost inanimate daughter of sorrows. The poetic paradoxes of his speech construct Cordelia as one who resolves contradiction,[3] which is her potential role in the narrative and her crucial function in the ideological coherence of the text:

> patience and sorrow strove
> Who should express her goodliest. You have seen
> Sunshine and rain at once: her smiles and tears
> Were like a better way: those happy smilets
> That played on her ripe lip seemed not to know
> What guests were in her eyes, which parted thence
> As pearls from diamonds dropped.
> (IV.iii.15–23)

With Cordelia's reaction pre-empted by the gentleman, the scene where Lear and Cordelia meet substitutes the pleasure of pathos for suspense. The imagery gives Cordelia's forgiveness divine sanction, and the realism of Lear's struggle for sanity closes off any responses other than complete engagement with the characters' emotions. Yet in this encounter Cordelia denies the dynamic of the whole play. Lear fears that she cannot love him:

> for your sisters
> Have, as I do remember, done me wrong.
> You have some cause, they have not.
> (IV.vii.73–5)

But Cordelia demurs with 'No cause, no cause'.

Shakespeare's treatment of this moment contrasts with that of the earlier chronicle play from which he took a number of details, including Lear kneeling and being raised. In the old play the scene is almost comic as Leir and Cordella kneel and rise in counterpoint to their arguments about who most deserves blame.[4] The encounter is used to sum up the issues and the old play allows Cordella a much more active role in weighing her debt to Leir. In Shakespeare's text, however, the spectacle of suffering obliterates the past action so that the audience with Cordelia will murmur 'No cause, no cause'. Rather than a resolution of the action, their reunion becomes an emblem of possible harmony, briefly glimpsed before the tragic debacle.

The deaths of Lear and Cordelia seem the more shocking for this moment of harmony but their tragic impact is also a function of thwarting the narrative expectation of harmony restored which is established by the text's folk-tale structure.[5] The folk-tale of the love test provides an underlying pattern in which harmony is broken by the honest daughter and restored by her display of forgiveness. The organisation of the Shakespearean text intensifies and then denies those expectations so as once more to insist on the connection between evil women and a chaotic world.

The penultimate scene opposes the ordered formality of the resolution of the Gloucester plot with the unseemly disorder of the women's involvement. The twice-repeated trumpet call, the arrival of a mysterious challenger in disguise, evoke the order of a chivalric age when conflict was resolved by men at arms. The women, however, act as disrupters of that order: Goneril attempts to deny the outcome of the tourney, grappling in an unseemly quarrel with Albany (V.iii.156–8) and their ugly deaths interrupt Edgar's efforts to close off the narrative with a formal account of his part in the story and Gloucester's death.

Thus the deaths of Lear and Cordelia are contrasted with and seem almost a result of the destructiveness of the wicked sisters. Albany says of them: 'This judgement of the heavens, that makes us tremble, / Touches us not with pity' (V.iii.233–4). The tragic victims, however, affect us quite differently. When Lear enters, bearing his dead daughter in his arms, we are presented with a contrasting emblem of the natural, animal assertion of family love, destroyed by the anarchic forces of lust and the 'indistinguished space of woman's will'. At this point in the play the most stony-hearted feminist could not withhold her pity even though it is called forth at the expense of her resistance to the patriarchal relations which it endorses.

The effect of these dramatic devices is to position the audience as a coherent whole, comfortably situated *vis-à-vis* the text. To attempt to shift that position by denying Lear's rights as a father and a man would be to deny the pity of Lear's suffering and the pleasurable reaffirmation of one's humanity through sympathetic fellow feeling. A feminist reading of the text cannot simply assert the countervailing rights of Goneril and Regan, for to do so would simply reverse the emotional structures of the play, associating feminist ideology with atavistic selfishness and the monstrous assertion of individual wills. Feminism cannot simply take 'the woman's part' when that part has been so morally loaded and theatrically circumscribed. Nor is any purpose served by merely denouncing the text's misogyny, for *King Lear*'s position at the centre of the Shakespeare canon is assured by its continual reproduction in education and the theatre and is un-likely to be shifted by feminist sabre-rattling.

A more fruitful point of entry for feminism is in the process of the text's reproduction. As Elizabeth Cowie and others have pointed out,[6] sexist meanings are not fixed but depend upon constant repro-duction by their audience. In the case of *King Lear* the text is tied to misogynist meaning only if it is reconstructed with its emotional power and its moral imperatives intact. Yet the text contains pos-sibilities for subverting these meanings and the potential for re-constructing them in feminist terms.

The first of these lies in the text's historical otherness; for in spite of constant critical assertion of its transcendent universality, specific connections can be shown between Shakespeare's text and contem-porary material and ideological conflict without presenting a merely reductive account of artistic production in terms of material circum-stances.[7]

Discussing the 'gerontocratic ideal', for example, Keith Thomas has noted that 'The sixteenth and seventeenth centuries are conspicu-ous for a sustained desire to subordinate persons in their teens and twenties and to delay their equal participation in the adult world

. . . such devices were also a response to the mounting burden of population on an unflexible economy'.[8] This gerontocratic ideal was not without contradiction, for the very elderly were removed from economic and political power and 'essentially it was men in their forties or fifties who ruled'.[9] Moreover the existence of this ideal did not obviate the need for careful material provision for the elderly. There is a certain poignancy in the details of wills which specify the exact houseroom and the degree of access to the household fire which is to be left to aged parents.[10] However, this suggests that Lear's and his daughter's bargaining over the number of his knights need not be seen as an egregious insult and that the generational conflict within the nuclear family could not be resolved by recourse to a simply accepted ideal of filial piety.

As a corrective to prevailing gloomy assessments of the happiness of the early modern family, Keith Wrightson has produced evidence of individuals who show considerable concern to deal with family conflict in a humane and flexible fashion.[11] But it is equally clear from his evidence that family relations were the focus of a great deal of emotional energy and the primary source both of pleasure and pain. This is also borne out in Michael MacDonald's account of a seventeenth-century psychiatric practice in which, as today, women were more susceptible to mental illness than men:

> Not all the stress women suffered was caused by physical illness . . . women were also more vulnerable than men to psychologically disturbing social situations. Their individual propensities to anxiety and sadness were enhanced by patriarchal custom and values that limited their ability to remedy disturbing situations . . . Napier and his troubled patients also believed that oppression made people miserable and even mad, but the bondage they found most troubling subordinated daughters to parents, wives to husbands rather than peasants to lords.[12]

This discussion of social history cannot propose an alternative 'interpretation' of the text or assert its true meaning in the light of historical 'facts'. Rather it indicates that the text was produced within the contradictions of contemporary ideology and practice and suggests that similar contradictions exist within the play. These contradictions could fruitfully be brought to bear in modern criticism and productions. The dispute between Lear and his daughters is in part concerned with love and filial gratitude but it also dramatises the tense relationship between those bonds and the material circumstances in which they function. Lear's decision to publish his daughter's dowries is so 'that future strife / May be prevented now': the connection between loving harmony and economic justice is the accepted factor which underlies the formal patterning of the opening scene and is disrupted only by Cordelia's asides which introduce a notion of love as a more individual and abstract concept, incompatible both with public declaration and with computation of forests, champains, rivers and meads. Cordelia's notion of love gained precedence in modern ideology but it seriously disrupts Lear's discussion of property and inheritance. When Lear responds with 'Nothing will come of nothing' his words need not be delivered as an angry calling to account: they could equally be presented as a puzzled reaction to an inappropriate idea. Moreover Cordelia is not opposing hereditary duty to transcendent love – she does not reply 'There's beggary in the love that can be reckoned'. When she expands on her first assertion her legal language suggests a preference for a limited, contractual relationship: 'I love your majesty / According to my bond, no more nor less' (I.i.94–5). The conflict between the contractual model and the patriarchal model of subjects' obligations to their king was at issue in contemporary political theory[13] and Cordelia's words here introduce a similar conflict into the question of obligations within the family.

When in Act II Lear again bargains with his daughters, a similar confusion between affective relations and contractual obligations is in play. Lear asserts the importance of the contractual agreement made with his daughters, for it is his only remaining source of power. Since they are now in control, Goneril and Regan can assert an apparently benign notion of service which does not depend on contract or mathematical computation:

> What need you five and twenty? ten? or five?
> To follow in a house where twice so many
> Have a command to tend you?
> (II.iv.259–62)

The emotional impact of the scene, which is its principal power in modern productions, simply confuses the complex relations between personal autonomy, property and power which are acted out in this confrontation. The scene could be directed to indicate that the daughters' power over Lear is the obverse of his former power over them. His power over them is socially sanctioned but its arbitrary and tyrannical character is clear from his treatment of Cordelia. Lear kneeling to beg an insincere forgiveness of Regan is no more nor less 'unsightly' than Goneril's and Regan's formal protestations to their father. Both are the result of a family organisation which denies economic autonomy in the name of transcendent values of love and filial piety and which affords no rights to the powerless within it. Such a production of meaning offers the pleasure of understanding in place of the pleasure of emotional identification. In this context Lear's speeches about nature and culture are part of an argument, not a *cri de coeur*; the blustering of his threats is no longer evidence of the destruction of a man's self-esteem but the futile anger of a powerful man deprived of male power.

Further potential for comically undermining the focus on Lear is provided by the Fool, who disrupts the narrative movement of the action, subverting if not denying the emotional impact of the scenes in which he appears. In an important sense the Fool is less an *alter ego* for Lear than for his daughters: like them he reminds Lear and the audience of the material basis for the change in the balance of power. However, where they exploit Lear's powerlessness with cruelty and oppression he denies that necessity by his continued allegiance. In modern productions this important channel for an alternative view of events is closed off by holding the Fool within the narrative, using him as a means to heighten the emotional appeal of Lear's decline.[14]

The potential for subversive contradiction in the text is, however, restricted to the first part. Lear's madness and the extrusion of Gloucester's eyes heavily weight the action towards a simpler notion of a time when humanity must perforce prey upon itself like monsters of the deep, denying comic recognition of the material facts of existence. Yet even Cordelia's self-denying love or Gloucester's stoic resignation are denied the status of ideological absolutes. The grotesque comic lie of Gloucester's fall from Dover cliff is hardly a firm basis for a belief in the saving power of divine providence and Cordelia's acceptance of her father's claims on her is futile because it is unsupported by material power.

A production of the text which would restore the element of dialectic, removing the privilege both from the character of Lear and from the ideological positions which he dramatises, is crucial to a feminist critique. Feminist criticism need not restrict itself to privileging the woman's part or to special pleading on behalf of female characters. It can be equally well served by making a text reveal the conditions in which a particular ideology of femininity functions and by both revealing and subverting the hold which such an ideology has for readers both female and male.

The misogyny of King Lear, both the play and its hero, is constructed out of an ascetic tradition which presents women as the source of the primal sin of lust, combining with concerns about the threat to the family posed by female insubordination. However the text also dramatises the material conditions which lie behind assertions of power within the family, even as it expresses deep anxieties about the chaos which can ensue when that balance of power is altered.

An important part of the feminist project is to insist that the alternative to the patriarchal family and heterosexual love is not chaos but the possibility of new forms of social organisation and affective relationships. However, feminists also recognise that our socialisation within the family and, perhaps more importantly, our psychological development as gendered subjects make these changes no simple matter.[15] They involve deconstructing the sustaining comforts of love and the family as the only haven in a heartless world. Similarly a feminist critique of the dominant traditions in literature must recognise the sources of its power, not only in the institutions which reproduce them but also in the pleasures which they afford. But feminist criticism must also assert the power of resistance, subverting rather than co-opting the domination of the patriarchal Bard.

From Jonathan Dollimore and Alan Sinfield (eds), *Political Shakespeare: New Essays in Cultural Materialism* (Manchester, 1985), pp. 98–108.

NOTES

[The above extract is from a longer essay entitled 'The Patriarchal Bard: Feminist Criticism and Shakespeare: *King Lear* and *Measure for Measure*'. The volume in which it appeared was the first book of cultural materialist criticism devoted to Shakespeare. In their Foreword the editors define the philosophy informing the collection as based on the belief that 'a combination of historical context, theoretical method, political commitment and textual analysis offers the strongest challenge' to conventional critical practice:

Historical context undermines the transcendent significance traditionally accorded to the literary text and allows us to recover its histories;

theoretical method detaches the text from immanent criticism which seeks only to reproduce it in its own terms; socialist and feminist commitment confronts the conservative categories in which most criticism has hitherto been conducted; textual analysis locates the critique of traditional approaches where it cannot be ignored. We call this 'cultural materialism'. (p. vii)

The concern, moreover, is not only with the distant history of Shakespeare's time, but with the modern cultural uses to which Shakespeare's plays have been put, and with finding ways of making them serve more progressive political ends in the present. Kathleen McLuskie's essay on *King Lear* exemplifies perfectly this double strategy of historicising the text as a warrant for reading it against the grain of its supposed original intent and subsequent conservative appropriation. Ed.]

1. Raymond Williams, *Modern Tragedy* (London, 1966), p. 45.

2. See *The True Chronicle History of King Leir*, in Geoffrey Bullough (ed.), *The Narrative and Dramatic Sources of Shakespeare*, VII (London, 1973), pp. 337–402.

3. The imagery of ll. 12–14 gives this resolution a political tinge; resolution is seen as subjection.

4. See *The True Chronicle History of King Leir*, in Geoffrey Bullough (ed.), *The Narrative and Dramatic Sources of Shakespeare*, VII (London, 1973), p. 393.

5. Freud in 'The Theme of the Three Caskets' accounts for the psychological power of the myth in terms of 'the three inevitable [sic] relations that a man has with a woman – the woman who bears him, the woman who is his mate and the woman who destroys him'. Lear's entrance with Cordelia dead in his arms is, for Freud, a wish-fulfilling inversion of the old man being carried away by death. See Ernest Jones (ed.), *The Collected Papers of Sigmund Freud*, IV (London, 1925), pp. 245–56.

6. 'The problem of stereotyping is not that it is true or false, distorting or manipulated, but that it closes off certain productions of meaning in the image' (Elizabeth Cowie, 'Images of Women', *Screen Education*, 23 [1977], 22).

7. Bullough has drawn attention to 'the remarkable historical parallel' of the case of Sir Brian Annesley, whose daughter Cordell took steps to prevent her sister declaring their father insane so that she could take over the management of his estate. Cordell Annesley's solution was that a family friend should be entrusted with the old man and his affairs. See Geoffrey Bullough (ed.), *The Narrative and Dramatic Sources of Shakespeare*, VII (London, 1973), p. 270.

8. Keith Thomas, 'Age and Authority in Early Modern England', *Proceedings of the British Academy*, 62 (1976), 214.

9. Ibid., 211.

10. Discussed in Margaret Spufford, *Contrasting Communities: English Villagers in the Sixteenth and Seventeenth Centuries* (Cambridge, 1974), p. 113.

11. See Keith Wrightson, *English Society 1580–1680* (London, 1982), ch. 4.

12. Michael MacDonald, *Mystical Bedlam: Madness, Anxiety and Healing in Seventeenth-Century England* (Cambridge, 1981), pp. 39–40.

13. See Gordon Schochet, *Patriarchalism in Political Thought* (Oxford, 1975).

14. For example, in the 1982–3 Royal Shakespeare Company production Antony Sher played the fool as a vaudeville clown, but the theatrical inventiveness of his double-act with Lear emphasised the closeness of their relationship with the fool as a ventriloquist's dummy on Lear's knee.

15. See Michele Barrett and Mary McIntosh, *The Anti-Social Family* (London, 1982).

4

The Theatre of Punishment

LEONARD TENNENHOUSE

I

King Lear perplexes readers in those places where what is done can only be for the purpose of purifying the iconography of the Elizabethan theatre. This is to suggest *King Lear* has proved troubling to critics mainly because of the political consequences which unfold when the monarch divests himself of the patriarchal prerogatives traditionally inhering in his body. This attempt on Lear's part to retain only this symbolic status as king initiates events which defy our notion of psychological motivation. For Shakespeare's audience these scenes must have been disturbing too. But the seventeenth-century theatre-goer would have been disturbed for the very reason that the political meaning of dramatic events was sharply apparent. For us, in contrast, that meaning has been lost over the course of time, its traces further obscured by several centuries of literary interpretation, and the behaviour displayed on the stage consequently cries out for a 'depth' interpretation.

Aside from its obvious kinship to such a work as *Gorboduc*, Shakespeare's play draws most heavily upon another Elizabethan source, *The True Chronicle Historie of King Leir*, for the Lear story. Sidney's account of the blind king of Paphlagonia in *The Countess of Pembroke's Arcadia* inspired much of the Gloucester story. Shakespeare obviously felt obliged to revise these Elizabethan materials for a historically later audience, for the Jacobean Lear forfeits the Crown's prerogative to control the exchange of daughters along with the power to distribute property. Gone, too, is an Elizabethan teleology that reunited an internally divided state by means of outside intervention. It is this notion of providence, among other things, that makes the source *King Leir* at one with other Elizabethan chronicle history plays. However outnumbered, the army of Gallia succeeds in the Elizabethan *Leir* when, as Cornwall says, 'The day is lost, our friends do all revolt, / And joyne against us with the adverse part . . .' (lines 2616–17).[1] In Shakespeare's revision of the story, however, neither Edmund nor Cordelia can be successful in these earlier terms. When they try to play the upstart challenger and redemptive outsider respectively, each fails to seize the kingdom. They collapse before the forces which providence has lined up in support of patriarchal power.

Shakespeare's most telling revision of Elizabethan materials has to do with the division of the kingdom and the events that unfold as a consequence, for it is with this that he raises the whole issue of what the monarchy is. In *King Leir* the crown is merely property: it can be divided, willed, used as surety for a loan, and – as the play takes pains to demonstrate – treated as dowry to be divided equally among the three daughters for their jointure. As property, it could be subjected to laws governing the distribution of property or even be seized by force. As in the history plays, the crown goes to whoever could seize the signs and symbols of kingship and also command popular support. Like the resolution of any other Elizabethan chronicle history, then, the outnumbered and undervalued King of Gallia successfully overcomes the combined British forces to win the kingdom for Leir; true power displays itself in the effective exercise of physical force through competition and is subsequently ratified by an outpouring of popular support for the displaced king.

The older play, of course, is a chronicle history and not a tragedy. Yet even when it entertains the possibility of a tragic complication, in doing so *Leir* takes a peculiarly Elizabethan turn. The threat to the kingdom, for one thing, is imagined as the dismemberment of the aristocratic body. Leir's prophetic dream of his murder reveals each of his daughters, in his words, 'brandishing a Faulchion in their hand, / Ready to lop a lymme off where it fell / and in their hands a naked poynyard, / Wherewith they stabd me in a hundred places . . .' (1490–3). As it is figured forth in terms of dismemberment, such a threat to the old king is overturned with Cordella's restoration of the wounded body to 'perfit health'. Cordella's return at the end of the play prophetically reunites various parts of the state that have been fractured by competition. By way of contrast, Shakespeare's Jacobean version of the story interrogates the very notion of

the Crown as a corporate essence in perpetuity. His Lear thus poses
a threat to legitimate authority that had never been at issue before.
Out of this historically later contest between the king's two bodies,
a Jacobean thematics can be said to emerge. The metaphysics of the
Crown itself is called into question so that it may be displaced onto
the state as a ubiquitous presence which exists prior to and
ontologically different from any of its natural embodiments.

II

When James came to the throne, in the words of Marie Axton:

> Poets and dramatists worked up pageants for James's coronation,
> translating into icons the legal theory which had supported the new
> King. Their pageant iconography declared that it was not the land, or
> the estates of Parliament, but the King who represented the power of
> government and the perpetuity of the realm.[2]

As the new phoenix as well as 'England's Caesar', James was celebrated as the literal embodiment of the Crown in perpetuity, in
contradiction to the facts of history. Writing of James's coronation
pageant, Jonathan Goldberg has suggested that the major trope of
this pageant – indeed of James's entire reign – was that of 'revival';
James encouraged a belief in 'the monarch's ability to live beyond
himself'.[3] He welcomed representations of himself as the British
equivalent of the Roman emperor, and coins were struck to emphasise this connection. He enjoyed the title of *Rex Pacificus* and was
represented as the prince of peace, the new Augustus. 'In a Roman
matrix', Goldberg argues, 'James generated his "style of gods",
claiming deity as the emperors had done before him.'[4] In this environment, poets, playwrights, members of court, and members of
parliament, along with all those who saw the pageants or read
accounts of them, would have been aware of a new insistence on the
iconic nature of the king's body. James himself maintained that bond
was a much more literal one than Elizabeth had believed. He claimed
not only to have the only body whose blood united all of Britain but
also to exist in unbroken continuity with the tradition of monarchy.
And this Stuart mythology extended beyond the first heady public
pageant for the new king. The same year *King Lear* was probably
produced, 1605, Anthony Munday's lord mayor's pageant, *The Triumphs of Re-United Britannia*, included an account of the myth of

Brutus and his founding of England in which the monarch was celebrated as 'our second *Brute*, Royall King *James*'.[5]

In the first scene of *King Lear*, no one suggests Lear has violated the most important prohibition of his culture. Nor does anyone suggest that Lear is destroying the whole iconography of nationalism centred in the monarch's body. But this is indeed the threat such behaviour on the part of a monarch actually poses, for the terrible consequences of violating the patriarchal prerogative subsequently play themselves out on the stage. As in *Othello*, so in *Lear*, too, the fundamental cultural truth that tragedy affirms remains largely unstated. It is defined through its violation. Like the Elizabethan drama which preceded it, *Lear* insists on the iconic nature of the monarch's body, but the basis for establishing that iconic bond has changed. There is nothing explicitly illegal in what Lear proposes in the opening scene. The will of the monarch is the law. When the will of the king is to divest monarchy of power, the carnage that ensues implies that it is a primal law of nature that has been violated. By dividing up the monarchy, the powers which had been united in the monarch are separated into functions each of which – curiously enough – loses its efficacy once isolated from the others. Kent provides a handy summary of those features once bound together in Lear:

> Royal Lear
> Whom I have ever honor'd as my king,
> Lov'd as my father, as my master follow'd,
> As my great patron thought on in my prayers. . . .
> (I.i.139–42)

When he disperses his patrimony, Lear acts as if patronage no longer originates in the monarch; when he denounces Cordelia and hands her over in a dowerless marriage, he effectively renounces his role as *pater familias*; when he banishes Kent, he overturns the principle of fealty; and – perhaps more seriously than these – when he determines the rules of inheritance according to his will and not according to the principle of primogeniture, he appears to deny the metaphysics of the body politic and the special status of the king's blood. By dismantling his iconic body, Lear disperses these powers in a way that pits them against one another. This initiates a series of conflicts which threaten the stability of the state as well as the coherence of its signs and symbols.

It is precisely this separation of forms of power that makes Lear's retainers – seemingly a minor element in the play – a major issue which divides Lear and his daughters. When he resigns his throne, the retainers operate only as the symbols of a power once located in Lear. Detached from the legitimate right to exercise power, they suddenly pose a potential threat to legitimate authority. Rather than point to the harmony of a social order that is centred in the king and the displays of his court, then, Lear's retainers take on the features of carnival and inversion. Goneril says to Lear, 'your insolent retinue / Do hourly carp and quarrel, breaking forth / In rank and not-to-be endur'd riots' (I.iv.202–4). As a rationale for stripping him of his retainers, she poses the problem in these terms:

> Here do you keep a hundred knights and squires,
> Men so disorder'd, so debosh'd and bold,
> That this our court, infected with their manners,
> Shows like a riotous inn. Epicurism and lust
> Makes it more like a tavern or a brothel
> Than a grac'd palace.
>
> (I.iv.241–6)

Rather than represent them in a stately processional mode, then, Goneril describes Lear's court in the very terms Shakespeare once used to represent Falstaff's carnivalesque excesses.

The history plays always included potentially disruptive forms of popular power marked by the features of carnival. Monarchs were successful to the degree they incorporated these carnivalesque elements within the official rituals of state. It has to be a significant moment, then, when the king's own retainers assimilate the dissolute features of a disruptive social force where once they would have opposed such a force in the name of political order. As the signs of state power, one finds that Lear's retainers exhibit a kind of invertibility which turns them back into the subversive forces of tavern and brothel that once opposed aristocratic signs of power. It is as if Shakespeare has allowed the components of kingship to devolve into the semiotic stuff of which they were made. But it is not in fact the inversion of patriarchal order that makes Lear's retainers so threatening. Shakespeare stresses that they have grown suddenly dangerous in that they threaten to revive an earlier form of monarchy. Goneril, for one, fears the retainers might exhibit fealty to the person of the monarch over and above the newer bureaucracy she has installed. To her such a possibility smacks of conspiracy against the state: 'Each buzz, each fancy, each complaint, dislike, / He may enguard his dotage with their pow'rs, / And hold our lives in mercy' (I.iv.325-7). To those who rule, signs of loyalty to the old king have become signs of illegitimate power.

Shakespeare appropriately links the king's retainers in metonymy with the disloyal Edgar. These two signs of legitimate authority – the embodiment of aristocratic blood in the legitimate heir and the display of a household retinue – come together as a narrative designed to explain the plot on Gloucester's life by his legitimate son:

> Regan What, did my father's godson seek your life?
> He whom my father nam'd, your Edgar?
> Glou. O lady, lady, shame would have it hid!
> Regan Was he not companion with the riotous knights
> That tended upon my father?
> Glou. I know not, madam. 'Tis too bad, too bad.
> Edmund Yes, madam, he was of that consort.
> Regan No marvel then, though he were ill affected:
> 'Tis they have put him on the old man's death,
> To have th' expense and waste of his revenues.
> (II.i.91-100)

These few statements concerning Lear's retainers may stand for the larger drama of disintegration of which they constitute but one part. As the material forms of state power are detached from their symbolic centre in the natural body of the monarch, their essential nature undergoes a sudden change, a change as sudden, that is, as the one which turns the king's retainers into a potential agency of misrule. His power having rested on land and title, when he renounces these, Lear also loses control over his daughters.

Violation of the principle of primogeniture, I have suggested, constitutes the most serious assault on the principle of patriarchy, for this violation challenges every Stuart king's right to sit. In particular, to deny primogeniture is to undermine the Stuart argument on the metaphysical body of power. In opposition to this argument, Lear behaves as if the sitting monarch alone determines the disposition of the crown without regard to primogeniture or to the laws of nature. This dissociation of kinship from kingship reverberates to the very core of Renaissance culture to challenge the belief which locates the metaphysical authority of the crown within the natural body of the ageing monarch. For this reason, as soon as Lear cancels out primogeniture, Gloucester finds Edgar's malevolence plausible. This story of the legitimate son turned against his father in rivalry no longer violates the law of nature once Gloucester construes nature itself not only as portending but even as authorising such a sundering of the patriarchal bond:

> These late eclipses in the sun and moon portend no good to us. Though the wisdom of nature can reason it thus and thus, yet nature finds itself scourg'd by the sequent effects. Love cools, friendship falls off, brothers divide: in cities, mutinies; in countries, discord; in palaces, treason; and the bond crack'd twixt son and father. This villain of mine comes under the prediction; there's son against father: the King falls from bias of nature; there's father against child.
>
> (I.ii.103–12)

Once Gloucester sees nature as a disorderly force which opposes the traditional order of state, he can not only misconceive the bastard as the legitimate son; he can also dispossess Edgar of birthright, blood, and family.

At this point, it should be noted that the crimes which make Lear's daughters monstrous are not, at least in the first half of the play, crimes of pollution. The crimes which make Goneril and Regan monsters are all crimes of ingratitude. Ingratitude, which might also describe Macbeth's offence, is characteristically a male crime arising from a patronage relationship in which the ungrateful client mistakes his patron's generosity for a lack of aristocratic largess. By making women into figures of 'monster ingratitude', Shakespeare both links them to and distinguishes them from those other women who are brutalised on the Jacobean stage. The fact that Lear's daughters are not initially subjected to spectacular scenes of torture for assaulting the king's body confirms again the political function such iconography served on the stage. The scene of punishment which fulfils the Jacobean pattern in this play is certainly the blinding of Gloucester. Cornwall gives the order, as Regan accuses the old duke of pollution.

> **Cornwall** Bind him, I say.
> **Regan**   Hard, hard. O filthy traitor.
> (III.vii.32)

Gloucester recognises his role in the drama which ensues – 'I am tied to th' stake, and I must stand the course' (III.vii.54), just as Cornwall plays out the part of his tormenter: 'Fellows, hold the chair, / Upon these eyes of thine I'll set my foot' (III.vii.67–8). Like Iago, Cornwall and Regan are writing their own death warrant on the body of their victim, but like Desdemona, Gloucester has offended a higher law. When he disowned his legitimate son and declared the bastard legitimate, Gloucester committed the same crime against the blood as that committed by the Duchess of Malfi or by Desdemona: he has included an extra member within the aristocratic body. In the scene of his punishment, then, Shakespeare completes the transposition begun when Lear's daughters became monsters of ingratitude. Having displaced the crime of ingratitude onto the female, Shakespeare locates pollution in the body of the male. This sexual transposition makes pollution and ingratitude into two forms of the same crime against the aristocratic body. Each one is a crime against patriarchy which explicitly challenges the metaphysics of the blood. By undergoing ritual punishment, Gloucester purifies the aristocratic body.

When Lear strips off his clothes to reveal himself as 'unaccommodated man', Shakespeare boldly reveals the natural body of the king as one that appears to bear little value in its own right. It has been stripped of retainers, patronage, patrilineal authority, the ability to raise an army, the power of the *pater familias*, and all the other features which attract the gaze of power. In and of itself, it is powerless. Lear has already equated clothing with his retainers, when he says to his daughter,

> Thou art a lady;
> If only to go warm were gorgeous,
> Why, nature needs not what thou gorgeous wear'st,
> Which scarcely keeps thee warm.
> (II.iv.267–70)

Observing this same principle, Shakespeare strips Lear of the symbolic surface he acquired by virtue of his blood and offers us a parodic version of kingship. He makes Lear hold a trial with a joint stool as defendant, for example, wander the countryside with a crown of wildflowers, and hold forth in a delirium on matters of government and the law. We can see how thoroughly Shakespeare has drained Elizabethan materials of their political power by such gestures. He does not consolidate power in a contender for the throne as the Elizabethan pattern would have had it. Instead, Shakespeare scatters the rituals of state after emptying them of all social content. To be sure, both *Gorboduc* and the Elizabethan *Leir* dramatise the conflicts arising from a divided kingdom. But theirs is just that, a kingdom internally divided, not one dispersed according to rules of kinship quite at odds with those which determine kingship.

Lear gives Albany and Cornwall territory, 'sway', 'revenue', and the execution of the rights and powers of the monarch. Attuned to Elizabethan representations of disorder, we might presume such behaviour would divide the kingdom against itself, but these are not the terms in which Shakespeare's Jacobean tragedy unfolds. He seems much more interested in depicting the consequences of severing the iconic bond between the powers inhering in the blood and the blood itself.

Detached from their legitimate source of power in his body, the instruments of state turn against the monarch. That they operate to subvert patriarchy creates a framework where the threat to legitimate power takes the form of pollution rather than dismemberment. By privileging kinship over kingship, Lear produces an unruly state where women can rule men, where daughters can rule their fathers, and where bastards can dispossess the aristocracy. That such disorder arises from the pollution of blood becomes explicit, finally, when the two unruly daughters lust for the bastard Edmund. And true to the logic of pollution too, *King Lear* itself enacts a purification of the blood that is first and foremost a purification of Shakespeare's sources. Shakespeare's play strips these sources of their Elizabethan features just as it strips Lear of all the cultural trappings of state power. Once scattered, the components of the monarch's body cannot be reassembled in quite the same way. We do not see contenders for the throne displaying and finally authorising their use of its power. In marked contrast with Elizabethan strategies, Shakespeare devalues the natural body of power in such a way as to lend state authority a metaphysical source.

Unlike the Elizabethan chronicle history of *King Leir*, the restoration of patriarchal authority does not evolve out of some struggle among Lear, his daughters, and their husbands to see who shall possess the land. Shakespeare declared his difference from the Elizabethan materials both by making Gloucester suffer the ritual punishment usually reserved for the female and also by making Gloucester the figure who initiates the repair of the metaphysics of patriarchy. The blinding of Gloucester allows the mystical bond to assert itself between father and legitimate son. Thus recentred in the father-son matrix, the drama unfolds which makes the political world coherent. 'Thy life's a miracle' (IV.vi.55), Edgar tells the blind man. But even as Edgar describes for him the supernatural form of intervention that prevented Gloucester's suicide, the son himself performs the miraculous rescue of the father before the audience's eyes. This is not to indicate duplicity or bad faith on Edgar's part, of course. The gesture simply makes Gloucester the object of his son's sense of patriarchal duty. Having invested him with such meaning, Shakespeare has Gloucester pay fealty in turn to King Lear. This scene makes certain one knows that Gloucester cannot address what he cannot see – the natural body of the monarch as the blind duke does homage to the disembodied voice of his 'royal lord'. Then Shakespeare brings Cordelia on stage to acknowledge Lear as her father.

It is worth noting what happens to Lear's unruly daughters as patriarchal order returns to the world. After the blinding of Gloucester, Shakespeare suddenly removes Regan and Goneril from the sphere of male patronage relations where they were represented as malcontents. He reinscribes them within more properly female roles where they become monstrous women. Thus he uses them to draw sexual differences, much as he does in Desdemona and Lady Macbeth; with the reassertion of patriarchy as a metaphysical principle, the two ambitious daughters are suddenly seized by desire for the bastard Edmund. Nor is there precedent for their inexplicable lust in the sources. It is a curious moment in the play when the daughters give themselves over to libidinous desires which had not been part of their character for the three acts preceding the onset of this passion. As they are redefined in Jacobean terms, furthermore, it is as if the political threat represented by their sexual rebellion has already found a resolution. All threats to patriarchy disappear as these women are stabbed and poisoned for harbouring illicit desire and, in the bastard's words, 'wedded' with him 'in death'.

As if it were not enough to have remodelled all this theatrical machinery in *Lear*, Shakespeare even revises the traditional Elizabethan contest between contenders for power. This scene operates according to the logic of purification as well, which is to say there is no contest at all. The duel is staged for only one reason: to display the dissymmetrical power relations between bastard and legitimate son. In acknowledging his defeat, Edmund also acknowledges the legitimacy of his utter subjection on the basis of blood when he interrogates Edgar, 'But what art thou / That hast this fortune on me? – If thou'rt noble, / I do forgive thee' (V.iii.165–7). Shakespeare gives Edgar the lines which define his power over Edmund as that of blood, and blood, as defined patrilineally: 'I am no less in blood than thou art, Edmund; / If more, the more th' hast wrong'd me. / My name is Edgar, and thy father's son' (lines 168–70). Shakespeare assures us that only those survive at the end of the play who have

maintained belief in the primacy of blood over all other signs, instruments, or manifestations of power. Edgar is not alone in this. Albany
remains true to the patriarchal principle throughout the play, for he
claims to recognise the aristocratic blood beneath Tom's disguise.
'Thy very gait', he tells Edgar, 'did prophesy / A royal nobleness'
(lines 176–7). Upon Cordelia's death, it is Albany who returns the
crown to Lear, renouncing his own claim with these words:

> . . . For us, we will resign
> During the life of this old majesty,
> To him our absolute power.
> (V.iii.299–301)

But if the patriarchal principle is really at stake, and if the play
dramatises the impossibility of separating kinship from kingship
for Britain to remain Britain, then why does Cordelia have to die?
The question is even more vexing when one realises that not one of
the historical sources felt obliged to kill her off in this apparently
gratuitous fashion. To the contrary, without exception they insist
that she restored her father to the throne and upon his death then
reigned for several years.

To ask why Cordelia, in my reading of the situation, has to die, is
virtually to provide the answer: because the patriarchal principle
itself rather than the identity of the monarch's natural body is in
question. England's kinship system allowed modification of strict
patrilineage that made the requisite term 'father'; the blood could be
– and Shakespeare's audience well knew it had recently been –
embodied in a female. But the relationship of power to gender is
obviously *not* the issue this play asks an audience to consider. Rather,
in re-establishing the bond between kinship and kingship, this play
wants us to think of them both in male terms. Thus the Gloucester/
Edgar relationship provides the site where the power of patriarchy
re-enters the world. For the same reason, Albany remains in line for
the throne even though he is not, strictly speaking, a blood relation,
and even though in *Gorboduc* Albany plays the malevolent character. No doubt his Scottish title made Shakespeare prefer Albany over
Cornwall as the one to survive, thus implicitly linking him to James
even though his birth does not make the duke a particularly strong
contender for the crown. Were Cordelia rather than Albany and
Edgar to remain at the end of the play, the crown would descend to
her upon Lear's death; either that or the play would challenge the

metaphysics of blood all over again in giving the crown to a male. It is more than coincidental, then – or rather it is coincidental in precisely the way that ideology arranges the coincidence of such events – that no direct heir to the throne of Britain remains alive at the end of *King Lear*. Under such conditions, the power of state reverts to a male. But still more important than this, for lack of a natural embodiment, power reverts back to its metaphysical source – the patriarchal principle itself. What matters most in maintaining the order of the state is loyalty to the principle of blood – the metaphysical body of power – and not the individual who wields it. For this is the form of power that Shakespeare displays by his revision of Elizabethan materials.

From Leonard Tennenhouse, *Power on Display: The Politics of Shakespeare's Genres* (London and New York, 1986), pp. 132–42.

NOTES

[The argument of this extract and of *Power on Display* as a whole is deeply indebted to the work of the French philosopher and social historian Michel Foucault. In *Discipline and Punish: The Birth of the Prison* (New York, 1979) Foucault develops from accounts of public executions the theory that the state used them to enforce its power not so much through the punishment itself as through the dramatic *spectacle* of punishment. Tennenhouse takes this as a cue to contend that in Shakespeare's drama 'stagecraft collaborates with statecraft in producing spectacles of power. The strategies of theatre resembled those of the scaffold as well as court performance . . . in observing a common logic of figuration that both sustained and testified to the monarch's power' (*Power on Display*, p. 15). Crucial to this 'logic of figuration' (or 'iconography') in *Lear* is the idea evolved by Elizabethan legal theory of the sovereign possessing two distinct bodies: a mortal 'body natural' and a deathless 'body politic'. As Marie Axton explains (quoted ibid., p. 102):

> The body politic was supposed to be contained within the natural body of the Queen. When lawyers spoke of this body politic they referred to a specific quality: the essence of corporate perpetuity. The Queen's natural body was subject to infancy, error, and old age; her body politic . . . was held to be unerring and immortal.

Tennenhouse's term 'the metaphysics of blood' designates the Elizabethan ideology fashioned to police the purity, and so ensure the security, of the royal and aristocratic blood-lines.

Textual references are to G. Blakemore Evans (ed.), *The Riverside Shakespeare* (Boston, 1972). Ed.]

1. *The True Chronicle Historie of King Leir*, in Geoffrey Bullough (ed.), *Narrative and Dramatic Sources of Shakespeare*, VII (New York, 1973).

2. Marie Axton, *The Queen's Two Bodies* (London, 1977), p. 131.

3. Jonathan Goldberg, *James I and the Politics of Literature* (Baltimore, 1983), p. 40.

4. Ibid., p. 46.

5. David M. Bergeron, *English Civic Pageantry, 1558–1642* (Columbia, Carolina, 1971), p. 144.

5

'King Lear': The Subversive Imagination

KIERNAN RYAN

QUESTIONING THE CONSENSUS

Viewed through the eyes of most orthodox and most radical critics of
Shakespeare alike, the vision of the tragedies appears profoundly
conservative. In the two dominant and complementary interpretive
manoeuvres, the tragedies are presented either as dramatising the
validity of the established social order and vindicating conventional
beliefs and values, or as reconciling us to what is perceived as our
intractably flawed human nature, and thus to the inescapable necessity of the given human condition, however monstrous and unbear-
able its cruelty and injustice. But whereas recent oppositional readings
have tended to treat the tragedies as insidious ideological illusions
ripe for dispassionate exposure,[1] the traditional critical response has
been only too eager to end up surrendering rational analysis to the
sway of the awesome and ineffable:

> What do we touch in these passages? Sometimes we know that all
> human pain holds beauty, that no tear falls but it dews some flower we
> cannot see. Perhaps humour, too, is inwoven in the universal pain, and
> the enigmatic silence holds not only an unutterable sympathy, but also
> the ripples of an impossible laughter whose flight is not for the wing
> of human understanding.

This is Wilson Knight in a relentlessly reprinted account of *King
Lear*.[2] The rapturous rhetoric may no longer be quite so fashionable
in Shakespeare criticism, but the substance of the passage remains

representative of the position from which a depressingly vast number of the standard books, essays and study-guides on the tragedies continue to be written. It is a position which in effect applauds Shakespearean tragedy for confirming that 'human pain' is universal, and therefore permanent and unavoidable; that the reasons for this pain are beyond human comprehension; and that the pain is somehow beautiful and necessary in a sense we cannot fathom.

A more sober statement of the same set of ideas is furnished by H. B. Charlton's likewise much anthologised study, *Shakespearian Tragedy*. The tragic hero's fate, we are told, 'springs irresistibly from the ultimate nature of things'. Shakespeare 'simply reveals his hero's death as the inevitable outcome of primary universal law. That is, indeed, the fundamental note of tragedy'. Moreover, as far as the effect on the audience or reader is concerned,

> intellectual acquiescence is all that is immediately required; one is aroused to feel that the action is inevitable, but reason cannot formulate the ultimate principles which make it inevitable. The riddle of the universe remains; and mystery is still one of the major threads in the web of human destiny.[3]

Nor is this stance peculiar to critics of Knight's and Charlton's generation. In Michael Long's much more recent study, *The Unnatural Scene*, for example, the author's distinctly modern critical idiom serves only to deliver the same basic punchline: 'Shakespearean tragedy sees the delimiting structuration of social and mental life as being *absolutely necessary and yet necessarily reductive*'.[4]

The notion that Shakespeare's tragedies depict as fixed and inexorable the destructive forces to which individuals find themselves subject, and that the wisdom they preach is submission to conditions human beings cannot change, crops up in a wide variety of critical disguises. The principal variation is the attempt to turn the tragedies into religious or secular morality plays. The success of this stratagem is testified to year after year in examination scripts at all levels. Shakespeare's tragedies are twisted into timeless spiritual narratives of fall, sacrifice and redemption or even temptation and damnation, into prescriptive illustrations of some comprehensive metaphysical plot imposed on human life; or they are press-ganged into labouring as little more than didactic secular parables, dramatised cautionary tales pointing up the prudence of obeying, and the folly of flouting, the overt or unspoken rules which secure the accustomed ordering of things.

The interpretations of the tragedies canonised in the standard critical editions and casebooks strive above all else to defuse these explosive plays by denying their depiction of reality as a changing social process made, and hence transformable, by men and women. Time and again the tragedies' dynamically concrete representation of life as a particular human history is obliterated. The plays are forced, against their grain, to testify to an underlying order of experience, whose universality and permanence mock the perception of destiny's social construction and the recognition of historical development as delusions. Such criticism drains the tragedies of their power both to arraign the alterable causes of injustice, violence and despair, and to expand our awareness of alternative sources of human motivation waiting in the wings of past and present events.

But if the tragedies are re-read from the perspective which this study proposes, it becomes impossible to continue claiming that their aim is to reconcile us to the ultimately purposeful pain and necessary defeat of the heroic figures they portray. Bradley's classic study somehow manages to discern in Shakespeare's tragedies reassuring fables in which virtue finally celebrates its Pyrrhic victory over evil, and 'what remains is a family, a city, a country, exhausted, pale, and feeble, but alive through the principle of good which animates it'.[5] While Willard Farnham takes refuge in the belief that Shakespeare 'purges our emotions of pity and fear by making us acquiesce without bitterness in catastrophe'.[6] But I would maintain that precisely the reverse is the case. Shakespeare's tragic vision affords no therapeutic catharsis, no soothing consolation or compensation for the inhuman suffering it dramatises. It furnishes every reason for resisting the complacent conclusion that this is how life has to be after all, its agonies and devastations to be borne patiently as the insuperable will of spiritual forces beyond our ken, or as rooted for some hidden but enriching reason in the very nature of mankind.

The present meaning and value of the tragedies stem rather from their refusal to resolve the intolerable contradiction between justified human desires and their unjustifiable suppression: the heartbreaking contradiction between what men and women want to be and could be, and what the particular social scenario into which they have been scripted by history cruelly condemns them to be, in spite of the superior selves and more satisfying lives struggling within them for realisation. Shakespearean tragedy is defined by its organising awareness of alternative potentiality; by its meticulous demonstration that what happens in these plays is the result of a specific constellation of particular conditions and pressures, and thus that the lives of human beings such as the protagonists exemplify could evolve along quite different lines under other conceivable circumstances. It is in the insistence on the conditional, contestable status of the lethal predicament which grinds down the protagonists, regardless of merit or their manifest potential to live otherwise, that the tragic quality of the drama finds expression.

Shakespeare's tragedies force us to confront without illusions the appalling cost in possible human justice and happiness of modes of thought and behaviour whose absorption condemns people to terrorise and even destroy not only others but themselves, making a mockery of whatever they might consciously intend. Shakespeare's great tragic protagonists are indeed 'fools of Time' (Sonnet 124),[7] but in the sense that they are all hoodwinked by history: overpowered by the prevailing social and ideological tides which sweep them unawares out of their depth, rather than by some metaphysically predestined misfortune or by some flaw, whether culpable, haphazard or innate, in the composition of their characters. Romeo and Juliet, Hamlet, Othello and Desdemona, King Lear, Macbeth, Antony and Cleopatra: all of them appear in retrospect as figures born before their time, citizens of an anticipated era whose utopian values their suffering discloses, pointing us towards more desirable versions of human existence yet to be scripted by history. Their tragedy is to find themselves stranded back in time, far from that foreshadowed future; marooned in a brutal and bewilderingly alien reality which has already contaminated their hearts and minds, and eventually crushes them completely.

'MEN / ARE AS THE TIME IS'

Shakespeare's revelation of the tragic gulf which divides how people could live from the lives their historical limits condemn them to endure receives its most compelling dramatisation in *King Lear*. Given that our world is one which swarms far less forgivably with millions more 'houseless heads and unfed sides' (III.iv.30), having ushered in an age when indeed 'Man's life is cheap as beast's' (II.iv.267) and 'Humanity must perforce prey on itself, / Like monsters of the deep' (IV.ii.49–50); and granted that we are ourselves the cast of what may yet turn out to be a real, humanly wrought tragedy of apocalyptic proportions – 'the promis'd end' for sure and no mere 'image of that horror' (V.iii.264,265) – the urgent bearing of *King Lear* on our own predicament, and hence the critical priorities which such a relevance dictates, should scarcely need spelling out.

Nor would they, were it not for the continued dominance of powerful recuperative readings such as that quoted above from Professor Wilson Knight, or that which is enshrined in the Riverside introduction to the play. The latter affords a salutary instance of the kind of sterile historicism which has lost all sense of why a past masterpiece like *Lear* might be worth studying by people living in the present. The opening manoeuvre contracts the play into an arid allegorical exemplification of Renaissance legal and political theories, reflecting in particular the doctrine of 'the King's two bodies'. The complex, concrete human experiences imaginatively figured by the tragedy recede before the schematised abstractions which the scholar-critic insists on exhuming and passing off as the real protagonists of the play. Thus Lear 'appears in the opening scene as Justice itself, illustrating . . . the two main branches of Justice according to Aristotle: Distributive, as when he portions out his kingdom, and Retributive, as when he punishes Cordelia for her lack of compliance'.[8]

The Medusan effect of this antiquarian view of *Lear* is compounded by forcing the tragedy to fit the equally petrified Christian formula of pride humbled into charity by a purgatorial experience, which culminates in the sublime reward of spiritual salvation. (Bradley thought the play might aptly be retitled 'The Redemption of King Lear'.[9]) This is the depressingly influential conception of the play promoted, for example, by the Arden editor, who regards Shakespeare's 'religious attitude' in *King Lear* as self-evident. This *Lear* is the story of a man who 'loses the world and gains his soul', and the central Christian message run by the tragedy emerges with dreary inevitability as the divine wisdom of passive endurance even in the face of the most indescribable inhumanity.[10]

But the illusion that what happens in *King Lear* mirrors some ultimately beneficent supernatural plan which 'shows you are above, / You justicers' (IV.ii.78–9) is expressly invoked by the play itself in order to be rudely shattered time and again by fresh horrors, the last and most excruciating being the sadistically gratuitous deaths of Cordelia and Lear himself. However, the opposite idea of Lear (popularised by Jan Kott[11]) as an existentialist vision of man's alienated plight in an arbitrary, meaningless universe, as the supreme text in the repertoire of the theatre of cruelty, gets equally short shrift from the play. Gloucester's celebrated absurdist reading of events – 'As flies to wanton boys are we to th' gods, / They kill us for their sport' (IV.i.36–7) – is ironically framed and deliberately disqualified within the tragedy. This is accomplished not only by Edmund's caustic demolition and brazen parody of his father's philosophy right at the start of the play (I.ii.118–49), but by the whole drama's scrupulously specific confirmation that everything which occurs, however horrific, follows all too clearly from the fact 'that men / Are as the time is' (V.iii.30–1) rather than as nature or the gods direct, whatever the characters themselves may blindly assert to the contrary.

In *King Lear* the assault on the traditional structures of social domination by a ruthlessly competitive and acquisitive individualism – the war Macbeth finds staged in his own mind – is imaginatively refracted through the parallel generational conflicts which rip the families of Lear and Gloucester apart. In the course of these conflicts both the old code based on service and the new self-serving realism are subjected to a searching dramatic evaluation, which faithfully registers the admirable and appealing as well as the ugly and pernicious qualities of the rival ideologies. At the close the plotline is pulled towards a routine re-establishment of feudality by the formal chivalric triumph of 'Legitimate Edgar' over 'the bastard Edmund' who holds 'the plague of custom' in contempt (I.ii.16,17,3). But the text ultimately urges us to reject both the waning and the waxing world-views it explores in favour of a perspective whose purchase on our imagination and moral sense is far more powerful: a perspective implicitly committed to equality, mutuality and co-operation rather than division, domination and exploitation.

It is Lear's violent dislocation from the social framework and the ideology which defined him as king that makes the growth and discovery of this standpoint possible. The meaning of that dislocation cannot begin to be fathomed by the countless interpretations, including George Orwell's stunningly uninspired reading,[12] which assume that the tragedy consists in Lear's being lured, by the flaws in his own personality, into the cataclysmic folly of surrendering his sovereignty. For to adopt this line means blocking out the entire point of *King Lear*, which subjects an all-powerful, patriarchal monarch to a traumatic experience whose consequences throw into question kingship as such and the unequal distribution of wealth and power on which it is predicated. The tragedy confounds conventional expectations by posing problems whose solution demands that we probe beyond the facts of Lear's personal fate as such to examine the codes which determine the form that fate takes. It compels us to dive deeper than a moralistic critique of the characters allows, to indict the internalised system of constraints which covertly denies them the option of being fully human.

Thus we watch Lear being stripped of his status and power, and hounded to an extremity of mental anguish at which he is brutally disabused, in his encounter with Poor Tom on the heath, of any lingering regal fantasy that his robes do not conceal the same 'unaccommodated man' and 'poor, bare, fork'd animal' (III.iv. 106–8) as the lowest and most wretched of the fellow creatures who were once his subjects. The scene enforces the arresting realisation that distinctions of rank ('Off, off, you lendings!', III.iv.108) have no natural or intrinsic authority at all. Lear's disillusioning 'madness' expels him into a licensed space outside the perceptual framework contrived by class society, a space in which he is soon joined by the blind Gloucester, once he too has learned to 'see . . . feelingly' (IV.vi.149). It is the space already fleetingly sprung open in the play's first scene by Cordelia, whose rebellious refusal to express her feelings in the language of her father's world summons the might of the unspoken to reject that world's coercive, quantifying definitions of love and relationship: '[Aside] What shall Cordelia speak? Love, and be silent' (I.i.62). And it is the space continually inhabited by the classless and timeless figure of the Fool, with whom Cordelia is subliminally identified at the end in Lear's line, 'And my poor fool is hang'd!' (V.iii.306).

Like Gobbo in The Merchant, and like Touchstone and Feste in their plays, the Fool furnishes a vital reflexive means of activating and monitoring our awareness of the fundamental issues at stake in King Lear. This is most apparent at the close of Act III, scene ii, at the turning-point of the tragedy, as Lear moves off with Kent to the hovel in the storm and the Fool tarries to address the audience directly:

> I'll speak a prophecy ere I go:
>   When priests are more in word than matter;
>   When brewers mar their malt with water;
>   When nobles are their tailors' tutors;
>   No heretics burn'd, but wenches' suitors;
>   Then shall the realm of Albion
>   Come to great confusion.
>   When every case in law is right;

> No squire in debt, nor no poor knight;
> When slanders do not live in tongues;
> Nor cutpurses come not to throngs;
> When usurers tell their gold i' th' field,
> And bawds and whores do churches build;
> Then comes the time, who lives to see't,
> That going shall be us'd with feet.
> This prophecy Merlin shall make, for I live before
> his time. [*Exit.*]
>
> (III.ii.80–95)

In these provocatively enigmatic, colloquial couplets, delivered in that richly ambivalent dramatic zone between the illusionistic play world and the reality of the audience, the Fool sardonically shuffles together bitter actualities and millenial possibilities, challenging us to discern and turn our minds to the tragic contradiction between history and utopia which pulses at the heart of *King Lear*.

The 'all-licens'd Fool' (I.iv.201) dissolves into the text once Lear has made the wise fool's role his own and invested himself with motley. Out on the heath in the storm Lear learns to feel what 'Poor naked wretches' feel (III.iv.28ff), to identify physically and emotionally with the 'houseless poverty' (III.iv.26) of the dispossessed and discounted, incarnate before him in the figure of Poor Tom. But in doing so he breaks through not to some primordial bedrock of human nature, eternally enduring beneath the surface of history, but to a way of seeing things which enables *us* to apprehend the need for human beings to reconstruct their lives together according to values which are the reverse of those responsible for the tragic conflicts and catastrophe.

King Lear edges us progressively into an understanding which turns the class-divided view of society, then as now, on its head. Lear's moving prayer that the rich and powerful may suffer a change of heart and 'shake the superflux' to the impoverished (III.iv.33–6), and Gloucester's no less compassionate plea concluding that 'distribution should undo excess, / And each man have enough' (IV.i. 66–71), mark decisive movements towards the play's extraordinary transvaluation of accepted values. But the philanthropic injunctions of both these celebrated speeches are limited by their tacit toleration of the hierarchical status quo, whose amelioration is sought merely in the divine reproof and moral rearmament of those who possess and rule, not in their abolition. The play as a whole goes much further. The point of complete breakthrough is reached in Lear's astonishing lines to Gloucester in Act IV, which Edgar's subsequent aside to the audience invites us to construe as 'matter and impertinency mix'd, / Reason in madness!' (IV.vi.174–5):

> **Lear** . . . A man may see how this world goes with no eyes. Look with thine ears; see how yond justice rails upon yond simple thief. Hark in thine ear: change places, and handy-dandy, which is the justice, which is the thief? Thou hast seen a farmer's dog bark at a beggar?
> **Glou.** Ay, Sir.
> **Lear** And the creature run from the cur?
> There thou mightst behold the great image
> Of authority: a dog's obey'd in office.
> Thou rascal beadle, hold thy bloody hand!
> Why dost thou lash that whore? Strip thy own back,
> Thou hotly lusts to use her in that kind
> For which thou whip'st her. The usurer hangs the cozener.
> Through tatter'd clothes small vices do appear;
> Robes and furr'd gowns hide all. Plate sin with gold,
> And the strong lance of justice hurtless breaks;
> Arm it in rags, a pigmy's straw does pierce it.
> None does offend, none, I say none, I'll able 'em.
>   (IV.vi.150–68)

That crucial last line is charged with the whole tragedy's recognition that its causes are housed beyond the conscious culpability of individuals in the iniquitous structures of economic, social and sexual relationship which breed the despair and ultimate devastation of exploiters and exploited alike. Much as many a critic would prefer it to, the tragedy refuses to halt at what might safely be applauded as a summons to Christian charity. It leaves us no choice but to identify the problem as the indefensible subjection of men and women to the injustices of a stratified society, and to seek the implied solution in the egalitarian standpoint created and vindicated by the play as a whole.

Through a relentless process of internal disruption and dislocation, *King Lear* wrests itself free of the presiding ideologies at war within its world, aligning itself instead with the mad, the blind, the beggared, the speechless, the powerless, the worthless: with all those 'Who with best meaning have incurr'd the worst' (V.iii.4) through their heroic failure to be 'as the time is' (V.iii.31), to think, feel and act as history dictates. For figures such as these, the play knows, there can be no place in a regime of whose values they are the living indictment, and which must therefore exile or destroy them. For the tragic protagonists of *King Lear*, 'Freedom lives hence' indeed, 'and banishment is here' (I.i.181) in history.

The close of the play addresses the brute fact of their obliteration with implacable honesty, making no soothingly redemptive sense of it whatsoever. For those who die, and for those who are left alive, there is no consolation, no paradoxical moral triumph in which to take comfort or find compensation. Broken and bewildered by the unremitting pain, Lear ends the play, like Cordelia, simply and irredeemably 'dead as earth' (V.iii.262), in a world where 'All's cheerless, dark, and deadly' (V.iii.291), and where the ring of Albany's reassurance that 'All friends shall taste / The wages of their virtue, and all foes / The cup of their deservings' (V.iii.303–5) is pathetically hollow. What survives, if we are ready to read the play this way, is our enhanced understanding of the mainsprings of the tragedy, and thus of the intolerable price still being paid in needless human suffering to keep our society divided.

From Kiernan Ryan, *Shakespeare* (Hemel Hempstead and Atlantic Highlands, NJ, 1989), pp. 44–51, 66–73.

NOTES

[My reading of *Lear* is part of a polemical book which argues that the most influential alternative accounts of Shakespeare now emerging have ironically conspired with conventional criticism to rob Shakespeare's drama of its subversive modern potential. Taking issue with established and oppositional views alike, it puts forward a radical humanist way of reading the plays from a standpoint in the present which is at once textually verifiable and historically legitimate. The book seeks to show how Shakespeare's comedies, tragedies and romances use the power historically inscribed in their language and form not merely to challenge the realities of Shakespeare's world, but to fire our imagination to question and change our own.

Textual quotations are from G. Blakemore Evans (ed.), *The Riverside Shakespeare* (Boston, 1972). Ed.]

1. See, for example, Leonard Tennenhouse, *Power on Display* (New York and London, 1986), ch. 3: 'The Theatre of Punishment: Jacobean Tragedy and the Politics of Misogyny'.

2. G. Wilson Knight, *The Wheel of Fire*, 4th revised edn (London, 1949), p. 176. The book is still selling, and this essay on *Lear* alone is further anthologised in at least three standard casebooks, likewise still in print:

Laurence Lerner (ed.), *Shakespeare's Tragedies: An Anthology of Modern Criticism* (Harmondsworth, 1963); Alfred Harbage (ed.), *Shakespeare: The Tragedies* (Englewood Cliffs, NJ, 1964); Frank Kermode (ed.), *Shakespeare: King Lear: A Selection of Critical Essays* (London, 1969).

3. H. B. Charlton, 'Humanism and Mystery', in Alfred Harbage (ed.), *Shakespeare: The Tragedies* (Englewood Cliffs, NJ, 1964), p. 10.

4. Michael Long, *The Unnatural Scene: A Study in Shakespearean Tragedy* (London, 1976), p. 35.

5. A. C. Bradley, *Shakespearean Tragedy* (London, 1904), p. 35.

6. Willard Farnham, 'The Tragic Qualm', in Alfred Harbage (ed.), *Shakespeare: The Tragedies* (Englewood Cliffs, NJ, 1964), p. 22.

7. The phrase adopted by Northrop Frye for the title of his *Fools of Time: Studies in Shakespearean Tragedy* (Oxford, 1967).

8. G. Blakemore Evans (ed.), *The Riverside Shakespeare* (Boston, 1972), p. 1251.

9. A. C. Bradley, *Shakespearean Tragedy* (London, 1904), p. 285.

10. Kenneth Muir (ed.), *King Lear*, The Arden Shakespeare, revised edn (London, 1972), pp. lii, l, lv.

11. '*King Lear*, or Endgame', in Jan Kott, *Shakespeare Our Contemporary* (London, 1964).

12. 'Lear, Tolstoy and the Fool', in George Orwell, *Shooting an Elephant* (London, 1950).

6

Language and Value in 'King Lear'

TERRY EAGLETON

King Lear opens with a bout of severe linguistic inflation, as Goneril and Regan rival each other in lying rhetoric. Goneril pitches her love for Lear beyond all language and value, and so ironically reveals this 'more than all' as just the resounding nothing that it is:

> Sir, I love you more than word can wield the matter;
> Dearer than eyesight, space, and liberty;
> Beyond what can be valued, rich or rare;
> No less than life, with grace, health, beauty, honour;
> As much as child e'er lov'd, or father found;
> A love that makes breath poor and speech unable;
> Beyond all manner of so much I love you.
>
> (I.i.54–60)

Goneril's love for Lear is indeed beyond value, since it doesn't exist; it is inarticulate not because it transcends meaning but because it has none. By representing her love as the negation of any particular object, she merely succeeds in cancelling it out, just as she uses language only to suggest its utter inadequacy. Goneril, whom Albany will later call 'Thou worse than any name' (V.iii.156), fails to see that definitions can be creative as well as restrictive, fashioning something from nothing. It is then up to Regan to negate her sister's negativity to imply an even more grandiose all, claiming, contradictorily, that Goneril has both defined her own love precisely and fallen woefully short.

Within this stage-managed charade, where 'all' has been so radically devalued, Cordelia's murmured 'Nothing' is the only sound currency. Cordelia is characteristically exact to maintain that she can say nothing to outdo her sisters, for who can trump 'all'? Lear warns her that nothing will come of this – 'Nothing will come of nothing. Speak again' (I.i.89) – but as usual he is mistaken: when meaning has been inflated beyond measure, nothing *but* nothing, a drastic reduction of signs to cyphers, will be enough to restabilise the verbal coinage. Only by a fundamental inversion and undercutting of this whole lunatic language game can the ground be cleared for a modest 'something' to begin gradually to emerge. That 'something' is in fact already figured in Cordelia's reply. With scrupulous precision, she informs Lear that she loves him 'According to my bond; no more nor less' (I.i.92), appealing away from the crazed subjectivism of the King's whimsical demand for love to the web of impersonal constraints and obligations of kinship. The other side of reckless inflation is the crass utilitarian exactitude with which Lear believes human love can be quantified; Cordelia counters the first with a more authentic precision, and the second, later in the play, with a forgiveness which is creative excess. Lear himself, of course, cannot see such precision as anything but paucity of spirit, gripped as he is by a semiotic crisis which spurs him to shed the substance of power while retaining 'The name, and all th'addition to a king', voiding the referent while clutching at the empty signifier. He trusts to the aura of a title, even as he credits lines drawn on a piece of paper: 'Of all these bounds, even from this line to this . . . We make thee lady.' No map can fully represent the terrain it signifies, just as Lear has struck his own title abstract, divorced it from material life.

Lear's paranoid drama, like the Malvolio-taunting scene of *Twelfth Night*, fashions a verbal nexus to which there is no 'outside', double-binding Cordelia so that to play her role or refuse it, speak or keep silent, become equally falsifying. (The Fool will later complain that he is whipped whether he speaks truth, lies or holds his peace.) France's gratuitous action of accepting Cordelia even when 'her price is fallen' makes something of nothing, cutting across Lear's world of precisely calculated imprecisions, but he can extricate Cordelia from the charade only in a way which that fiction can nullify as beggarly sentimentalism. When social reality has become mystified to its core, truth can lie only beyond its boundaries, as France lies beyond the extreme limit of Britain (Dover cliff). But such truth can therefore also be neutralised as marginal aberration. Cordelia consequently disappears into the future of the play, and truth becomes a simple inversion of whatever Lear affirms: Cordelia, France comments, is 'most rich, being poor', just as Kent finds that 'Freedom lives hence, and banishment is here'. We shall see later that the truth of a false condition can be articulated only in the discourse of madness, in a language which raises political insanity to the second power, parodying and redoubling it so as to deconstruct it from the inside. There can be no straight talking, no bold gesture of unmasking, which will not be absorbed and reinflected by the nexus of delusion, becoming yet another mask and falsehood in its turn; only the coupling of two negatives can hope to produce a positive.

In severing himself from Cordelia, spokeswoman for the material bonds of kinship, Lear cuts himself off from his own physical life, leaving his consciousness to consume itself in a void. In madness, as in sleepwalking, the mind ranges impotently beyond the body's limits, capable of destroying its substance: Edgar declares that he eats poisonous matter when seized by devils. Lear's mind is so tormented by his daughters' cruelty that his body is impervious to the storm which assails it: ' . . . When the mind's free / The body's delicate; this tempest in my mind / Doth from my senses take all feeling else, / Save what beats there' (III.iv.11–14). Body and consciousness, once disjointed, are each reduced to a kind of nothing: the former becomes an insentient blank, the latter, unmoulded by material constraint, emptily devours itself. Gloucester, confronted with Lear's agony, yearns to unhinge his own mind and body:

> The King is mad; how stiff is my vile sense,
> That I stand up, and have ingenious feeling
> Of my huge sorrows! Better I were distract;
> So should my thoughts be sever'd from my griefs,
> And woes by wrong imaginations lose
> The knowledge of themselves.
>
> (IV.vi.279–84)

What Gloucester will finally learn, once blindness has thrust the brute fact of his body into consciousness, is not to give the body the slip but to 'see feelingly', to allow sight (the symbol of a potentially unbridled self) to be constrained from within by the compassionate senses. Gloucester's body becomes his mode of communication with the material world (he 'smell[s] his way to Dover'), more solidly reliable than the verbal trickery of his bastard son. At the extreme outer limit of political society – on Dover cliff – those fictions can be induced by the fruitfully deceitful ministrations of Edgar to keel over into a kind of truth. This painful rediscovery of the body is what Lear must also learn. To regain touch with the harsh materiality of things, to discover that one is nothing in comparison with all one had imagined, is in that very act to become something:

> To say 'ay' and 'no' to everything that I said! 'Ay' and 'no' too was no good divinity. When the rain came to wet me once, and the wind to make me chatter; when the thunder would not peace at my bidding; there I found 'em, there I smelt 'em out. Go to, they are not men of their words. They told me I was everything; 'tis a lie – I am not ague-proof.
>
> (IV.vi.)

To say 'ay' and 'no' to everything is say nothing; Lear has 'smelt out' this truth, absorbed it through the stuff of the ambivalently linking, limiting body, whose stringent boundaries the storm has thrown into exposure. To know your own nothingness is to become something, as the Fool is wiser than fools because he knows his own folly and so can see through theirs.

To be purely bodily, like the non-linguistic animals, is to be essentially passive, a prey to the biological determinations of one's nature. Goneril and Regan, despite a ruthless activism which springs from being unbounded by sensuous compassion, are fundamentally passive in this sense, unable after their initial dissembling to falsify what they are. In this sense they are the true sisters of Cordelia, who is likewise unswervingly faithful to her own being. Edmund sees himself as equally fixed by nature ('I should have been that I am, had the maidenliest star in the firmament twinkled on my bastardising' [I.ii]), but by reflecting sardonically on his own determinants he is able to escape a blind enslavement to them. He is a self-creating opportunist who can manipulate others' appetites to his own advantage precisely because he knows his own so well. Like Iago, he moves primarily at the level of mystifying language, hostile to physical affinities, intent on rupturing the relations between his father and brother. By consciously appropriating what one ineluctably is, it is possible in part to transcend limit; and this is also true of Edgar and Kent, who deliberately embrace the wretchedness and delusion through which Lear is blindly forced, submitting to degrading limit in order finally to surpass it. The play seeks to distinguish the creative passivity of being constrained in the flesh by the needs of others, from the destructive passivity of being a mere function of one's appetites. For consciousness to be wholly bound by the body is to be a bestial slave to limit; to be purely active, however, is to over-reach those physical bonds for the vacuous freedom of an exploitative individualism. Both modes of being are a kind of nothing, and 'something' emerges in the play only elusively, glimpsed fitfully in the dialectic between them. The paradox which *King Lear* explores is that it is 'natural' for the human animal to transcend its own limits, yet this creative tendency to exceed oneself is also the source of destructiveness. Being 'untrue' to their own nature is natural to human beings: what we call culture or history is an open-ended transformation of fixed boundaries, a transcendence of mere appetite or rich surplus over precise measure. But when this process transgresses the body's confines too far, it violates the bonds of sensuous compassion and begins to prey on physical life itself. A hubristic, overweening consciousness must then be called sharply to order, shrunk back violently within the cramped frontiers of creaturely existence. The problem is how to do this without extinguishing that authentic self-exceeding which distinguishes an animal with history from other natural species.

One can pinpoint this difficult dialectic as the problem of respecting a norm or measure while simultaneously going beyond it. Excess may swamp such measure with its own too much, toppling over by a curious logic into less than anything; yet such superfluity is also precisely that which marks off men and women from the inhuman precision of beasts, or indeed of Goneril and Regan. The sisters fail to understand why their father should require a retinue of knights, and looking at Lear's gang of macho ruffians one can see their point. Lear's reply, however, is telling:

> O, reason not the need! Our basest beggars
> Are in the poorest thing superfluous.
> Allow not nature more than nature needs,
> Man's life is cheap as beast's.
> (II.iv.263–6)

There is no *reason* why human beings should delight in more than is strictly necessary for their physical survival; it is just structural to the human animal that demand should outstrip exact need, that culture should be of its nature excessive. It is this capacity for a certain lavish infringement of exact limit which distinguishes humankind, just as the play's first scene reveals the same capacity to lie at the source of what makes humans immeasurably more destructive than any other species. Surplus is radically ambivalent, not least in economic life.

Too many material possessions blunt one's capacity for fellow feeling, swaddling one's senses from exposure to the misery of others. If one could truly *feel* that wretchedness, register it sharply on the senses, then one would be moved to share one's surplus with the poor in a fundamental, irreversible redistribution of wealth:

> Take physic, pomp;
> Expose thyself to feel what wretches feel,
> That thou mayst shake the superflux to them,
> And show the heavens more just . . .
> (III.iv.34–7)

> Let the superfluous and lust-dieted man
> That slaves your ordinance, that will not see
> Because he does not feel, feel your power quickly;
> So distribution should undo excess,
> And each man have enough.
> (IV.i.68–72)

Against this image of a destructive surplus is balanced Cordelia's forgiveness of her father, a gratuitous excess of the strict requirements of justice. It is a kind of nothing, a refusal to calculate debt, out of which something may come.

What is superfluous or excessive about human beings, *King Lear* suggests, is nothing less than language itself, which constantly outruns the confines of the body. 'The worse is not,' declares Edgar, 'So long as we can say "This is the worst"' (IV.i.28–9). By naming an ultimate limit, speech transcends it in that very act, undoing its own pronouncement by its own performance. Language is the edge we have over biology, but it is a mixed blessing. Goneril and Regan's speech is rigorously exact, pared to the purely functional: Goneril tells Edmund to 'spare speech' when she uses him as a messenger. The disguised Kent's language is as parodically plain as Edgar's is elaborately confusing; Oswald's foppish idiom incites Kent (whose reports are said to be 'nor more nor clipp'd, but so') to spurn him as an 'unnecessary letter'. Language, like much else in the play, has a problem in pitching itself at the elusive point between too much and too little – except, perhaps, in the formally precise yet generously affectionate discourse of Cordelia. Cordelia blends largesse and limitation on her first appearance in the play, when she reminds Lear that her love, though freely given, must be properly divided between himself and her future husband; and the same balance is present in her combination of physical rootedness and freedom of spirit. In this sense, she symbolically resolves many of the play's formal antinomies.

The only problem, however, is that she dies. Edgar's closing injunction – 'Speak what we feel, not what we ought to say' – is no trite tag, denoting as it does that organic unity of body and language, that shaping of signs by the senses, of which Cordelia is representative; but the play has also demonstrated that to speak what one feels is no easy business. For if it is structural to human nature to surpass itself, and if language is the very index and medium of this, then there would seem a contradiction at the very core of the linguistic animal which makes it 'natural' for signs to come adrift from things, consciousness to overstep physical bonds, values to get out of hand and norms to be destructively overridden. It is not, after all, simply a matter of reconciling fixed opposites: it is a matter of regulating what would seem an ineradicable contradiction in the material structure of the human creature. *King Lear* is a tragedy because it stares this contradiction full in the face, aware that no poetic symbolism is adequate to resolve it.

From Terry Eagleton, *William Shakespeare* (Oxford, 1986), pp. 76–83.

NOTES

[In the Preface to the book from which this excerpt is taken Eagleton frankly disclaims any attempt at a historical study of his subject, describing his project as rather 'an exercise in political semiotics, which tries to locate the relevant history in the very letter of the text' (p. ix). This turns out to mean an unashamed endeavour to reinterpret Shakespeare's drama in the light of modern poststructuralist theories of language, desire, law and the body. Or, as Eagleton teasingly puts it:

> Though conclusive evidence is hard to come by, it is difficult to read Shakespeare without feeling that he was almost certainly familiar with the writings of Hegel, Marx, Nietzsche, Freud, Wittgenstein and Derrida. Perhaps this is simply to say that though there are many ways in which we have thankfully left this conservative patriarch behind, there are other ways in which we have yet to catch up with him. (pp. ix–x)

For a lucid and witty exposition of the poststructuralist assumptions and deconstructive approach organising his reflections on *Lear*, see Eagleton's own *Literary Theory: An Introduction* (Oxford, 1983), ch. 4. The final chapter of the same book explains why Eagleton finds nothing anomalous in a Marxist like himself pirating the discourse of an ostensibly alien theoretical stance:

> Any method or theory which will contribute to the strategic goal of human emancipation, the production of 'better people' through the socialist transformation of society, is acceptable. Structuralism, semiotics, psychoanalysis, deconstruction, reception theory and so on: all of these approaches, and others, have their valuable insights which may be put to use. (Ibid., p. 211)

Textual references are to Peter Alexander (ed.), *William Shakespeare: The Complete Works* (London, 1951). Ed.]

7

The Absent Mother in 'King Lear'

COPPÉLIA KAHN

Fleeing Goneril's 'sharp-tooth'd unkindness', Lear arrives at Gloucester's house in search of Regan, still hoping that she will be 'kind and
comfortable', although she was inexplicably not at home when he
called before. He finds his messenger in the stocks, a humiliation that
he rightly takes as directed at him personally. At first he simply
denies what Kent tells him, that Regan and her husband did indeed
commit this outrage. Then he seeks to understand how, or why. Kent
recounts the studied rudeness, the successive insults, the final sham-
ing, that he has endured.

For a moment, Lear can no longer deny or rationalise; he can only
feel – feel a tumult of wounded pride, shame, anger, and loss, which
he expresses in a striking image:

> O! how this mother swells upward toward my heart!
> *Hysterica passio*! down, thou climbing sorrow!
> Thy element's below.
>
> (II.iv.56–8)[1]

By calling his sorrow hysterical, Lear decisively characterises it as
feminine, in accordance with a tradition stretching back to 1900 BC
when an Egyptian papyrus first described the malady. Fifteen hundred years later in the writings of Hippocrates, it was named, and
its name succinctly conveyed its aetiology. It was the disease of
the *hyster*, the womb. From ancient times through the nineteenth
century, women suffering variously from choking, feelings of suf-

focation, partial paralysis, convulsions similar to those of epilepsy, aphasia, numbness, and lethargy were said to be ill of hysteria, caused by a wandering womb. What sent the womb on its errant path through the female body, people thought, was either lack of sexual intercourse or retention of menstrual blood. In both cases, the same prescription obtained: the patient should get married. A husband would keep that wandering womb where it belonged. If the afflicted already had a husband, concoctions either noxious or pleasant were applied to force or entice the recalcitrant womb to its proper location.[2]

In Shakespeare's time, hysteria was also called, appropriately, 'the mother'. Although Shakespeare may well have consulted a treatise by Edward Jordan called *A Brief Discourse of a Disease Called the Suffocation of the Mother*, published in 1603, like anyone in his culture he would have understood 'the mother' in the context of notions about women. For hysteria is a vivid metaphor of woman in general, as she was regarded then and later, a creature destined for the strenuous bodily labours of childbearing and childrearing but nonetheless physically weaker than man. Moreover, she was, like Eve, temperamentally and morally infirm: – skittish, prone to err in all senses. Woman's womb, her justification and her glory, was also the sign and source of her weakness as a creature of the flesh rather than the mind or spirit. The very diversity of symptoms clustering under the name of hysteria bespeaks the capricious nature of woman. And the remedy – a husband and regular sexual intercourse – declares the necessity for male control of this volatile female element.[3]

Psychoanalysis was born, one might say, from the wandering womb of hysteria. Anna O., the star of *Studies in Hysteria*, published by Freud and Joseph Breuer in 1895, was its midwife. It was she who named psychoanalysis 'the talking cure' and in a sense even discovered it. Afflicted with a veritable museum of hysterical symptoms, when Breuer visited her she spontaneously sank into a rapt, semiconscious state in which she insisted on talking about what bothered her, thus showing the way to free association as the distinctly psychoanalytic technique of treating mental disorders. For psychoanalysis and hysteria both, the discovery that its strangely disparate physical symptoms were in fact symbolic representations of unconscious mental conflict constituted a crucial breakthrough. Relocating the cause of hysteria in the head instead of in the womb, Breuer and Freud were able to make sense of it, treat it, and, to an extent, cure it. Yet, in the Viennese women they treated, we can see that hysteria does indeed come from the womb – if we understand the womb as a metaphor for feelings and needs associated with women. As Dianne Hunter suggests, what Anna O. talked out was her specifically *female* subjectivity.[4] She expressed through the body language of her paralysed arm, her squint, and her speech disorders the effects on her as a woman of life in a father-dominated family and a male-dominated world that suppressed the female voice. The matrix of her disease was both sexual and social: the patriarchal family.

Because the family is both the first scene of individual development and the primary agent of socialisation, it functions as a link between psychic and social structures and as the crucible in which gender identity is formed. From being mothered and fathered, we learn to be ourselves as men and women. The anthropologist Gayle Rubin describes psychoanalysis as 'a theory of sexuality in human society . . . a description of the mechanisms by which the sexes are divided and deformed, or how bisexual androgynous infants are transformed into boys and girls . . . a feminist theory manqué'.[5] A great Shakespearean critic, C. L. Barber, calls psychoanalysis 'a sociology of love and worship within the family'.[6] Freud, of course, viewed this family drama from the standpoint of a son; he conceived the development of gender as governed primarily by relationship with the father. Because Freud grounds sexual differentiation in the cultural primacy of the phallus, within the context of a family structure that mirrors the psychological organisation of patriarchal society, he enables us to deconstruct the modes of feeling, the institutions, and the social codes in which much if not most of English literature is embedded.

But to use one of Freud's favourite metaphors, to excavate patriarchal sensibility in literature, we must sift through more than one layer. In the history of psychoanalysis, the discovery of the Oedipus complex precedes the discovery of pre-oedipal experience, reversing the sequence of development in the individual. Similarly, patriarchal structures loom obviously on the surface of many texts, structures of authority, control, force, logic, linearity, misogyny, male superiority. But beneath them, as in a palimpsest, we can find what I call 'the maternal subtext', the imprint of mothering on the male psyche, the psychological presence of the mother whether or not mothers are literally represented as characters.[7] In this reading of *King Lear*, I try, like an archaeologist, to uncover the hidden mother in the hero's inner world.

Now, it is interesting that there is no literal mother in *King Lear*. The earlier anonymous play that is one of Shakespeare's main sources opens with a speech by the hero lamenting the death of his 'dearest Queen'.[8] But Shakespeare, who follows the play closely in many respects, refers only once in passing to this queen. In the crucial cataclysmic first scene of his play, from which all its later action evolves, we are shown only fathers and their godlike capacity to make or mar their children. Through this conspicuous omission the play articulates a patriarchal conception of the family in which children owe their existence to their fathers alone; the mother's role in procreation is eclipsed by the father's, which is used to affirm male prerogative and male power.[9] The aristocratic patriarchal families headed by Gloucester and Lear have, actually and effectively, no mothers. The only source of love, power, and authority is the father – an awesome, demanding presence.

But what the play depicts, of course, is the failure of that presence: the failure of a father's power to command love in a patriarchal world and the emotional penalty he pays for wielding power.[10] Lear's very insistence on paternal power, in fact, belies its shakiness; similarly, the absence of the mother points to her hidden presence, as the lines with which I began might indicate. When Lear begins to feel the loss of Cordelia, to be wounded by her sisters, and to recognise his own vulnerability, he calls his state of mind *hysteria*, 'the mother', which I interpret as his repressed identification with the mother. Women and the needs and traits associated with them are supposed to stay in their element, as Lear says, 'below' – denigrated, silenced, denied. In this patriarchal world, masculine identity depends on repressing the vulnerability, dependency, and capacity for feeling which are called 'feminine'.

Recent historical studies of the Elizabethan family, its social structure and emotional dynamics, when considered in the light of psychoanalytic theory, provide a backdrop against which Lear's family drama takes on new meaning as a tragedy of masculinity.[11] Recently, several authors have analysed mothering – the traditional division of roles within the family that makes the woman primarily responsible for rearing as well as bearing the children – as a social institution sustained by patriarchy, which in turn reinforces it.[12] Notably, Nancy Chodorow offers an incisive critique of the psychoanalytic conception of how the early mother-child relationship shapes the child's sense of maleness or femaleness. She argues that the basic masculine sense of self is formed through a denial of the male's initial connection with femininity, a denial that taints the male's attitudes toward women and impairs his capacity for affiliation in general. My interpretation of *Lear* comes out of the feminist re-examination of the mothering role now being carried on in many fields, but it is particularly indebted to Nancy Chodorow's analysis.

According to her account, women as mothers produce daughters with mothering capacities and the desire to mother, which itself grows out of the mother-daughter relationship. They also produce sons whose nurturant capacities and needs are curtailed in order to prepare them to be fathers. A focus on the primacy of the mother's role in ego-formation is not in itself new. It follows upon the attempts of theorists such as Melanie Klein, Michael and Alice Balint, John Bowlby, and Margaret Mahler to cast light on that dim psychic region which Freud likened to the Minoan civilisation preceding the Greek, 'grey with age, and shadowy and almost impossible to revivify'.[13] Chodorow's account of the mother-child relationship, however, challenges the mainstream of psychoanalytic assumptions concerning the role of gender and family in the formation of the child's ego and sexual identity.

Because I find family relationships and gender identity central to Shakespeare's imagination, the most valuable aspect of Chodorow's work for me is its comparative perspective on the development of gender in the sexes. For both, the mother's rather than the father's role is the important one, as crucial to the child's individuation (development of a sense of self) as to the child's sense of gender. It is only for the purpose of analysis, however, that the two facets of identity can be separated. Both sexes begin to develop a sense of self in relation to a mother-woman. But a girl's sense of femaleness arises *through* her infantile union with the mother and later identification with her, while a boy's sense of maleness arises *in opposition* to those primitive forms of oneness. According to Robert Stoller, whose work supports Chodorow's argument, 'Developing indissoluble links with mother's femaleness and femininity in the normal mother-infant symbiosis can only augment a girl's identity', while for a boy, 'the whole process of becoming masculine . . . is endangered by the primary, profound, primal oneness with mother'.[14] A girl's gender identity is reinforced but a boy's is threatened by union and identification with the same powerful female being. Thus, as Chodorow argues, the masculine personality tends to be formed through denial of connection with femininity; certain activities must be defined as masculine and superior to the maternal world of childhood, and women's activities must, correspondingly, be denigrated. The process of differentiation is inscribed in patriarchal ideology, which polarises male and female social roles and behaviour.[15]

The imprint of mothering on the male psyche, the psychological presence of the mother in men whether or not mothers are represented in the texts they write or in which they appear as characters, can be found throughout the literary canon. But it is Shakespeare who renders the dilemmas of manhood most compellingly and with the greatest insight, partly because he wrote at a certain historical moment. As part of a wide-ranging argument for the role of the nuclear family in shaping what he calls 'affective individualism', Lawrence Stone holds that the family of Shakespeare's day saw a striking increase in the father's power over his wife and children. Stone's ambitious thesis has been strenuously criticised, but his description of the Elizabethan family itself, if not his notion of its place in the development of affective individualism, holds true.[16]

Stone sums up the mode of the father's dominance thus:

> This sixteenth-century aristocratic family was patrilinear, primo-genitural, and patriarchal: patrilinear in that it was the male line whose ancestry was traced so diligently by the genealogists and heralds, and in almost all cases via the male line that titles were inherited; primogenitural in that most of the property went to the eldest son, the younger brothers being dispatched into the world with little more than a modest annuity or life interest in a small estate to keep them afloat; and patriarchal in that the husband and father lorded it over his wife and children with the quasi-absolute authority of a despot.[17]

Patriarchy, articulated through the family, was considered the natural order of things.[18] But like other kinds of 'natural order', it was subject to historical change. According to Stone, between 1580 and 1640 two forces, one political and one religious, converged to heighten paternal power in the family. As the Tudor-Stuart state consolidated, it tried to undercut ancient baronial loyalty to the family line in order to replace it with loyalty to the crown. As part of the same campaign, the state also encouraged obedience to the *paterfamilias* in the home, according to the traditional analogy between state and family, king and father. James I stated, 'Kings are compared to fathers in families: for a king is truly *parens patriae*, the politic father of his people.'[19] The state thus had a direct interest in reinforcing patriarchy in the home.

Concurrently, Puritan fundamentalism – the literal interpretation of Mosaic law in its original patriarchal context – reinforced patriarchal elements in Christian doctrine and practice as well. As the head of the household, the father took over many of the priest's functions, leading his extended family of dependents in daily prayers, questioning them as to the state of their souls, giving or withholding his blessing on their undertakings. Although Protestant divines argued for the spiritual equality of women, deplored the double standard, and exalted the married state for both sexes, at the same time they zealously advocated the subjection of wives to their husbands on the scriptural grounds that the husband 'beareth the image of God'. Heaven and home were both patriarchal. The Homily on the State of Matrimony, one of the sermons issued by the crown to be read in church weekly, quotes and explicates the Pauline admonition, 'Let women be subject to their husbands, as to the Lord; for the husband is the head of the woman, as Christ is the head of the church.'[20] In effect, a woman's subjection to her husband's will was the measure of his patriarchal authority and thus of his manliness.

The division of parental roles in childrearing made children similarly subject to the father's will. In his study of Puritan attitudes toward authority and feeling, David Leverenz finds an emphasis on the mother's role as tender nurturer of young children, as against the father's role as disciplinarian and spiritual guide for older children. Mothers are encouraged to love their children openly in their early years but enjoined to withdraw their affections 'at just about the time the father's instructional role becomes primary'. Thus the breaking of the will is accomplished by the father, rather than by both parents equally. This division of duties, Leverenz holds, fostered a pervasive polarity, involving 'associations of feared aspects of oneself with weakness and women, emphasis on male restraint and the male mind's governance of female emotions, the separation of "head" from "body", . . . a language of male anxiety, rather than of female deficiency.'[21]

A close look at the first scene in *King Lear* reveals much about lordliness and the male anxiety accompanying it. The court is gathered to watch Lear divide his kingdom and divest himself of its rule, but those purposes are actually only accessory to another that touches him more nearly: giving away his youngest daughter in marriage. While France and Burgundy wait in the wings, Cordelia, for whose hand they compete, also competes for the dowry without which she cannot marry. As Lynda Boose shows, this opening scene is a variant of the wedding ceremony, which dramatises the bond between father and daughter even as it marks the severance of that bond. There is no part in the ritual for the bride's mother; rather, the bride's father hands her directly to her husband. Thus the ritual articulates the father's dominance both as procreator and as authority figure, to the eclipse of the mother in either capacity. At the same time, the father symbolically certifies the daughter's virginity. Thus the ceremony alludes to the incest taboo and raises a question about Lear's 'darker purpose' in giving Cordelia away.[22]

In view of the ways that Lear tries to manipulate this ritual so as to keep his hold on Cordelia at the same time that he is ostensibly giving her away, we might suppose that the emotional crisis precipitating the tragic action is Lear's frustrated incestuous desire for his daughter. For in the course of winning her dowry, Cordelia is supposed to show that she loves her father not only more than her sisters do but, as she rightly sees, more than she loves her future husband; similarly, when Lear disowns and disinherits Cordelia, he thinks he has rendered her, dowered only with his curse, unfit to marry – and thus unable to leave paternal protection. In contrast, however, I want to argue that the socially-ordained, developmentally appropriate surrender of Cordelia as daughter-wife – the renunciation of her as incestuous object – awakens a deeper emotional need in Lear: the need for Cordelia as daughter-mother.

The play's beginning, as I have said, is marked by the omnipotent presence of the father and the absence of the mother. Yet in Lear's scheme for parcelling out his kingdom, we can discern a child's image of being mothered. He wants two mutually exclusive things at once: to have absolute control over those closest to him and to be absolutely dependent on them. We can recognise in this stance the outlines of a child's pre-oedipal experience of himself and his mother as an undifferentiated dual unity, in which the child perceives his mother not as a separate person but as an agency of himself, who provides for his needs. She and her breast are a part of him, at his command.[23] In Freud's unforgettable phrase, he is 'his majesty, the baby'.[24]

As man, father, and ruler, Lear has habitually suppressed any needs for love, which in his patriarchal world would normally be satisfied by a mother or mothering woman. With age and loss of vigour, and as Freud suggests in 'The Theme of the Three Caskets', with the prospect of return to mother earth, Lear feels those needs again and hints at them in his desire to 'crawl' like a baby 'toward death'.[25] Significantly, he confesses them in these phrases the moment after he curses Cordelia for her silence, the moment in which he denies them most strongly. He says, 'I lov'd her most, and thought to set my rest / On her kind nursery' (I.ii.123–4).

When his other two daughters prove to be bad mothers and don't satisfy his needs for 'nursery', Lear is seized by 'the mother' – a searing sense of loss at the deprivation of the mother's presence. It assaults him in various ways – in the desire to weep, to mourn the enormous loss, and the equally strong desire to hold back the tears and, instead, accuse, arraign, convict, punish, and humiliate those who have made him realise his vulnerability and dependency. Thus the mother, revealed in Lear's response to his daughters' brutality toward him, makes her re-entry into the patriarchal world from which she had seemingly been excluded. The repressed mother returns specifically in Lear's wrathful projections onto the world about him of a symbiotic relationship with his daughters that recapitulates his pre-oedipal relationship with the mother. In a striking series of images in which parent-child, father-daughter, and husband-wife relationships are reversed and confounded, Lear re-enacts a childlike rage against the absent or rejecting mother as figured in his daughters.

Here I want to interject a speculation inspired by Stone's discussion of the custom of farming children out to wet nurses from birth until they were twelve to eighteen months old; at that time they were restored to the arms of their natural mother, who was by then a stranger to them.[26] Many if not most people in the gentry or aristocracy of Shakespeare's day must have suffered the severe trauma of maternal deprivation brought on by the departure of the wet nurse. We know the effects of such a trauma from the writings of John Bowlby: a tendency to make excessive demands on others, anxiety and anger when these demands are not met, and a blocked capacity for intimacy.[27] Lear responds to the loss of Cordelia, the 'nurse' he rejects after she seems to reject him, by demanding hospitality for his hundred knights, by raging at Goneril and Regan when they refuse him courtesy and sympathy, and by rejecting human society when he stalks off to the heath. After the division of the kingdom, he re-enters the play in the fourth scene with this revealing peremptory demand: 'Let me not stay a jot for dinner; go, get it ready' (I.iv.9–10): he wants food, from a maternal woman. I believe that Lear's madness is essentially his rage at being deprived of the maternal presence. It is

tantalising, although I can imagine no way of proving it, to view this
rage as part of the social pathology of wet-nursing in the ruling
classes.

The play is full of oral rage: it abounds in fantasies of biting and
devouring, and more specifically, fantasies of parents eating children
and children eating parents. The idea is first brought up by Lear
when he denies his 'propinquity and property of blood' with Cordelia;
that is, he denies that he begot her, that he is her father, as he also
denies paternity of Regan and Goneril later. He assures her,

> The barbarous Scythian,
> Or he that makes his generation messes
> To gorge his appetite, shall to my bosom
> Be as well neighbour'd, pitied, and reliev'd,
> As thou my sometime daughter.
> (I.i.116–20)

The savagery of the image is shocking; it indicates Lear's first step
toward the primitive, infantile modes of thinking to which he surren-
ders in his madness. When Cordelia doesn't feed him with love, he
thinks angrily of eating *her*. Lear again voices this complex conjunc-
tion of ideas about maternal nurture, maternal aggression, and aggression against the mother when he looks at Edgar's mutilated
body, bleeding from its many wounds, and remarks,

> Is it the fashion, that discarded fathers
> Should have thus little mercy on their flesh?
> Judicious punishment! 'twas this flesh begot
> Those pelican daughters.
> (III.iv.72–5)

Lear seems to think that Edgar first transgressed against his father by
'discarding' him as Regan and Goneril discarded Lear, and that
Edgar's father then got back at his child, his 'flesh', *in* the flesh, as
Lear would like to do. But this fantasy of revenge calls forth an
answering fantasy of punishment against his own flesh – a punishment he deserves for begetting children in the first place. The image
of the pelican may have been suggested to Shakespeare by this
passage in a contemporary text, which I will quote because it elu-
cidates both the reciprocating spiral of aggression and revenge and
the close identification between parent and child, which possesses
Lear's mind:

> The Pellican loueth too much her children. For when the children be
> haught, and begin to waxe hoare, they smite the father and mother in
> the face, wherefore the mother smiteth them againe and slaieth them.
> And the thirde daye the mother smiteth her selfe in her side that the
> bloud runneth out, and sheddeth that hot bloud upon the bodies of
> her children. And by virtue of the bloud the birdes that were before
> dead, quicken againe.[28]

The children strike their parents, the mother retaliates, then wounds
herself that the children may nurse on her blood. 'Is't not', Lear
asks, 'as this mouth should tear this hand / For lifting food to 't?'
(III.iv.15–16) referring to 'filial ingratitude'. His daughters are the
mouths he fed, which now tear their father's generous hand; but at
the same time, he is the needy mouth that would turn against those
daughters for refusing to feed him on demand. Lear's rage at not
being fed by the daughters whom, pelican-like, he has nurtured, fills
the play. It is mirrored in Albany's vision of all humanity preying
upon itself, like monsters of the deep (IV.ii.46–9), a vision inspired
by the reality of Goneril turning her father out in the storm and
shortly confirmed by the more gruesome reality of Regan and Cornwall tearing out another father's eyes.

Bound up with this mixture of love and hate, nurture and aggression, is Lear's deep sense of identification with his daughters as born
of his flesh. When Goneril bids him return to Regan's house rather
than disrupt her own, his first thought is absolute separation from
her, like his banishment of Cordelia: 'We'll no more meet, no more
see one another'. But immediately he remembers the filial bond, for
him a carnal as much as a moral bond:

> But yet thou art my flesh, my blood, my daughter;
> Or rather a disease that's in my flesh,
> Which I must needs call mine: thou art a boil,
> A plague-sore, or embossed carbuncle,
> In my corrupted blood.
>
> (II.iv.223–7)

Gloucester echoes the same thought when he says wryly to Lear on
the heath, 'Our flesh and blood, my lord, is grown so vile, / That it
doth hate what gets it' (II.iv.149–50).

Children are products of an act that, in Elizabethan lore, was
regarded as the mingling of bloods. In the metaphor of Genesis,
repeated in the Anglican wedding service, man and wife become 'one
flesh'. With regard to mother and children, however, the fleshly bond

is not metaphorical but literal. Lear (like Gloucester) ignores the mother-child fleshly bond and insists that his children are, simply, *his* 'flesh and blood'. In the pelican image, he assimilates maternal functions to himself, as though Goneril and Regan hadn't been born of woman. Like Prospero, he alludes only once to his wife, and then in the context of adultery. When Regan says she is glad to see her father, he replies

> if thou shouldst not be glad
> I would divorce me from thy mother's tomb,
> Sepulchring an adultress.
>
> (II.iv.131–3)

These lines imply, first, that Lear alone as progenitor endowed Regan with her moral nature, and second, that if that nature isn't good, she had some other father. In either case, her mother's only contribution was in the choice of a sexual partner. Thus Lear makes use of patriarchal ideology to serve his defensive needs: he denies his debt to a mother by denying that his daughters have any debt to her, either.

Lear's agonising consciousness that he did indeed produce such monstrous children, however, persists despite this denial and leads him to project his loathing toward the procreative act onto his daughters, in a searing indictment of women's sexuality:

> The fitchew nor the soiled horse goes to 't
> With a more riotous appetite.
> Down from the waist they are centaurs,
> Though women all above:
> But to the girdle do the Gods inherit,
> Beneath is all the fiend's: there's hell, there's darkness,
> There is the sulphurous pit – burning, scalding,
> Stench, consumption; fie, fie, fie! pah, pah!
>
> (IV.vi.124–31)

Even if he did beget these daughters, Lear implies, he's not answerable for their unkindness, because they are, after all, women – and women are tainted, rather than empowered as men are, by their sexual capacities. Thus he presses into service another aspect of patriarchal ideology, its misogyny, to separate himself from any feminine presence.

To return for a moment to the social dimensions of Lear's inner turmoil, it is important here that generational conflicts entwine with and intensify gender conflicts. Lear and his daughters, Gloucester and his sons are pitted against one another because the younger generation perceives the authority of the elder as 'the oppression of aged tyranny' (I.ii.47–52). Stephen Greenblatt remarks that this period has 'a deep gerontological bias', revealed in numerous claims that 'by the will of God and the natural order of things, authority belonged to the old'. At the same time, however, sermons, moral writings, and folk tales of the kind on which *King Lear* is based voice the fear that if parents hand over their wealth or their authority to their children, those children will turn against them.[29] The common legal practice of drawing up maintenance agreements testifies that this fear had some basis in actual experience. In such contracts, children to whom parents deeded farm or workshop were legally bound to supply food, clothing, and shelter to their parents, even to the precise number of bushels of grain or yards of cloth. Thus the law put teeth into what was supposed to be natural kindness. Lear's contest of love in the first scene functions as a maintenance agreement in that he tries to bind his daughters, by giving them their inheritance while he is still alive, into caring for him. This generational bargain is then complicated by the demands proper to gender as well – the father's emotional demand that his daughters be his mothers and perform the tasks of nurture proper to females.

Regan and Goneril betray and disappoint Lear by not being mothers to him, but in a deeper, broader sense, they shame him by bringing out the woman in him. In the following speech, Shakespeare takes us close to the nerve and bone of Lear's shame at being reduced to an impotence he considers womanish:

> You see me here, you Gods, a poor old man,
> As full of grief as age; wretched in both!
> If it be you that stirs these daughters' hearts
> Against their father, fool me not so much
> To bear it tamely; touch me with noble anger,
> And let not women's weapons, water-drops,
> Stain my man's cheeks! No, you unnatural hags,
> I will have such revenges on you both
> That all the world shall – I will do such things,
> What they are, yet I know not, but they shall be
> The terrors of the earth. You think I'll weep;
> No, I'll not weep;
> I have full cause of weeping, but this heart
> Shall break into a hundred thousand flaws
> Or ere I'll weep.
>   (II.iv.274–88)

He calls his tears 'women's weapons' not only as a way of depre‿
ing women for using emotion to manipulate men but also because he
feels deeply threatened by his own feelings. Marianne Novy has
argued that Lawrence Stone, in calling attention to the 'distance,
manipulation, and deference' that characterised the Elizabethan family, identified 'a cultural ideal of Elizabethan society . . . a personality
type that on the one hand kept feelings of attachment and grief under
strict control, but on the other was more ready to express feelings of
anger'. 'The model', she comments, 'was primarily a masculine ideal.'[30]
In agreeing, I would suggest that this masculine ideal was produced
by the extreme sexual division of labour within the patriarchal
family, which made women at once the source and the focus of a
child's earliest and most unmanageable feelings.

Despite a lifetime of strenuous defence against admitting feeling
and the power of feminine presence into his world, defence fostered
at every turn by prevailing social arrangements, Lear manages to let
them in. He learns to weep and, though his tears scald and burn like
molten lead, they are no longer 'women's weapons' against which he
must defend himself. I will conclude this reading of the play by
tracing, briefly, Lear's progress toward acceptance of the woman in
himself, a progress punctuated by his hysterical projections of rage at
being deprived of maternal nurture. In the passage that I just quoted,
as he turns toward the heath, Lear prays that anger may keep him
from crying, from becoming like a woman. He also, in effect, tells us
one way to read the storm – as a metaphor for his internal emotional
process: 'I have full cause of weeping, but this heart / Shall break into
a hundred thousand flaws / Or ere I'll weep' (II.iv.286–8). Shakespeare portrays the storm as the breaking open of something en-
closed, a break that lets out a flood of rain; it thus resembles Lear's
heart cracking, letting out the hungry, mother-identified part of him
in a flood of tears. Lear exhorts the winds to crack their cheeks and
the thunder to crack Nature's moulds and spill their seeds; he envi-
sions 'close pent-up guilts' riven from 'their concealing continents'
(II.ii.1–9, 49–59). He wants the whole world struck flat and cleft
open, so that the bowels of sympathy may flow. What spills out of
Lear at first is a flood of persecutory fantasies. He sees everyone in
his own image, as either subjects or agents of persecution. Only
daughters like his, he thinks, could have reduced Poor Tom to naked
misery; Poor Tom and the Fool are, like him, stern judges bringing
his daughters to trial. Gloucester is 'Goneril, with a white beard', and
then, someone who might weep along with Lear although he has
only the case of eyes.

are allows Lear to feel the weeping woman in
is need for Cordelia and his guilt for the wrong he
s and excoriates a world full of viperish women.
ear's indictments of women during Acts III and IV
lustful mistresses of Poor Tom's sophisticated past,
the wea~~~~ ackets and rustling silks, as well as the real Regan
tearing out Gloucester's eyes, and the real Goneril, stealthy and
lustful, seducing Edmund and sloughing off Albany. It is as though
Shakespeare as well as his hero must dredge up everything horrible
that might be imagined of women and denounce it before he can
confront the good woman, the one and only good woman, Cordelia.

Cordelia's goodness is as absolute and inexplicable as her sisters'
reprovable badness, as much an archetype of infantile fantasy as they
are. When she re-enters the play, she is described as crying with pity
for her father's sufferings, yet in her tears she is still 'queen over her
passion'. Whereas Lear thought weeping an ignoble surrender of his
masculine authority, Cordelia conceives her tears as a source of
power:

> All blest secrets,
> All you unpublished virtues of the earth,
> Spring with my tears; be aidant and remediate
> In the good man's distress!
>
> (IV.iv.15–18)

In these scenes Cordelia becomes, now in a benign sense, that
daughter-mother Lear wanted her to be. Like the Virgin Mary, she
intercedes magically, her empathy and pity coaxing mercy from
nature. Yet finally, as the Doctor's words imply, she can only be 'the
foster-nurse' of Lear's repose.[31]

Lear runs from the attendants Cordelia sends to rescue him, who
appear just after he poignantly evokes the crying infant as a common
denominator of humanity:

> Thou must be patient; we came crying hither.
> Thou know'st, the first time that we smell the air
> We wawl and cry . . .
> When we are born, we cry that we are come
> To this great stage of fools.
>
> (IV.vi.178–80, 182–3)

Here he comes closest to admitting his vulnerability, but he must
immediately defend against it and see the proffered help as a threat.
Stanley Cavell has argued that the reluctance to be recognised by

those whom they love most, which characterises Lear, Kent, Edgar and Gloucester, lies at the heart of this play; he holds that they are reluctant because they feel that their love bespeaks a demeaning dependency.[32] I agree – and I regard that embarrassed shrinking from recognition as part of a masculine identity crisis in a culture that dichotomised power as masculine and feeling as feminine.

And so Lear exits running in this scene, asserting his kingship ('Come, come, I am a king') but behaving like a mischievous child who makes his mother run after him ('Come, and you get it, you shall get it by running', IV.vi.199, 201–2). When he reappears, he is as helpless as a child, sleeping and carried in by servants. He awakes in the belief that he has died and been reborn into an afterlife, and he talks about tears to Cordelia:

> Thou art a soul in bliss, but I am bound
> Upon a wheel of fire, that mine own tears
> Do scald like molten lead.
> (IV.vii.45–7)

These are the tears of ashamed self-knowledge, manly tears caused by a realisation of what his original childish demands on his daughters had led to. In this scene, which I want to compare with the next scene with Cordelia, Lear comes closer than he ever does later to a mature acceptance of his human dependency. He asserts his manhood, and admits Cordelia's separateness from him at the same time that he confesses his need for her: he can say 'I am a very foolish fond old man' and yet also declare, 'For (as I am a man) I think this lady / To be my child Cordelia' (IV.vii.59, 69). I want to pause at those three words 'man', 'lady', and 'child'. Lear acknowledges his manhood and his daughter's womanhood in the same line and the same breath. He can stop imagining her as the maternal woman that he yearned for and accept his separateness from her. Yet he also calls her his child, acknowledging the bond of paternity that he denied in the first act. He need not be threatened by her autonomy as a person nor obsessed by the fleshly tie between them as parent and child.

Lear's struggle to discover or create a new mode of being based on his love for Cordelia continues to his last breath. Imagining their life together in prison, he transcends the rigid structure of command and obedience that once framed his world:

> Come, let's away to prison:
> We two alone will sing like birds i' th' cage;
> When thou dost ask me blessing, I'll kneel down

And ask of thee forgiveness. So we'll live,
And pray, and sing, and tell old tales, and laugh at gilded
    butterflies . . .

                                                    (V.iii.8–11)

Parent and child are equal, the gestures of deference that ordinarily denote patriarchal authority now transformed into signs of reciprocal love. Moreover, Lear now views all power from a quasi-divine perspective that charmingly deflates pretension or ambition as mere toys, while nevertheless carrying a certain grandeur of its own. On the other hand, Lear's characteristically fierce defensiveness continues to shape his fantasy, which is provoked by Cordelia's request that they confront their enemies: 'Shall we not see these daughters and these sisters?' The prospect of facing his bad mothers as well as his good mother impels Lear to conceive of Cordelia and himself as forming an impregnable dyad bound together by a complete harmony of thought and feeling more than by the circumstances of captivity. If he did agree to meet Regan and Goneril, he would have to abandon the fantasy that one good woman like Cordelia can triumph over or negate her evil counterparts, as well as the fantasy that a prison can be a nursery in which Cordelia has no independent being and exists solely for her father as part of his defensive strategy against coming to terms with women who are as human, or as inhuman, as men.

Cordelia's death prevents Lear from trying to live out his fantasy, and perhaps discover once again that a daughter cannot be a mother.[33] When he enters bearing Cordelia in his arms, he is struggling to accept the total and irrevocable loss of the only loving woman in his world, the one person who could possibly fulfil needs that he has, in such anguish, finally come to admit. No wonder that he cannot contemplate such utter, devastating separateness, and in the final scene tries so hard to deny that she is dead. At the end of *King Lear*, only men are left. It remains for Shakespeare to re-imagine a world in his last plays in which masculine authority *can* find mothers in its daughters, in Marina, Perdita, and Miranda – the world of pastoral tragicomedy and romance, the genres of wish-fulfilment, rather than the tragic world of *King Lear*.

From Margaret Ferguson, Maureen Quilligan and Nancy Vickers (eds), *Rewriting the Renaissance* (Chicago and London, 1986), pp. 33–49.

NOTES

[The above volume in which Coppélia Kahn's essay first appeared is a multi-disciplinary collection of essays which, in the words of the editors, 'invite the reader to consider historical documents and aesthetic works no longer as isolated objects of specialised study but now as parts of a social text – a text constituted not only by economic forces and class ideologies but also by the complex ideologies of sexual difference' (p. xxxi). Kahn belongs to that movement within feminist scholarship and criticism which challenges the accepted version of the literary canon by reading canonical texts like *King Lear* in heretical ways. Her subtle alliance of the usually estranged perspectives of psychoanalysis, textual interpretation and social history yields a feminist account of *Lear* instructively at odds with that of Kathleen McLuskie in this volume. It also produces a radically different view of *Lear*'s concern with male anxiety from that elaborated in Stephen Greenblatt's essay below. Ed.]

I am grateful to David Leverenz and Louis Adrian Montrose for their sensitive comments on drafts of this essay.

1. This and all subsequent quotations are taken from Kenneth Muir (ed.), *King Lear* (Cambridge, Mass., 1952).

2. See Ilza Veith, *Hysteria: The History of a Disease* (Chicago, 1965).

3. As Veith (ibid.) shows, during the Middle Ages hysteria had ceased to be known as a disease and was taken as a visible token of bewitchment. Jordan wrote his treatise to argue for a distinction between the two. Both his work and the pamphlet by Samuel Harsnett denouncing the persecution of witches (from which Shakespeare took much of Poor Tom's language) have the effect of pointing up parallels between hysteria and witchcraft as deviant kinds of behaviour associated with women, which are then used to justify denigrating women and subjecting them to strict control. In her essay on the literary and social forms of sexual inversion in early modern Europe whereby women took dominant roles and ruled over men, Natalie Zemon Davis notes that such female unruliness was thought to emanate from a wandering womb and comments, 'The lower ruled the higher within the woman, then, and if she were given her way, she would want to rule over those above her outside. Her disorderliness led her into the evil arts of witchcraft, so ecclesiastical authorities claimed'. See 'Women on Top', in Davis's *Society and Culture in Early Modern France* (Stanford, Calif., 1975), p. 125. Hilda Smith notes that a gynaecological text published in 1652 calls the entire female sexual structure 'The Matrix', subordinating female sexuality to its reproductive function; see her 'Gynaecology and Ideology in Seventeenth-Century England', in Berenice Carroll (ed.), *Liberating Women's History* (Urbana, Illinois, 1976), pp. 97–114. For a theory of hysteria as a disorder that 'makes complex use of contem-

poraneous cultural and social forms', see Alan Krohn, *Hysteria: The Elusive Neurosis* (New York, 1978).

4. Dianne Hunter, 'Psychoanalytic Intervention in the History of Consciousness, Beginning with O', in Shirley Nelson Garner, Claire Kahane and Madelon Sprengnether (eds), *The (M)Other Tongue: Essays in Feminist Psychoanalytic Interpretation* (Ithaca, NY, 1985). Freud suggests that attachment to the mother may be 'especially intimately related to the aetiology of hysteria, which is not surprising when we reflect that both the phase and the neurosis are characteristically feminine': 'Female Sexuality' (1931), in *The Standard Edition*, 24 vols (London, 1953–), vol. 21, pp. 223–45.

5. Gayle Rubin, 'The Traffic in Women: Notes on the "Political Economy" of Sex', in Rayna Reiter (ed.), *Toward an Anthropology of Women* (New York, 1975), pp. 184–5.

6. C. L. Barber, 'The Family in Shakespeare's Development', in Murray Schwartz and Coppélia Kahn (eds), *Representing Shakespeare: New Psychoanalytic Essays* (Baltimore, 1980), p. 199.

7. See my article 'Excavating "Those Dim Minoan Regions": Maternal Subtexts in Patriarchal Literature', *Diacritics* (Summer 1982), 32–41, which contains a much condensed version of this essay. The idea of a maternal subtext was first suggested to me by Madelon Gohlke's essay '"I wooed thee with my sword": Shakespeare's Tragic Paradigms', in Murray Schwartz and Coppélia Kahn (eds), *Representing Shakespeare: New Psychoanalytic Essays* (Baltimore, 1980). She writes of a 'structure of relation' in which 'it is women who are regarded as powerful and men who strive to avoid an awareness of their vulnerability in relation to women, a vulnerability in which they regard themselves as "feminine"' (p. 180).

8. *The True Chronicle Historie of King Leir*, in Geoffrey Bullough (ed.), *Narrative and Dramatic Sources of Shakespeare*, VII (New York, 1973), pp. 337–402.

9. In his brilliant and wide-ranging essay '"Shaping Fantasies": Figurations of Gender and Power in Elizabethan Culture', in Margaret W. Ferguson, Maureen Quilligan and Nancy Vickers (eds), *Rewriting the Renaissance* (Chicago and London, 1986), pp. 65–87, Louis Adrian Montrose explicates the patriarchal ideology threaded through *A Midsummer Night's Dream*, whereby the mother's part in procreation is occluded and men alone are held to 'make women, and make themselves through the medium of women'. He interprets this belief as 'an overcompensation for the *natural* fact that men do indeed come from women; an overcompensation for the cultural facts that consanguineal and affinal ties *between* men are established through mothers, wives, and daughters'.

10. Murray Schwartz explored this idea in a series of talks given at the Centre for the Humanities, Wesleyan University, February–April 1978.

11. Lawrence Stone's *The Family, Sex and Marriage in England, 1500–1800* (New York, 1978) offers a picture of Elizabethan filial relationships which is both highly suggestive for readings of Shakespeare and much at variance with him; see especially pp. 151–218. For a convenient summary of Stone's account of the Elizabethan patriarchal family, see his essay 'The Rise of the Nuclear Family in Early Modern England', in Charles E. Rosenberg (ed.), *The Family in History* (Philadelphia, 1975), pp. 25–54.

12. Adrienne Rich, *Of Woman Born: Motherhood as Experience and Institution* (New York, 1976); Dorothy Dinnerstein, *The Mermaid and the Minotaur: Sexual Arrangements and Human Malaise* (New York, 1976); Nancy Chodorow, *The Reproduction of Meaning: Psychoanalysis and the Sociology of Gender* (Berkeley and Los Angeles, 1979). My article 'Excavating "Those Dim Minoan Regions"' mentioned above (note 7) is in part a review of these books.

13. Sigmund Freud, 'Female Sexuality' (1931), in *The Standard Edition*, 24 vols (London, 1953–), vol. 21, p. 228.

14. Robert Stoller, 'Facts and Fancies: An Examination of Freud's Concept of Bisexuality', in Jean Strouse (ed.), *Women and Analysis: Dialogues on Psychoanalytic Views of Femininity* (New York, 1974), p. 358.

15. For a reading of Shakespeare in light of this differentiation and the ideology connected with it, see my *Man's Estate: Masculine Identity in Shakespeare* (Berkeley and Los Angeles, 1981).

16. See reviews by E. P. Thompson, *Radical History Review*, 20 (1979), 42–50; Alan MacFarlane, *History and Theory*, 18 (1979), 103–26; Randolph Traumbach, *Journal of Social History*, 13 (1979), 136–43; Richard T. Vann, *Journal of Family History*, 4 (1979), 308–15.

17. Lawrence Stone, *The Crisis of the Aristocracy, 1558–1641*, abridged edn (New York, 1967), p. 271.

18. This and the following paragraph appear in my *Man's Estate: Masculine Identity in Shakespeare* (Berkeley and Los Angeles, 1981), pp. 13–14.

19. Quoted from C. H. McIlwain (ed.), *Political Works of King James I* (Cambridge, Mass., 1918), p. 307; cited in Lawrence Stone, 'The Rise of the Nuclear Family in Early Modern England', in Charles E. Rosenberg (ed.), *The Family in History* (Philadelphia, 1975), p. 54.

20. 'An Homily of the State of Matrimony', in John Griffiths (ed.), *The Two Books of Homilies Appointed to be Read in Churches* (Oxford, 1859), p. 505.

21. David Leverenz, *The Language of Puritan Feeling: An Exploration in Literature, Psychology and Social History* (New Brunswick, NY, 1980), p. 86. Leverenz gives a fuller and more psychologically astute interpretation of child-rearing than does Stone. Though he is specifically concerned with the Puritan family, he relies on the same sources as Stone – Elizabethan and Jacobean manuals of child-rearing and domestic conduct, holding that 'almost any point made in Puritan tracts can be found in non-Puritan writings' (p. 91).

22. Lynda Boose, 'The Father and the Bride in Shakespeare', *PMLA*, 97 (1982), 325–47.

23. For a subtle and lucid account of pre-oedipal experience, see Margaret S. Mahler, Fred Pine and Anni Bergman, *The Psychological Birth of the Human Infant: Symbiosis and Individuation* (New York, 1975), pp. 39–120.

24. Sigmund Freud, 'On Narcissism' (1914), in *The Standard Edition*, 24 vols (London, 1953–), vol. 14, pp. 69–102.

25. Sigmund Freud, 'The Theme of the Three Caskets', ibid., vol. 12, pp. 289–300.

26. Lawrence Stone, *The Family, Sex and Marriage in England, 1500–1800* (New York, 1978), pp. 106–9.

27. John Bowlby, *Attachment and Loss*, 2 vols (New York, 1969).

28. *Batman upon Bartholeme* (1582), cited in Kenneth Muir (ed.), *King Lear* (Cambridge, Mass., 1952), p. 118. 'The kind life-rend'ring pelican' was a familiar image of Christ in the Middle Ages, wounding herself with her beak to feed her children. Even today, the blood bank of the city of Dublin, administered by an organisation called 'Mother and Child', is known as 'the Pelican'. (I am indebted to Thomas Flanagan for this information.)

29. Stephen J. Greenblatt, 'The Cultivation of Anxiety: King Lear and his Heirs', *Raritan* (1982), 92–114 [reprinted in this volume: see essay 11. Ed.]

30. Marianne Novy, 'Shakespeare and Emotional Distance in the Elizabethan Family', *Theatre Journal*, 33 (1981), 316–26.

31. See C. L. Barber, 'The Family in Shakespeare's Development: Tragedy and Sacredness', in Murray Schwartz and Coppélia Kahn (eds), *Representing Shakespeare: New Psychoanalytic Essays* (Baltimore, 1980) for the idea that 'the very central and problematical role of women in Shakespeare – and the Elizabethan drama generally – reflects the fact that Protestantism did away with the cult of the Virgin Mary. It meant the loss of ritual resource for dealing with the internal residues in all of us of the once all-powerful and all-inclusive mother' (p. 196).

32. Stanley Cavell, 'The Avoidance of Love', in *Must We Mean What We Say?* (Cambridge, 1976).

33. This reading of the play suggests that Shakespeare departed from his sources and let Cordelia die because he wanted to confront as starkly as possible the pain of separation from the mother.

8

Retrospective: 'King Lear' on St Stephen's Night, 1606

LEAH MARCUS

During the early years of Stuart rule, the Project for Union was so prominent in public discourse that it provided an uncommonly rich matrix for theatrical topicality. Local reading of several of Shakespeare's plays would yield interesting results in terms of James I's project for Great Britain – *The Winter's Tale* most notably, perhaps, but also *King Lear*. *King Lear* is a play for which we have more than one early text. It therefore allows us to observe some of the subtle local differences about which we can only speculate in the case of *Cymbeline*. I would like to consider one specific *King Lear* – the *King Lear* published in the Pied Bull quarto (1608) as having been *'played before the Kings Maiestie at Whitehall vpon S. Stephans night in Christmas Hollidayes'* in the year 1606.[1] The title page claims fidelity to that performance and sets forth its special institutional and liturgical context: *King Lear* was played at court before King James I; it was played on the night of the Feast of St Stephen. We can supply the additional information that St Stephen's Day was one of the official 'red letter' days of the Anglican church, which had King James himself as its head. What might that particular localisation mean in terms of the contemporary meaning of the play?

Several recent critics have pointed out *King Lear's* immersion in contemporary materials relating to the Union of the Kingdoms.[2] Like the much earlier tragedy *Gorboduc* performed before Queen Elizabeth in the 1560s, *King Lear* in both the quarto and folio versions can easily be interpreted as a dramatisation of the perils of division. Both texts of *King Lear* portray a series of catastrophes unleashed by an ageing monarch's decision to segment Britain into three parts, and those three parts can easily enough be identified with England, Scotland, and Wales. But neither text of the play offers a straightforward identification of either King Lear or his enemies with the 'Jacobean line'. Of the two versions of the play, the quarto is more permeated with local details relating to the Project for Union. In the 1608 version of Gloucester's initial speech, for example, he refers to the recent 'diuision of the kingdomes' (p. 664); the plural 'kingdomes' is puzzling in terms of the Britain of King Lear, extremely evocative in terms of the divided Britain of James I. The folio reads instead 'diuision of the Kingdome', muting some of the contemporary resonance of the phrase by altering the plural to a singular. But if the 1608 quarto version is richer in topical details evoking the royal Project for Union, it is also richer in particularised materials which can easily be interpreted as criticism of King James I.

The quarto *King Lear* includes several fleeting references to issues of royal prerogative which are not to be found in the folio. The 'abuse' of royal monopolies had come up repeatedly in connection with James's high notions of his own prerogative. His Project for Union and his wholesale granting of monopolies to royal favourites were, for his critics, but two aspects of the same broad encroachment upon traditional 'liberties'. Both royal programmes were contested during the first decade of his reign in terms of the same set of legal principles about the limitation of royal authority. In the quarto *King Lear* the fool brings up the monopoly system, taunting his royal master for giving away his land and rents to his daughters. The fool is a royal favourite who might be considered a prime candidate for monopoly, but he cannot claim sole right to his folly: 'No faith, Lords and great men will not let me, if I had a monopolie out, they would haue part an't, and lodes too, they will not let me haue all the foole to my selfe, they'l be snatching' (p. 672). That speech, with its implication that the whole royal system of monopolies is built upon (royal) folly, is omitted from the folio and its immediate context is altered.

There are similar differences later on. In the quarto *King Lear*, the stage directions for Lear's appearance during the battle between Albany and Cordelia's forces read 'Enter Lear mad'. His first words are, 'No they cannot touch mee for coyning, I am the king himselfe'

(p. 695). In terms of Jacobean theory, the mad king speaks the truth. The king's absolute authority to coin money came up many times in contemporary debate in connection with James's more controversial assertions of royal prerogative.[3] In the folio version, the speech is subtly different. The stage direction does not call for Lear to enter 'mad' and the key word 'coining' is altered to the more general and neutral word 'crying':

> *Enter Lear.*
> [**Edgar**]   But who comes heere?
>   The safer sense will ne're accommodate
>   His Master thus.
> **Lear**   No, they cannot touch me for crying. I am the King himselfe.
> (TLN 2526–31)

An attribute associating King Lear specifically with King James I is neutralised into a trait Lear shares with all humanity.

The most flamboyant difference between the quarto and the folio *King Lear*s is that the mock trial in the hovel is entirely missing from the folio version. That scene, too, is full of pregnant references to issues of royal prerogative. By 1606, when *King Lear* was performed at court, James I had already encountered severe opposition to his highhanded notions about the power of royal prerogative to override legal and legislative curbs upon it. He regularly used the Court of Chancery, which operated as a court of equity according to his beloved civil law, to circumvent challenges to royal authority which emanated from the courts of common law. By 1606, Chancery had already demonstrated its receptivity to James's ideas about absolutism.[4] In the quarto *King Lear*, the wronged king attempts to create a commission of judges very much like a Chancery commission to pronounce on the justice of his daughters' behaviour. In the eye of the storm and in the height of his madness, he appoints Edgar in disguise as Tom o' Bedlam as his first 'robbed man of Iustice' and the fool as his second: '& thou his yokefellow of equity, bench by his side, you are ot'h commission, sit you too' (p. 687). In contemporary England, 'yokefellows of equity' were judges in the Court of Chancery.

When *King Lear* was performed at court during the Christmas holidays of 1606, the Parliament over which James I stormed like Jove with his thunderbolts was in session albeit recessed for the holidays; the Union of the Kingdoms and the naturalisation of the Scots were at the centre of parliamentary debate. James had ordered English and Scottish parliamentary commissions to meet jointly under Lord Chancellor Ellesmere (head of Chancery) to weigh the impediments to union and he was already proposing to submit the project to the courts.[5] In 1608, when the quarto *King Lear* was published, the case of the Post Nati had been tried in the Court of Chancery and the Lord Chancellor himself had issued a lengthy opinion on the Post Nati's right to citizenship on the basis of civil law and equity. The 'royal commission' of the hovel Lear appoints to 'arraign' and try those daughters who have stripped him of his authority and exacerbated the 'diuision of the Kingdomes' is a madman's eerie echo of James I's actual tactics – in the matter of Great Britain and on numerous other occasions – for attempting to work his will upon recalcitrant subjects who committed more minor versions of the same infractions. By omitting the trial scene entirely, the folio version of the play skirts the interesting and uncomfortable problem of its insistent Stuart referentiality.

The pattern of alteration between quarto and folio is too regular to be a matter of mere chance. If we gauge authorial intent by collecting textual instances that appear to push meaning in a single direction, then what is at issue here is a matter of intent. It is not, however, clear whose intent is in question. Sometimes – to my mind implausibly, given the quarto's association with the court of James – the 'intent' behind the alterations has been taken to be that of the official censor. We have no date for the composition of the folio *King Lear*, but editorial opinion is now inclined to place it later than the quarto version. If the revisions were made by Shakespeare, 1609–10 appears one likely period.[6] That would place the folio *Lear* in much the same contemporary milieu as the *Cymbeline* seen by Simon Forman, and create the interesting possibility that the two plays were 'cleansed' of their intense Stuart topicality at about the same time. But the fact is that we do not know certainly when, why, or by whom the alterations were made, or even whether the folio version was revised from the quarto. I would be loath to insist that the quarto had to come first, or that it is a more authentic *King Lear* because it is 'the Originall'. There is no reason to regard one text as more 'Shakespeare' than the other, or to assume that the alterations can be accounted for solely on the basis of either censorship or aesthetic considerations. By 1623, when the First Folio was published, many of the topical details evoking the king's Project for Union – details which provide such a striking localisation of the quarto version – would in any case have lost some of their urgency. By 1623, James I had also taken strong steps to reform the monopoly system and the quarto reference to abuse would therefore have lost some of its heat.[7] What we have in the 1608 quarto and the 1623 folio are two 'local' versions of *King Lear* among other possible versions which may have existed in manuscript, promptbook, or performance without achieving the fixity of print. One of our two *King Lear*s is more closely tied than the other to a particular contemporary occasion.

What are we to make of the fact that the *Lear* most closely identified with the court of James I is also the *Lear* with the most potentially damaging references to specific royal policies? It is possible, of course, that some of the phrases we read in the printed quarto text were discreetly omitted from the performance before James. But we have no reason to suppose that they were. The common assumption that Stuart kings would never have suffered flouting before their face is not borne out by the evidence: there are many other instances of open criticism of the monarch and royal policies in masques and sermons at court. At Whitehall, as in the public playhouses, censorship was local and sporadic. Whether potentially damaging comments were suppressed or tolerated or even welcomed in royal entertainments was in large part a function of the specific conditions that surrounded each case.[8] We have no compelling grounds for contesting the quarto's claim to be the *King Lear* performed at court. The editorial tendency in recent years has been to elevate the status of the quartos, to give them far more textual credibility than Heminge and Condell's dark innuendo in the First Folio about 'stolne and surreptitious copies' would suggest they deserve. I will work on the assumption that the play performed at court on St Stephen's Night, 1606, followed the playtext we have reasonably closely. Even if there were significant alterations for performance, the title-page advertisement made it likely that 1608 readers, at least, would have bought and perused the quarto in the expectation that they were getting the court version of *King Lear*.

Steven Urkowitz, Michael Warren, and others have made valuable observations about differences in large structure between the quarto and the folio *Lear*s. The quarto version is slower-moving and more meditative, with frequent 'cameo' speeches of moral reflection which arrest the progress of the plot; it is also less ambiguous in its portrayal of the moral nature of characters like the duke of Albany – closer, in short, to the structure of a traditional morality play.[9] It was performed at court at a time when the nation was blanketed in propaganda for the Union and Parliament was heatedly arguing the matter. Many of its strongest and most evocative ideas take on special local significance within the almost inescapable context of the contemporary debate.

Like pamphlets and speeches in support of the Union of the Kingdoms, *King Lear*'s major protagonists argue vehemently for a doctrine of essences – a set of knots 'too intrinse t'unloose' between members of a family, a nation.[10] By assuming that he can divide up his kingdoms, shed his 'body politic' while keeping the 'name and all the additions to a King' (p. 666), Lear has performed just the kind of hideous dismemberment of his sacred royal identity that King James and his advisers warned the nation so vehemently against. As in pro-Union arguments growing out of the contemporary debate, the division of the kingdoms in *King Lear* is associated with cosmic portents of chaos, the disruption of families and larger political alliances: it is a fragmentation at once psychic (expressed through Lear's madness) and political. All of these related catastrophes can be associated with the familiar set of interconnected paradigms which we used to call the Elizabethan 'world picture'. But considering the play in terms of the parliamentary and public debate shows how fragile such ideals were in terms of contemporary credence – how easily assimilated to the 'Jacobean line', how easily contested by those who sought a less unitary, less authoritarian model of the state under the monarch. In *King Lear*, James I's notions about the organicism of Britain under the king as head are themselves placed on trial.

There are other ways in which the play's dominant ideas can be linked to the climate of contemporary debate. Let us take, for example, the parliamentary leitmotif from 1606–7 of James I as Jove the Thunderer, who would rain down his terrible punishments if the Project for Union were not expedited. The image of Jove – the storm, the implacable justice of his bolts from heaven – is extremely prominent in the play, as variations of the same topical motif were in masques and other court iconography associated with the Union. The chief victim of the 'sulpherous and / Thought executing fires, vaunt-currers to / Oke-cleauing thunderboults' that shake the divided Britain of *King Lear* is the monarch who has initiated the 'diuision of the Kingdomes'. King Lear opens himself willingly to the bolts of Jove as though to acknowledge that he has deserved the god's 'all shaking thunder' (p. 683) for his crime against Great Britain.

The play's repeated motif of the casting off of good, 'legitimate' offspring also reverberates with ideas about the Union. In England in

1606, the king's supporters were arguing that the 'mark of the stranger' be effaced from the Scots, that they be received as legitimate subjects, elevated from their outcast beggary and given the kind of welcome in England that King James himself had received. The duke of Albany, who bears a Scottish title, is more sympathetically presented in the quarto than in the folio.[11] At a time when parliamentarians and others were venting strong prejudice against the king's northern subjects, expecting them to swarm across the border and engulf English prosperity if allowed the slightest favour, *King Lear* could easily be interpreted as an extended political exemplum promoting charity toward the Scots. A king becomes a beggar, looks for succour and is denied it, as a result of the 'unnatural' division he has earlier unleashed: he becomes, in contemporary terms, an outcast 'Scot' himself, suffering the same scanted courtesy to which King James's northern subjects had been unjustly treated in England.

At court in 1606, the play's moral message about hospitality toward the poor and the castoff would have been immeasurably strengthened by the announced liturgical context – at least for those viewers who reverenced the teachings of the church. St Stephen's Day (December 26) was, of all the days of the year, the holiday most associated with the granting of traditional hospitality; it later became known as Boxing Day. On the Feast of St Stephen, as in the more recent carol of King Wenceslaus, the high were to look out in pity upon the tribulations of the low. On that day, poor boxes in which cash donations had been collected all year would be broken open and the money distributed. Poor people would gather in groups and proceed from house to house asking for a charity which could be denied only at the peril of those within. Wealthy individuals who participated in the spirit of the day took pride in having an estate on St Stephen's filled with as many guests as the 'howse wolld holld'.

In some places, 'Stephening' – the demanding of holiday charity – took on a highly aggressive cast. One parish in the seventeenth and early eighteenth centuries preserved records of Stephening and its demise. At Drayton Beauchamp, Buckinghamshire, on the Feast of St Stephen, all the parishioners were traditionally treated to 'open house' by the local rector at his own expense. When one parsimonious rector tried to evade his traditional responsibility on the feast day by shutting his doors and hiding inside his house, angry parishioners scaled the walls, broke through the roof, and emptied out his larder, claiming their traditional privilege of hospitality in honour of St Stephen. The parish custom was quickly reinstated and continued sporadically until 1834, when government commissioners appointed to inquire 'concerning charities' investigated Drayton Beauchamp and ruled that there was no 'legal proof' requiring the tradition's continuance.[12]

According to a popular saying, 'Blessed be St Stephen / There's no fast upon his even'.[13] Shakespeare's play depicts the inconceivable. On the night of St Stephen, 1606, *King Lear* enacted repeated violations of the festival 'law' against fasting. In the liturgical lessons proper for the Feast of St Stephen, the idea of bending to succour the less fortunate, of shedding 'pompe' to 'take physicke' and 'feele what wretches feele' (p. 685) occurs again and again. 'He that by usurie and uniust gaynes geathereth ryches: he shall lay them in stoare for a man that wyl pitie the poore.' 'He that wyl be ryche al to soone, hath an euyl eye: and consydereth not that pouertie shal comme upon hym.' 'He that giveth unto the poore, shall not lacke; but he that hideth his eyes from them, shall have many a curse.'[14]

It is easy to see how such a liturgical context – inescapable for anyone who went to church on the holiday as English subjects were required to – would frame the play itself, 'solve' and disentangle some of its interpretive cruxes. King Lear and his retainers have been rich but have become poor, and like the poor on Stephen's Night, they boisterously demand hospitality of the daughters who have suddenly 'gathered riches' through the king's abdication. Both their need and even a measure of aggression in demanding that it be met are 'licensed' by the liturgy and customs of the day. But Goneril and Regan repeatedly shut them out, advising Gloucester as well to 'shut vp your doores' against the king and his 'desperate traine' (p. 682). Gloucester passively allows the holiday violation to be perpetrated; one of the consequences of his act (at least in terms of the play's festival context in performance) is that he himself is blinded by the very guests he preferred above the needy. Denied hospitality by the 'hard house, more hard then is the stone whereof tis rais'd', Kent resolves to 'returne and force their scanted curtesie', according to the traditional liberty of Stephening (p. 684.) But the doors of the great ones remain shut. Only a hovel is open. In the quarto, the pattern of scanted Stephening receives particular emphasis if only because King Lear is given more extended contact with the company of outcasts who have, like him, been shut out of the hospitality of the night. He is shown physically supported by the lowly.[15] He reduces himself more, calling himself in one famous speech a 'poore old fellow', which is far more shockingly base than the folio version – 'You see me heere (you Gods) a poore old man' – but also more evocative of the holiday theme of kinship with the unfortunate. In the 'friendship' of the hovel in the quarto version, King Lear actually puts 'cold' hospitality on trial in accordance with liturgical precept and the doctrine of due reverence: 'He that giveth unto the poore, shall not lacke; but he that hideth his eyes from them, shall have many a curse.'

It is also easy to see how the play's lesson about succour for the needy and downtrodden could be given moral 'application', according to the Jacobean line, as reproof against those in the English Parliament and elsewhere who, like Goneril and Regan in the play, were hard-heartedly denying the nation's obligatory hospitality to the needy Scots. The preservation of old holiday customs was a very important policy matter for King James I. He had already issued royal proclamations calling for the keeping of open house during the Christmas season according to the traditional 'laws' of hospitality; a decade or so later, he would codify his position in the *Book of Sports*.[16] And yet, in his own kingdom, in the matter of the Post Nati, the poor continued to be kept out; his parliamentary supporters argued in vain that it is better to give than to receive.[17] *Cymbeline*'s worthy, legitimate, outcast figure of Posthumus would have recognised the hostile moral world of *King Lear*. The 1606 *King Lear* performed before King James I was, in contemporary political terms, a demand for what had not been offered generously and freely, a morality play enforcing the king's arguments for naturalisation and acceptance of the alien on the basis of liturgical and customary holiday injunctions.

What are we to make of the elements of the quarto *King Lear* that appear to criticise King James I and his notions of prerogative – the very notions which stood behind such arbitrary gestures as his attempt to enforce holiday hospitality by royal decree? To a degree, these elements take on an aura of ritual humiliation on the part of one of the powerful in connection with the holiday's strong message of *Deposuit potentes*. The liturgy for the day calls for just such self-abasement in kinship with the lowly on grounds that, as one verse of the lesson proper for St Stephen's puts it, 'Somme one commeth out of prison, and is made a king; and another which is borne in the kingdome, commeth unto pouertie'.[18] The wheel of fortune repeatedly referred to in the playtext can turn, then turn again. By watching a play that made rather obvious references to his political failings, James could be interpreted as 'taking physic' himself, displaying a comely willingness to enter into the charitable spirit of the day, which he was imposing on everyone else.

There was also local potential for the transmission of a stronger political message through the play's associations between festival folly and the dispersal of legal authority. St Stephen, the first martyr, was condemned to death by Judaic legalists for his arguments that the Mosaic code had to give way to the new Christian dispensation. His story from the Book of Acts was read as part of the liturgy for the day. In a parallel with St Stephen himself, *King Lear* displays a monarch martyred for his faith in extralegal charity and brother-hood. According to such a line of interpretation, King Lear would be less a negative antitype than an analogue of James I. In early Stuart England ideas about transcending the strictures of law (particularly the common law) and appeals to larger notions of brotherhood, equity, and charity were strongly associated with King James in his various battles with Parliament and the courts. The play undermines the rule of law in accordance with traditional holiday ideas about Christmas 'misrule' and the overthrow of all manner of legal hege-monies. Through his presence at the performance of *King Lear*, James I provided a 'perspective' on the play from which it could be read as both a royal acknowledgement of the king's 'sins of state' and a dispersal of just the type of legal authority which sought to under-cut his absolutism. In keeping with the example of St Stephen, James I could be interpreted, through his very tolerance of the play's critique, as forgiving his enemies – at least to the extent that public acknowledgement of hostile criticism can be taken as a kind of forgiveness.

There are, of course, other possibilities for interpretation set in motion by the quarto's liturgical and political context. As commen-tators have noted, the play can easily be taken as glancing at James's more personal foibles: his immoderate love of hunting, boisterous conviviality, and indulgence of his favourites; his sudden attacks of rage and recurrent fits of the 'mother'.[19] To the extent that James himself in his 'body natural' replicated the flaws of King Lear, it could be argued that he, too, had been subjected to intolerable affronts, rendered unnaturally impotent and divided from himself, by his subjects' continuing fragmentation of his very essence through their inhospitality toward the Union. The continuing suspension of the royal project, from such a perspective, could be taken as an explanation of all manner of royal failings. The king could not show himself in the full glory and perfection of his 'body politic' because his subjects would not allow him to be fully whole as himself – at one in 'body natural', 'body politic', and nation.

At court on St Stephen's Night, 1606, the presence of the king presiding over the performance and the play's many resonances with the liturgy for the day to some extent dampened *King Lear*'s potential for undoing the royal 'line'. In the public theatre and on a more neutral date, a similar performance might well appear seditious, or at least highly volatile in terms of its topical associations. For readers of the 1608 quarto, the play's lessons in Stuart political morality would have been less visible and clear-cut than in performance at court, since readers would not, in all likelihood, encounter the play on St Stephen's Night itself. But some of the holiday 'message' would have lingered about that particular playtext because of the elaborate specificity of its title page. For anyone who remembered what St Stephen's Day was about (and who could possibly forget?) the quarto *Lear* was framed within a markedly conservative ceremonial context.

It would, of course, have been perfectly possible to reject the holiday message. There were many well-to-do Jacobeans who made a point of scanting their 'obligatory' holiday hospitality on the basis of economic and religious principle. If anything, James's insistence on imposing the old forms made some people more hostile to them. The extent to which either readers or viewers 'applied' the holiday lesson correctly in terms of the Stuart line would depend, in large measure, on their pre-existing predilection for reverence toward the authority of church and state. Liturgical framing always carries with it an element of tautology. The Stuart line in *King Lear* would carry special credence only for those dutiful subjects who were already receptive to it. For those who were not, the play potentially opened itself to all manner of dissonant interpretation, even (as in Stephen Greenblatt's reading of the play) to the evacuation of the very traditions and unities that the court *King Lear* reinforced.[20]

The 'official' *Lear* of the quarto is not the only possible *Lear*, or even the only *Lear* that could have been read out of that specific festival occasion. Like *Cymbeline* and many other plays we call Shakespeare, it was generically unstable – labelled a 'Chronicle Historie' in the quarto, a tragedy, along with *Cymbeline*, in the folio. My purpose in focusing on the royal *Lear* as opposed to others is not to declare a preference for it but to stress, yet once more, the importance of localisation for defining parameters of meaning. A play which was orthodox in one setting could have been unorthodox in another. Shakespeare's 'double writing' of key scenes gave the theatre the 'high prerogative' of subtly altering a play's meaning in performance. The fact that there existed an 'unauthorised' court version of *King Lear* in print after 1608 might have helped contain the play's obvious potential for interrogating Stuart orthodoxy. And yet, depending on the performance and the circumstances surrounding it, the play's energies could easily be opened out into a field of freer signification which, by its very scattering of the 'unauthorised' liturgical reading, would weaken the Jacobean line. The *King Lear* of most modern editions is a different *King Lear* still. By interlayering the quarto and folio versions, editors have established 'authoritative' versions of the playtext but also created new areas of ambivalence and instability which do not exist in either text considered separately. To which *King Lear* can we assign the Man Himself? Whether or not Shakespeare was a 'King's Man' is a question which cannot be answered for All Time and in broadly general terms.

From Leah Marcus, *Puzzling Shakespeare* (Berkeley, Los Angeles and London, 1988), pp. 148–59.

NOTES

[In the study from which this essay is taken Leah Marcus describes her project as 'the localisation of Shakespeare' (p. 32). The aim she shares with a range of new-historicist scholars is to hasten 'the demise of the transcendent Bard' (p. 25) by restoring his drama to a revamped version of its original milieu, and thus exploding the myth of Shakespeare's being, in Ben Jonson's celebrated phrase, 'not of an age, but for all time!' ('To the Memory of My Beloved, the Author, Mr William Shakespeare').

Marcus's localisation of *King Lear* involves three points of historical reference which require elucidation. By 'the Jacobean line' is meant simply the prospect of an unbroken line of royal succession which the advent of James in 1603 had brought to the monarchy for the first time since the reign of Henry VIII. 'The Project for Union' was James's own cherished dream of creating Great Britain through the union of England and Scotland, an endeavour in which he found himself persistently frustrated by an uncooperative Parliament. (The Union of the Kingdoms was finally achieved only in 1707.) The 'Post Nati' were, as Marcus explains,

> all those Scotsmen born after James had ascended the English throne, theoretically uniting the kingdoms. James had proclaimed them citizens of Britain and according to Roman law they were already citizens, yet in England they were deprived of any recourse at law. The case of the Post Nati concerned a dispute over land titles and hinged

on whether a Scotsman born since the proclamation of union had the right to defend his ownership of property held in England in a court of English law.

(p. 124)

The case was settled in favour of the Post Nati in 1608.

The question of the quarto and folio versions of *King Lear* is discussed under Further Reading: see below, pp. 180–1. Ed.]

1. Here and throughout the discussion my text is the facsimile of the Pied Bull quarto in Michael J. B. Allen and Kenneth Muir (eds), *Shakespeare's Plays in Quarto* (Berkeley, 1981). Page numbers in the text will be to this edition. We surmise that 1606 was the year of performance because the quarto was entered in the Stationer's Register in 1607.

   For topical readings of *The Winter's Tale* in terms of the Project for Union, see Glynne Wickham, *Shakespeare's Dramatic Heritage* (New York, 1969); 'Riddle and Emblem: A Study in the Dramatic Structure of *Cymbeline*', in John Carey (ed.), *English Renaissance Studies Presented to Dame Helen Gardner* (Oxford, 1980), pp. 94–113; 'From Tragedy to Tragi-Comedy: *King Lear* as Prologue', *Shakespeare Survey*, 26 (1973), 33–48. There are also suggestive hints in David M. Bergeron, *Shakespeare's Romances and the Royal Family* (Lawrence, Kansas, 1985), p. 157.

2. I am indebted in particular to Annabel Patterson, *Censorship and Interpretation* (Madison, Wisc., 1984), pp. 58–73; Marie Axton, *The Queen's Two Bodies* (London, 1977), pp. 131–47; Steven Urkowitz, *Shakespeare's Revision of King Lear* (Princeton, 1980); and Gary Taylor and Michael Warren (eds), *The Division of the Kingdoms: Shakespeare's Two Versions of King Lear* (Oxford, 1983).

3. See Margaret Judson, *The Crisis of the Constitution* (1949; reprinted New York, 1964), pp. 25–7, 145; for uses of the idea in contemporary pageantry, see my 'City Metal and Country Mettle', in David M. Bergeron (ed.), *Pageantry in the Shakespearean Theatre* (Athens, Georgia, 1985), pp. 26–47.

4. See, for general discussion, George W. Keeton, *Shakespeare's Legal and Political Background* (London, 1967); O. Hood Phillips's survey, *Shakespeare and the Lawyers* (London, 1972), pp. 89–90; and C. H. McIlwain (ed.), *The Political Works of James I* (Cambridge, Mass., 1918), Appendix B, pp. lxxxviii–ix.

5. See James F. Larkin and Paul L. Hughes (eds), *Stuart Royal Proclamations*, vol. 1 (Oxford, 1973), pp. 92–3.

6. See John Kerrigan's essay 'Revision, Adaptation and the Fool in *King Lear*', and Gary Taylor's essay '*King Lear*: The Date and Authorship of the Folio Version', both in Gary Taylor and Michael Warren (eds), *The*

Division of the Kingdoms: Shakespeare's Two Versions of King Lear (Oxford, 1983), pp. 195–243 and 351–468. Possible reasons behind the alterations are discussed by Taylor, who argues for artistic motives in his essay 'Monopolies, Show Trials, Disaster and Invasion: *King Lear* and Censorship', ibid., pp. 75–119; and by Annabel Patterson in *Censorship and Interpretation* (Madison, Wisc., 1984), pp. 61–71; she contests Taylor's dismissal of censorship or the fear of it as a motivating factor behind the alterations.

I am also indebted to my former colleague Richard Knowles, who has supplied me with enough evidence against Urkowitz and Taylor's bibliographical arguments to convince me that I do not have enough expertise to enter that particular fray. See Knowles's reviews of Urkowitz in *Modern Philology*, 79 (1981–82), 197–200; and of Taylor and Warren in *Shakespeare Quarterly*, 36 (1985), 115–20.

7. See, for example, his heated speech against monopolies recounted in Lady Evangeline de Villiers (ed.), *The Hastings Journal of the Parliament of 1621*, vol. 20 (London, 1953), pp. 27–9. At the beginning of the reign, James had revoked existing monopolies, but it soon became clear that he was sweeping away the old ones to make room for his own. See James F. Larkin and Paul L. Hughes (eds), *Stuart Royal Proclamations*, vol. 1 (Oxford, 1973), pp. 11–14; but also the more favourable account in R. C. Munden, 'James I and "the growth of mutual distrust"', in Kevin Sharp (ed.), *Faction and Parliament: Essays in Early Stuart History* (Oxford, 1978), pp. 50–3.

8. I have made a detailed argument for this proposition in *The Politics of Mirth: Jonson, Herrick, Milton, Marvell and the Defence of Old Holiday Pastimes* (Chicago and London, 1986); both there and in the present discussion I am also strongly indebted to Philip J. Finkelpearl, '"The Comedians' Liberty": Censorship of the Jacobean Stage Reconsidered', *English Literary Renaissance*, 16 (1986), 123–38; and to Stephen Orgel's statement of the problem in 'Making Greatness Familiar', in David M. Bergeron (ed.), *Pageantry in the Shakespearean Theatre* (Athens, Georgia, 1985), pp. 19–25.

9. See Steven Urkowitz, *Shakespeare's Revision of King Lear* (Princeton, 1980) and all the essays in Gary Taylor and Michael Warren (eds), *The Division of the Kingdoms: Shakespeare's Two Versions of King Lear* (Oxford, 1983). As my discussion will make clear, however, I do not regard either text we have as definitive in the sense that these careful scholars claim for it.

10. The quarto version of the phrase reads 'Like Rats oft bite those cordes in twaine, / Which are to intrench, to inloose' (p. 677). The wording is interesting because it can be interpreted as a highly equivocal reference to the matter of essences: something tied together is either to be further tied ('intrenched') or loosened. The reading is admittedly shaky and, in

this case, I am willing to go along with modern editors who argue that the quarto version is probably garbled. I would accept a reading closer to the folio version, 'Like Rats oft bite the holy cords atwaine, / Which are t'intrince, t'vnloose' (Charlton Hinman [ed.], *The First Folio of Shakespeare* [New York, 1968], lines 1147–8).

11. See Steven Urkowitz, *Shakespeare's Revision of King Lear* (Princeton, 1980), pp. 80–128; and Randall McLeod, 'Gon. No more, the text is foolish', in Gary Taylor and Michael Warren (eds), *The Division of the Kingdoms: Shakespeare's Two Versions of King Lear* (Oxford, 1983), pp. 153–94. But see also Marion Trousdale's critique of the critical assumptions behind the differentiations in 'A Trip through the Divided Kingdom', *Shakespearean Quarterly*, 37 (1986), 218–23.

12. See the descriptions of the holiday in R. Chambers, *The Book of Days* (London, n.d.), vol. 2, pp. 763–5; and Margaret Hotine, 'Two Plays for St Stephen's Day', *Notes and Queries*, 227 (1982), 119–21. The carol of King Wenceslaus dates only from the nineteenth century. See Percy Dearmer et al., *The Oxford Book of Carols* (London, 1928), p. 271.

13. W. Carew Hazlitt, *Faiths and Folklore: A Dictionary of National Beliefs, Superstitions and Popular Customs* (London, 1905), vol. 2, p. 564.

14. Like Margaret Hotine, to whose work I am indebted for the parallels, I have used the 1559 *Book of Common Prayer*, but I have also checked the cited passages against the 1604 *Book of Common Prayer*. Biblical passages are from Hotine's citations of the Bishop's Bible version. There is another discussion of the liturgical context of *King Lear* in R. Chris Hassel, Jr, *Renaissance Drama and the English Church Year* (Lincoln, Nebraska, 1979), p. 28, which points out the play's use of the holiday motif of forgiveness of one's enemies. That idea will be brought up below.

15. See in particular Roger Warren, 'The Folio Omission of the Mock Trial: Motives and Consequences', in Gary Taylor and Michael Warren (eds), *The Division of the Kingdoms: Shakespeare's Two Versions of King Lear* (Oxford, 1983), pp. 45–57. Warren's major argument for the omission is on theatrical grounds – the scene slowed the play down too much. Given the festival context of the quarto version, I would suggest that much more was at stake. In the court setting, the slower quarto version might have been more moving and effective than the swifter and more perfunctory folio version.

16. See James F. Larkin and Paul L. Hughes (eds), *Stuart Royal Proclamations*, vol 1 (Oxford, 1973), pp. 103–4, and the similar order for the spring holidays, ibid., pp. 21–2. See also my more extended discussion in *The Politics of Mirth: Jonson, Herrick, Milton, Marvell and*

the Defence of Old Holiday Pastimes (Chicago and London, 1986), pp. 1–85.

17. Arthur Wilson, *The History of Great Britain* (London, 1653), p. 35.

18. Margaret Hotine, 'Two Plays for St Stephen's Day', *Notes and Queries*, 227 (1982), 120. See also Joseph Wittreich, *'Image of that Horror': History, Prophecy and Apocalypse in King Lear* (San Marino, Calif., 1984), pp. 16–33, 57–8 and 114–22.

19. See the rather massive evidence collected by Annabel Patterson, Gary Taylor and Marie Axton, all cited in note 2 above; Margaret Hotine has shown parallels between Lear's fits and a hallucinatory disorder suffered by James I in 'Lear's Fit of the Mother', *Notes and Queries*, 226 (1981), 138–41.

20. See Stephen Greenblatt, 'Shakespeare and the Exorcists', in Patricia Parker and Geoffrey Hartman (eds), *Shakespeare and the Question of Theory* (New York, 1985), pp. 163–87; and, for another fine essay that discusses similar issues of evacuation and deidealisation, Franco Moretti, '"A Huge Eclipse": Tragic Form and the Deconstruction of Sovereignty', in Stephen Greenblatt (ed.), *The Power of Forms in the English Renaissance* (Norman, Okla., 1982), pp. 7–40.

9

The Popular Voice of 'King Lear'

ANNABEL PATTERSON

If *Macbeth* displays to a degree unusual to Shakespeare a set of topics linked by their known pertinence to James I, *King Lear*, which probably shares the same compositional timeframe, comes perilously close to presenting a fictional portrait of the king himself. Ostensibly archaic in its historical location in 844 BC (approximately 800 years before the reign of Macbeth, and 800 after the events represented in *Coriolanus*), the play offered for inspection a disastrous representative of monarchy, and one who shared with the current monarch a striking number of characteristics, so striking, in fact, that it is hard to imagine the resemblance would have gone unnoticed by the censors. The difficulty is compounded by the fact that *King Lear* was, according to the 1608 Quarto, 'Played before the Kings Maiestie at Whitehall upon S. Stephans night in Christmas Hollidayes', an occasion which the Stationers' Register for 26 November 1607 identifies as 'Christmas Last'.

We know, in other words, that on 26 December 1606 King James was regaled by a play whose protagonist was an elderly monarch whose hobby was hunting, whose retinue was distinctive in its foregrounding of a Fool, who during the central acts is evidently insane, and whose authoritarian views ultimately destroyed himself and his entire family. While James himself was only forty in 1606, he prided himself on having ruled Scotland since the age of fifteen, and represented himself to his new subjects as 'an old, experienced king, needing no lessons'.[1] In July 1604 Count Beaumont wrote to Henry

IV of France that the 'king is for ever following the chase in order to divert his spirit';[2] and Archie Armstrong, who accompanied James from Scotland, had already established himself as the 'all-licens'd Fool' of Goneril's complaint (I.iv.209) who treated the king and men of high rank with astonishing familiarity. With these keys to identity firmly established in the first act, the audience would quickly have realised that the archaic setting was a ruse to permit analysis of a particular style and ideology of monarchy, one that was not only, with James's accession, suddenly topical, but that was also, given the king's preference for publishing his views, a matter already of public record.[3]

The Jacobean audience, also, would probably have not been discouraged from considering the Lear/James analogy by the fact that the pre-Arthurian monarch of the chronicles had a different familial situation from their own. Indeed, the play's very first lines would have momentarily suggested a still closer relationship. When Kent opens by remarking to Gloucester, 'I thought the King had more affected the Duke of Albany than Cornwall', his hearers could immediately have assumed, as Glynne Wickham suggested, some reference to Prince Henry, the current Duke of Cornwall, and his brother Charles, Duke of Albany until November 1605.[4] By contrast, in the old play, *The True Chronicle History of King Leir*, probably in print in the summer of 1605, the two husbands are registered as the Kings of Cornwall and Cambria. When the kingdom is divided between sisters, and the Dukes are re-entered in the playtext as merely the husbands of Goneril and Regan, the audience has been misled. At the very least, this ruse would have encouraged a flexible hermeneutics, a wary approach to the play's exceptionally complex representational structure.

As I have argued elsewhere, the theme of rival sons connected *King Lear* to the contemporary debate, initiated by James himself, on the relationship between England and Scotland, whose Union under himself James had made his reign's inaugural project.[5] On 18 November 1606, a little over a month before the royal performance of *King Lear*, James opened the third session of Parliament with a speech urging decision on the Union issue, and reassuring his subjects that 'he did so equally esteem these Two Kingdoms, betwixt which he was so equally divided, as Two Brothers, and as if they had equal Parts of his Affections . . . and after him there could never be any so equally and so amply *affected* to them both.'[6] In the light of this speech, Kent's opening words, 'I thought the King had more *affected* the Duke of Albany than Cornwall' and Gloucester's reply that 'in the division of the kingdom, it appears not which of the Dukes he values most', is manifestly misaligned as a key to the story of 844 BC, but rather more intelligible in the context of Christmas 1606, when the discourse of the day was of fathers, sons and divided inheritances.

There seems little doubt that the Union issue was one major form of the topicality in which *King Lear* is saturated, although, given the reversed mirror in which the issue is visible, it is impossible to decide what solution Shakespeare recommended. Evidently, the play includes a critique of the authoritarian, patriarchal and constitutionally absolutist *theories* of James himself, and at the same time reveals the distinction between absolutist theory and its practice, which in *King Lear* is clearly ineffective. The speech in which Lear gives away the 'name, and all th'addition to a king' (I.i.138), lays open to inspection the tautological structure of the Jacobean language of power, a grandiose and inflationary rhetoric that attempted to make the fact of 'rule' seem more than an accident of birth. And, differently again, the play provides echoes of James's other voices, the querulous voice of well-meaning ('I am a man more sinned against than sinning', III.ii.59; 'Your old kind father, whose kind heart gave all', III.ii.19); and even the voice of criticism well-taken, of reforms intended:

> O! I have ta'en
> Too little care of this.
> (III.iv.32–3)

It is the representation of these voices (in characterological terms, Lear's humanisation) that permits the audience to transfer its sympathy back to the king, and to perceive the system that he represents, however flawed, as more capable of amendment than the aggressive, voracious and essentially unstructured alternative of Edmund, Goneril and Regan. At the level, then, of the Union issue whose language and central metaphors the play incarnates, undecidability reigns.

But after the first act the Union issue disappears, though its familial forms remain. What replaces it, extending topicality's range from the narrowly specific to the broadest and deepest of contemporary concerns, is a critique of the socioeconomic system of Jacobean England. Nor can the force of this critique be restricted to Jacobean England, still less to the opening years of James's reign:

it was reinvoked, as we shall see, by James Agee as the inaugural premise of *Let Us Now Praise Famous Men,* his extraordinary study of American rural poverty in the Depression. Historicity, then, may itself encourage transhistoricity, even or especially when what is transferred to later cultures is the clash of human with economic values and structures.

It has become something of a commonplace in discussions of *King Lear* that it represents the transition from a feudal economy or culture to a nascent capitalism; or, in a slightly different vocabulary, the decline of a moral in the face of a market economy.[7] But the argument that Lear, Kent, and perhaps Cordelia act out the old feudal values or configure (semi-allegorically) a Moral Economy is deeply unpersuasive. Edmund, Goneril and Regan, the figures who supposedly represent the approach of capitalist values, in no way differ from aristocratic predators anywhere in Shakespeare's canon; while it is Lear himself, by promoting a land transfer tax to be paid in professions of love, who introduces marketability into a simple because arbitrary principle of aristocratic inheritance. As for a Moral Economy, if conceived as an earlier stage of mutual benevolence between a feudal aristocracy and clergy and a grateful, humble and obedient peasantry, such a conception could have been no more plausible to Shakespeare than the spectre of a free market regulated only by laws internal to itself, in which no controls could be posited on possessive individualism. Rather, he would have shared in an increasingly articulate body of opinion, articulate in the debates of the Jacobean parliament, that the system combined or should combine elements of morality with economic pragmatism. For the first few years of James's reign saw a distinct change in the fiscal role of parliament, whose previously limited concern with taxation was developed under James (and against his will) into a coherent theory of economic justice.

We will return in the next chapter to parliament's role in regulating the economy, especially as it was brought into sharp focus by the Midlands Rising, producing newly theoretical address to the problems of wealth's distribution. But already in the parliamentary sessions prior to *King Lear,* economics had been made the subject of the day. In the first Jacobean parliament, the Union issue brought immediately to the forefront an old grievance, old in the sense that James had inherited it from his Tudor predecessors, especially Elizabeth: monopolies, or private patents assigned by the monarch for the control of specific products, such as imported wines, salt or starch, to members of their court whom they wished to reward or control. At the end of her reign Elizabeth had acceded to complaints against the procedure, and in her last parliament of 1601, in the aftermath of the Essex rebellion, agreed to issue a proclamation against it. When James succeeded, however, many patents were still extant, and others were distributed in the first rush of liberality (what James called his Christmas) to his Scottish followers. The theme of economic rivalry between English and Scottish, therefore, when it surfaced in the 1604 parliament because James himself provoked it, was merely the hook that drew along with it a group of other fiscal grievances, including wardships, purveyance, the king's personal extravagance, and the hated monopolies, whose connection was made only beneath the debating surface. Loosely grouped under the heading of 'grievances', these issues were posed as the *other* subject of the reign's opening parliament, a subject on which the Commons required satisfaction if the king were ever to accomplish his own darling project, the Union.

Even one of the more conservative historians of this period, J. P. Kenyon, who began with the opinion that the 1604 parliament emitted ' a perpetual rumble' of unfocused discontent which only occasionally 'came to a head on some general issue', came later to the view that economic issues resulted in the formation of a more or less consolidated opposition.[8] Certainly, by the 1610 session, in which Salisbury attempted to resolve the fiscal impasse once and for all by proposing, unsuccessfully, the Great Contract, the nature of the parliament's interest in the economy had been greatly clarified. The symptomatic issue was now 'impositions', Salisbury's solution to the royal deficit by arbitrarily placing new taxes on imports. But the real issue was the mutual recognition by both king and parliament that they had entered an arena of contractual relationships, governed by a logic of reciprocal exchange. In a speech of 21 March, which was largely an exercise in unconstrained patriarchal and absolutist rhetoric, the king nevertheless requested the parliament to 'see how great my wants are' and declared both his willingness to deal and his recognition that absolutist theory should not always be put into practice: 'What a king will do upon bargain is one thing and what on his prerogative is another thing.'[9] The opening premise of *King Lear* is likewise the arrival of the deal, of a newly contractual approach to governance, and to the distribution of wealth. In the initial exchange of land for professions of affection, and even in Lear's own sinister and mistaken threat to Cordelia: 'Nothing will come of nothing',

Shakespeare might be thought to register a warning against the era of the fiscal bargain.

Yet as soon as the division of the kingdom is completed, the emphasis shifts. Lear learns the contractual relationship between power and responsibility for the powerless, and something about the role of need in establishing economic value. The Fool's gibe about monopolies (I.iv.158-9), interestingly omitted from the Folio, is not a casual and hence dispensable topicality, but the opening gambit in an analysis of class and economic difference that the Folio, if anything, intensifies. The Fool assumes that monopolies are the privilege of 'lords and great men'; his remark coordinates with Kent's complaint against Oswald, 'That such a slave as this should wear a sword' (II.ii.73), and Gloucester's complaint against Cornwall that putting Kent in the stocks is inappropriate to his earl's rank ('Your purpos'd low correction / Is such as basest and contemned'st wretches / For pilf'rings and most common trespasses /Are punish'd with' II.ii.142–5). And while Kent's and Gloucester's complaints are against social mobility, upwards and downwards, and therefore conservative, others on the same moral side as they have a more flexible sociology. Edgar's impersonation of a Bedlam beggar, whose models were themselves, in order to 'enforce charity', forced to impersonate the mad (II.iii.20),[10] is an example of willed or provisional topsy-turveydom. The transgressive aspect of Edgar's disguise can be better understood in terms of socioeconomic history than (*pace* Stephen Greenblatt) echoes of Samuel Harsnett and the exorcism debate.[11] The Fool's song, 'Come over the bourn, Bess', is found also in the old, black-letter play, *The longer thou livest, the more Foole thou art*, where 'Morus' is introduced "synging the foote of many songes, as fooles were wont'. And the 'foote' as the sign of transgressive foolishness reappears in *King Lear* in what must be seen as a meta-textual crux, when Goneril, resenting the impediment of her marriage to Albany, complains to Edmund in successively symbolic stages: 'My foote usurps my body' (in the uncorrected first Quarto), 'A foole usurps my bed' (in the corrected Quarto), 'My foote usurps my head', in the second and third Quartos, and finally in the Folio, 'My Fool usurps my body' (IV.ii.28). Foot, fool and usurpation of a proper space thereby converge in the text's own uncertainty.

But we do not need to rely on the antics of the text for this play's radicalism. As Richard Strier remarks, one of the most politically significant moments occurs at the level of violent physical action, when Cornwall's servant attempts to prevent him from blinding

Gloucester, and is stabbed in the back by Regan, exclaiming, with the full weight of outraged decorum, 'A peasant stand up thus!' (III.vii.79).[12] Not only does this moment, as Strier argues, present the 'most radical possible sociopolitical act in a way that can only be interpreted as calling for his audience's approval', it reintroduces precisely that ancient populism for which the term 'peasant' was now already cultural shorthand, a point reinforced for Shakespeare's audience by the fact that Cornwall insults his servant by calling him 'villain', the stigmatised echo of 'villein'.

And, although Shakespeare's audiences could not have known it, a special value attaches also to the Fool's request to know whether 'a madman be a gentleman or a yeoman', and his own conflation of the choice, 'He's a yeoman that has a gentleman to his son; for he's a mad yeoman that sees his son a gentleman before him' (III.vi.9–14). The family predicament speaks obliquely of Shakespeare's own and his father's situation, and for that famous application in 1596, when Shakespeare purchased for John Shakespeare, yeoman, for a gentleman's coat of arms: 'Gold, on a bend sables, a spear of the first steeled argent', with a motto, 'Non Sanz Droit', not without right.[13]

These positions on rank, though presented dialectically, lead inevitably to Lear's great speech of social inversion, which the Folio accentuates by adding the injunction, 'Change places', the heart of a radical theory of economic change and exchange:

> What! art mad? A man may see how this world goes with no eyes. Look with thine ears: see how yond justice rails upon yond simple thief. Hark, in thine ear: [change places, and,] handy dandy, which is the justice, which is the thief?
>
> (IV.vi.151–6)

Social mobility, expressed earlier in the upstart Oswald and the humiliation of Kent, in the yeoman whose ambitious son (unlike Shakespeare) leaves him behind in his climb towards gentrification, implies its own extreme conclusion. If men can change places on the social hierarchy, then those places have no absolute value, and complete inversion becomes, to the seeing ear of madness, utterly thinkable. The echo of Bottom's mingle-mangle of the organs of perception is surely as intentional here as is Lear's recapitulation of Hamlet's 'madness', the scandal of speaking the not immemorial forms of popular protest. But in Lear's case the scandal is the greater, since it is now the king himself, 'the great image of Authority' (IV.vi.160) who speaks in the popular voice.

The central scenes on the heath, then, situate gibes at monopolies or the excessive distribution of knighthoods in a far more radical argument, showing them to be not casual throwaways, but the building blocks of an emergent structural analysis of power and class relations. And in the Fool's prophecy, added in the Folio, this analysis is enigmatically performed in terms of the relationship between church, aristocracy, law, finance and the human body:

> When priests are more in word than matter;
> When brewers mar their malt with water;
> When nobles are their tailors' tutors;
> No heretics burn'd, but wenches' suitors;
> When every case in law is right;
> No squire in debt, nor no poor knight;
> When slanders do not live in tongues;
> Nor cut-purses come not to throngs;
> When usurers tell their gold i' th' field;
> And bawds and whores do churches build;
> Then shall the realm of Albion
> Come to great confusion.
> (III.ii.81–92)

It is not clear whether these distorted relationships are the cause or the consequence of the moral failings of greed, lechery and linguistic corruption; but no one, reading or hearing the last two lines, could avoid the knowledge that Lear's Fool speaks to a national problem, the state of Albion-England both as it is and as it might be if the 'when-then' tensions in the poem, themselves formulae inherited from radical prophecy and medieval social satire, are not resolved in favour of change for the better.[14]

And as in 1604 onwards James I had been responsible for raising those structural relations to the level of consciousness by attempting to theorise them, so in *King Lear* the king himself incorporates that coming to consciousness. Lear begins the analysis out of self-interest, with a critique of Regan's invocation of 'need' as a principle to deny him his retinue. His recognition that if each were to receive only according to his most basic needs he would be reduced to the level of the brute (II.iv.265–9) is a first step in his elementary thinking about the ways in which wealth is distributed. It is, of course, vitiated both in moral and practical terms by his current belief (soon to be shattered by contact with Poor Tom) that 'our basest beggars' already have those basic needs satisfied, and that to introduce the principle, 'to each according to his need', would require them to turn in their 'superfluous' goods. Yet this misconception prepares for his later recognition before the hovel on the heath that 'the art of our necessities is strange, /And can make vile things precious' (III.ii.70–1), simultaneously an acceptance of need as the source of value (if what we most need is shelter from the elements, the worst kind of shelter will outvalue the most precious clothing) and it leads ironically to his determination to 'shake the superflux', that is, the superfluous wealth that he knows the economy produces, to the 'wretches' whose condition he now experiences. The abstract conception of need, then, previously a mere strategy in his argument with Regan, has been rendered concrete (and its meanness admonished) by empirical evidence.

Following *Hamlet's* opening challenge, 'Stand and unfold *yourself*', Lear's demand, 'Expose *thyself* to feel what wretches feel', also acquires the status of metacommentary. Self-exposure in *King Lear*, however, is emphatically not a matter of subjective disclosure. Rather, it is the social outreach required for discovering the spirit of the moral economy embedded, always already, in the economic system. For Lear, this outreach is required 'to show the gods more just'. Much later, a secular interpretation revealed more precisely how self-exposure is the point of intersection between humanist values and empirical method. This point was defined by the documentary realism and poetic structure of Agee's *Let Us Now Praise Famous Men*, which offered the American public the most intimate view of the life of Alabama sharecroppers in the late 1930s, a view acquired by Agee's sharing for several weeks their shack and pitiful diet. It was no coincidence that the first words of Agee's project are those of Lear in his madness:

> Poor naked wretches, wheresoe'er you are,
> That bide the pelting of this pitiless storm,
> How shall your houseless heads and unfed sides,
> Your loop'd and window'd raggedness, defend you
> From seasons such as these? O! I have ta'en
> Too little care of this! Take physic, pomp;
> Expose thyself to feel what wretches feel,
> That thou may'st shake the superflux to them,
> And show the heavens more just.[15]

Agee's dilemmas in carrying his project to completion may also illuminate Shakespeare's, as the evolution of Roosevelt's New Deal may retroactively provide a model for the first decade of James's reign, unlikely though the comparison may seem. The book was the chance product of Walker Evans' appointment as 'roving social historian' of the Farm Security Administration and Agee's assignment to write a sociological article for *Fortune* magazine. The material they collected was destined never to be published by *Fortune*, since while they worked in Alabama Henry Luce decided to change the magazine's course, from support of New Deal policies to a more conservative agenda; but even before this occurred, Agee was consumed by guilt about his own procedures, recognising the aspect of exploitation involved in the assignment. In his 'Preamble' to the book that was eventually published by Houghton Mifflin in 1941, Agee called it 'obscene' that a journal, operating for profit, could propose:

> to pry intimately into the lives of an undefended and appallingly damaged group of human beings, an ignorant and helpless rural family, for the purpose of parading the nakedness, disadvantage and humiliation of these lives before another group of human beings, in the name of science, of 'honest journalism' (whatever that paradox may mean).

In order to deal with that guilt, Agee and Evans reconceived their role as that of holy spies,[16] witnesses or secret agents of the forces of good, a role that Agee conceived, again in terms of *King Lear*, as that of Edgar in his disguise as Poor Tom. In a poem that he wrote for Evans, subsequently added to the preliminaries of *Let Us Now Praise Famous Men*, Agee proposed that they go on their assignment as:

> Spies, moving delicately among the enemy,
> The younger sons, the fools,
> Set somewhat aside the dialects and the stained skins of feigned madness,
> Ambiguously signal, baffle, the eluded sentinel.

The poem advises Edgar to bring his father to his awakening, but himself to withdraw 'undisclosed'; and it concludes with the statement that it is not yet 'that naked hour when armed, / Disguise flung flat, squarely we challenge the field', for the world is still governed by the ruthless, 'Still captive the old wild king'.

From the beginning, *Let Us Now Praise Famous Men* obeys this poem's prescriptions. Among the most ambiguous of Agee's signals is the placing of Lear's speech on the heath opposite another famous radical text, the Communist Manifesto's call to action: 'Workers of the world, unite and fight. You have nothing to lose but your chains, and a world to win.' And beneath *that* quotation appeared the following disclaimer:

> These words are quoted here to mislead those who will be misled by them. They mean, not what the reader may care to think they mean, but what they say. . . for in the pattern of the work as a whole, they are, in the sonata form, the second theme; the poetry facing them [the quotation from *Lear*] is the first. In view of the average readers' tendency to label, and of topical dangers to which any man, whether honest, intelligent, or subtle, is at present liable, it may be well to make the explicit statement that neither these words nor the authors are the property of any political party, faith or faction.

The reader might well react to this opening like the Porter in *Macbeth*: 'it sets him on and it takes him off; it persuades him and disheartens him; makes him stand to and not stand to; in conclusion, equivocates' (II.ii.33–8).

The mention of sonata form, moreover, speaks to the way that *Let Us Now Praise Famous Men* succumbed to the idea of the artefact. The very respect that Agee developed for the sharecroppers, for the simplicity and authenticity of their lives and possessions, was processed as aesthetic appreciation of the worn, the bare, the marginal, or, as Lear put it, 'unaccommodated man'. And in proportion as Agee knew his project was aesthetically and ethically complex,[17] he was completely unable to take his own advice and 'undisclosed, withdraw'. The book is filled with himself, his ruminations on truth, beauty, and the role of the writer in society. He included, as part of this self-examination, his responses to a questionnaire distributed in 1939 by the *Partisan Review* to a number of American writers; and in response to the question, 'Do you think there is any place in our present economic system for literature as a profession?', replied in the negative:

> A good artist is a deadly enemy of society; and the most dangerous thing that can happen to an enemy, no matter how cynical, is to become a beneficiary. No society, no matter how good, could be mature enough to support a real artist without mortal danger to that artist. Only no one need worry: for this same good artist is about the one sort of human being alive who can be trusted to take care of himself.
>
> (p. 355)

As Agee's reading of *King Lear* is eccentrically acute, the predicament here both lamented and celebrated was one he shared, probably, with Shakespeare. Particularly in his intuition that the artist with a social conscience is the younger son, the fool, the feigned madman, Edgar as Poor Tom, Agee both found a metaphor for his own strategic adoption of the sharecroppers' way of life, and grasped in his own ahistorical manner the radical analysis that Shakespeare performed, in disguise, on the economic structure of his own society. That disguise was, like Edgar's, 'to take the basest and most poorest shape / That ever penury, in contempt of man, / Brought near to beast' (II.iii.7–9), that is to say, as a playwright, to take up the case of society's victims, but, by the grace of the dramatic metaphor, to do so 'undisclosed'. Yet Agee's remarks on the 'mortal danger' to the artist of patronage, of becoming society's beneficiary, must also be pertinent to *King Lear*, given that one of the few facts we have of its social existence is the record of that court performance on St Stephen's Night, December 1606, when Shakespeare's play was offered to James I. Leah Marcus may well be correct in reading that emphatic dating as a key to the tone of that one command performance; there is much in *King Lear*, whether or not it was written for this occasion, that fits the festival of St Stephen, whose primary message was charity: 'He that giveth unto the poore, shall not lacke; but he that hideth his eyes from them, shall have many a curse.'[18] And it would certainly be possible to argue that James I was thereby admonished to avoid the fate of Lear, by adopting Lear's hard-learned wisdom.

The fact remains, however, that the play as a whole does not remain faithful to that message, not, at least, at the deep structural level of socioeconomic analysis. For Lear *recovers* from his wisdom-as-madness, and takes nothing from it into his reconciliation with Cordelia that is not a purely domestic intelligence. In fact, in a speech that reveals the source of Agee's concept of holy spying, 'the old wild king' that Agee remembered disappears; or, rather, is domesticated. For when Lear and Cordelia are captured by Edmund's army, Lear responds with political cynicism and privatisation:

> We two alone will sing like birds i' th' cage:
> When thou dost ask me blessing, I'll kneel down,
> And ask of thee forgiveness: so we'll live,
> And pray, and sing, and tell old tales, and laugh
> At gilded butterflies, and hear poor rogues
> Talk of court news; and we'll talk with them too,

Who loses and who wins; who's in, who's out;
And take upon's the mystery of things,
As if we were God's spies.

(V.iii.9–17)

The temptation to withdraw from the 'general' (in Hamlet's sense) to the particular, from structural analysis to subjective concerns, is as candidly identified here as it was in *Hamlet*.

Is this, then, to be construed as Shakespeare's temptation also, his conclusion that the hope of changing places is, after all, a delusion from which we should recover? I doubt it. Such a conclusion is barely compatible with his most transgressive strategy so far, to make the king his own most powerful social critic. And if the play retreats finally into the domestic and familial, as a shelter from sociopolitical awareness, one of Shakespeare's motives may well have been the need for 'moving delicately among the enemy', and with ambiguous signals, to baffle the eluded sentinel.

From Annabel Patterson, *Shakespeare and the Popular Voice* (Oxford, 1989), pp. 106–16.

NOTES

[Annabel Patterson's Foreword to the study from which this excerpt comes declares her purpose to be threefold. The first objective is to challenge the widely held opinion that Shakespeare's view of the 'common' people ranged from amused indulgence of their antics to outright derision. The second is to reassess Shakespeare's social vision from the standpoint of modern theories of popular culture and popular protest. And the third is to attack head-on 'certain fashionable forms of anti-humanism which have seriously inhibited our capacity to talk sensibly about literature, not least because of their own secret elitism' (p. 5). Patterson's assertion of her defiantly unfashionable stance is worth quoting at length:

> this book calmly reinstates certain categories of thought that some have declared obsolete: above all the concepts of authorship, which itself depends on our predicating a continuous, if not a consistent self, of self-determination and, in literary terms, of intention . . . it is an ironic comment on the literary institution that those who have been most anxious to align Shakespeare with their own ideas of social hierarchy have happily attributed intentions to him; whereas those who deplore the alignment have feared, because of the avant-garde

proscriptions against talking about authors or intentions, to meet them on their own ground.

(p. 4)

Patterson has no such fear and boldly seeks to recover from the texts and their contexts Shakespeare's intentional critique of hierarchy from a popular point of view. Central to her case is her reading of *King Lear*, 'a play whose focus on "unaccommodated man" certainly requires understanding in terms of a new theoretically self-conscious humanism' (p. 5). Ed.]

1. Cited in J. P. Kenyon, *The Stuarts*, revised edn (Glasgow, 1970), p. 35.

2. See Frederick von Raumer, *History of the Sixteenth and Seventeenth Centuries*, 2 vols (London, 1835), vol. 2, p. 207. Gary Taylor reprints the king's hunting itinerary from November 1604 to December 1605 in 'King Lear and Censorship', in Gary Taylor and Michael Warren (eds), *The Division of the Kingdoms* (Oxford, 1983), p. 104. And in 1608 Nicholas Breton's pamphlet, *A Murmurer*, indicates that the king's hunting had already become a popular grievance, occasioning the 'murmuring' against which Breton argued: 'Doeth he hunt and delight in Dogges? better to nourish dogs, who shew but their nature . . . then to maintain those monsters of men, that contrary to the nature of men, will murmure at the welfare of their Master' (B6r/v). That Lear was a hunter was, however, already traditional.

3. As in Hamlet's mention of the 'late innovation' that had forced the players to travel, Gloucester's references (in I.ii.106–7) to 'these late eclipses in the sun and moon' encouraged a sense of contemporaneity, given that England had experienced eclipses of the moon and sun in September and October 1605 respectively.

4. See Glynne Wickham, 'From Tragedy to Tragi-Comedy: *King Lear* as Prologue', *Shakespeare Survey*, 26 (1973), 36.

5. See my *Censorship and Interpretation* (Madison, Wisc. 1984), pp. 64–73.

6. *Journals of the House of Commons*, 1, 315.

7. See especially Paul Delaney, '*King Lear* and the Decline of Feudalism', *PMLA*, 92 (1977), 429–40; Rosalie Colie, 'Reason and Need: *King Lear* and the "Crisis" of the Aristocracy', in Rosalie Colie and F. T. Flahiff (eds), *Some Facets of King Lear* (Toronto, 1974), pp. 189–216, an application of Lawrence Stone's theories which pits old aristocrat Lear against new man Edmund, yet attempts to locate both in 'a profound critique of the habits of quantification induced by a commercial revolution' (p. 190).

8. J. P. Kenyon, *The Stuarts*, revised edn (Glasgow, 1970), pp. 8, 37.

9. See Elizabeth Reid Foster (ed.), *Proceedings in Parliament, 1610* (New Haven, 1966), pp. 103, 105.

10. Paul Slack cites, among various types of vagrants recorded, 'counterfeit Bedlams'. See 'Vagrants and Vagrancy in England 1598–1634', *Economic History Review*, 27 (1974), 364.

11. [See Stephen Greenblatt, 'Shakespeare and the Exorcists', in Patricia Parker and Geoffrey Hartman (eds), *Shakespeare and the Question of Theory* (New York, 1985), pp. 163–87. Ed.]

12. Richard Strier, 'Faithful Servants: Shakespeare's Praise of Disobedience', in Heather Dubrow and Richard Strier (eds), *The Historical Renaissance: New Essays on Tudor and Stuart Literature and Culture* (Chicago, 1988), p. 199.

13. See Samuel Schoenbaum, *William Shakespeare: A Compact Documentary Life* (Oxford, 1977), pp. 227–32.

14. For the most extensive discussion of the Fool's prophecy and its relation to earlier forms of protest, including the *Piers Plowman* tradition, see Joseph Wittreich, Jr, *'Image of that Horror': History, Prophecy and Apocalypse in King Lear* (San Marino, Calif., 1984), pp. 60–74. Wittreich refutes the position of P. W. K. Stone in *The Textual History of King Lear* (London, 1980), pp. 119–21, that the prophecy should be discarded as non-Shakespearean on qualitative grounds and, because it is clearly topical, assumed to have been added 'for a purely theatrical purpose', probably by an actor.

15. James Agee and Walker Evans, *Let Us Now Praise Famous Men* (Boston, 1939, reprinted 1960), p. xviii.

16. See Laurence Bergreen, *James Agee: A Life* (Harmondsworth, 1984), p. 164.

17. For a subtle account of *Let Us Now Praise Famous Men* that attempts to relate its aesthetic and political parameters, and to explain its strangenesses as postmodernism *avant la lettre*, see T. V. Reed, 'Unimagined Existence and the Fiction of the Real: Postmodernist Realism in *Let Us Now Praise Famous Men*', *Representations*, 24 (1988), 156–76. It says something about Foucault's notion of a discursive formation that Agee's work, which received, as Reed points out (p. 173), its first full recognition during the civil rights movement of the 1960s, is now being rediscovered again.

18. Leah Marcus, *Puzzling Shakespeare* (Berkeley and Los Angeles, 1988), p. 238. [The allusion is to the account of *King Lear* by Leah Marcus which is reprinted in this volume: see essay 8. Ed.]

10

Perspectives: Dover Cliff and the Conditions of Representation

JONATHAN GOLDBERG

THE WAY TO DOVER

Act III of *King Lear* opens with a description that a nameless gentle-man makes to the disguised Kent, a description of Lear blasted 'with eyeless rage' (III.i.8).[1] Before we are offered the horrific spectacle of the king raging on the heath, we have this image of the king whom the storm would 'make nothing of' (III.i.9). And virtually simultane-ously, before the full force of Lear's expulsion from Gloucester's home becomes apparent, the possibility that the movement of the play contains within it a counterforce is voiced by Kent. It crystallises around Dover. Kent responds to the gentleman's annihilative vision; of his nothing he would make something, offering the hope of secrets to be revealed – the restorative forces of France, the return of Cordelia, the regaining of identity. Kent sends the gentleman, forti-fied with these hopeful words, with tokens 'to Dover' (III.i.36); as if to answer the blinding storm and its 'eyeless rage', he assures him of the possibility that he will 'see Cordelia' (III.i.46) there. A compen-satory pattern, initiated in this interchange and focused on the word *Dover*, continues in the scenes that follow.

Thus, just as we are offered *Dover* as the possibility of a happy ending before Lear's agony on the heath, the word appears again after Lear has endured the storm. Gloucester directs Kent to 'drive toward Dover . . . where thou shalt meet / Both welcome and protection' (III.vi.89–90). The king is borne sleeping to the place where he can escape the plots of death that threaten him. That direction and the reiteration of *Dover*, however, are even more forceful in the scene that follows, Gloucester's blinding at the hands of Regan and Cornwall. Shatteringly, the path of escape from 'eyeless rage' becomes the path to its realisation. It is because Gloucester has sent the king to Dover that he suffers the inquisition of Cornwall and Regan:

> **Cornwall**   Where hast thou sent the king?
> **Gloucester**   To Dover.
> **Regan**   Wherefore to Dover? Wast thou not charged at peril . . .
> **Cornwall**   Wherefore to Dover? Let him answer that.
> **Gloucester**   I am tied to th' stake, and I must stand the course.
> **Regan**   Wherefore to Dover?
> **Gloucester**   Because I would not see thy cruel nails
> Pluck out his poor old eyes
>
> (III.vii.50–7)

The pathos of the escape to Dover emerges in the repeated question, 'wherefore to Dover?' Wherefore, indeed.

When Gloucester has endured what he would not see, Regan sends him to 'smell / His way to Dover' (III.vii.93–4). Gloucester's path, doubling Lear's, collapses the antinomy of 'eyeless rage' and the hope of recovery. Gloucester emblematises, literalises, and makes fully horrific a path of fulfilled desire – the desire not to see. The desire and hope constellated around Dover sickens. In the next scene, Edgar, disguised as Poor Tom, meets his father with his bleeding eyes, and Gloucester asks him to lead 'i' th' way to Dover' (IV.i.43). 'Know'st thou the way to Dover?' (IV.i.55), he asks, and asks again, 'Dost thou know Dover?' (IV.i.71). To Edgar's affirmative response, the old man describes the cliff that is his utmost desire, a verge from whose dizzying height he expects no return.

Either way – as the place where Lear will see Cordelia, or the place where Gloucester will have the satisfaction of suicide – in these reiterations of *Dover*, the word names a site of desire, the hope for recovery or, at least, repose, restoratives to answer 'eyeless rage', or the final closing of the eyes in a sleep without end. Lear will awaken in Cordelia's sight, perceiving himself deprived of that ultimate rest: 'You do me wrong to take me out o' th' grave' (IV.vii.45).

Before that, Edgar will have fulfilled Gloucester's request in a way that as strongly undercuts any hope that Dover might embody. For, after Gloucester's reiterated questions to Edgar, the word *Dover* never recurs in *King Lear*. Instead of the place, we arrive at Dover Cliff only in the lines that Edgar speaks to his father in IV.vi. In 'Shakespeare Imagines a Theatre',[2] Stephen Orgel argues persuasively for the imaginative weight and force of these lines, and I will not repeat his observations here. It suffices to say that Dover Cliff exists only in Edgar's lines and nowhere else in the play. The refusal to allow the word *Dover* to arrive at the place it (apparently) names, the failure, in other words, for signifier to reach signified – the failure of the sign – establishes the place that *Dover* occupies in the text. It is the place of illusion – the illusion of the desire voiced by Kent or Gloucester, the illusion of recovery *and* the illusion of respite and end. Yet, to come to the central point that I wish to make here, Edgar's lines describing Dover Cliff establish themselves as illusion by illusionistic rhetoric. His description answers to a particular mode of seeing, and the limits that *Dover* represents in the text are the limits of representation themselves. Paradoxically, a speech that represents space in a realistic mode points to the incapacity of the stage – and of language – to realise what the lines represent.

PERSPECTIVES

Here are Edgar's lines:

> Come on, sir; here's the place. Stand still. How fearful
> And dizzy 'tis to cast one's eyes so low!
> The crows and choughs that wing the midway air
> Show scarce so gross as beetles. Halfway down
> Hangs one that gathers samphire – dreadful trade;
> Methinks he seems no bigger than his head.
> The fishermen that walk upon the beach
> Appear like mice; and yond tall anchoring bark,
> Diminished to her cock; her cock, a buoy
> Almost too small for sight. The murmuring surge
> That on th' unnumb'red idle pebble chafes
> Cannot be heard so high. I'll look no more,
> Lest my brain turn, and the deficient sight
> Topple down headlong.
>
> (IV.vi.11–24)

The lines come ten lines into a scene in which the information given is, at best, ambiguous, Gloucester insisting that the ground he treads is flat, and that he can hear no sea roaring. There is no evidence to his imperfect senses that he approaches the verge that suddenly looms in Edgar's lines; as Orgel argues, the evidence of the audience's eyes and ears would confirm Gloucester's denials. Still, an audience would also know that were we to witness a scene at Dover Cliff, Shakespeare's stage would have no way of representing that event save in the language of those on stage who could testify to such an arrival; in this scene, only Edgar could report the evidence of sight. The stage would be, whether we were at Dover Cliff or not, flat; language would tell us to see it otherwise.

Such had been Shakespeare's practice elsewhere. Thus, the Chorus before *Henry V* directly addressed the audience on the question of what the stage might represent and the possible transformation that the 'wooden O' (Prologue, 12) could undergo, bringing something out of nothing. The limits of representation is the theme of the prologue to the play. Although he desires to show a 'swelling scene' (Prologue, 4), all the Chorus can give is the 'great accompt'(Prologue, 17), 'flat unraised spirits' (Prologue, 9) in 'little place' (Prologue, 16) offering themselves and their words to the multiplying capacity of the audience: 'Piece out our imperfections with your thoughts: / Into a thousand parts divide one man / And make imaginary puissance' (Prologue, 23–5). The Chorus describes here a Shakespearean transaction regularly enacted: to allow the force of imagination to go beyond the limits possible on the stage, and to take what the mind makes as the goal at which representation aims. Representation strives to be presentation; the audience credits the illusion as real event.[3]

Allowing words to become events on stage through the transformative capacity of images is the crucial Shakespearean metamorphosis to which the Chorus alludes. Banquo outside Inverness stops to observe birds building nests in the castle walls:

> This guest of summer,
> The temple-haunting martlet, does approve
> By his loved mansionry that the heaven's breath
> Smells wooingly here. No jutty, frieze,
> Buttress, nor coign of vantage, but this bird
> Hath made his pendant bed and procreant cradle.

Where they most breed and haunt, I have observed
The air is delicate.

(I.vi.3–10)

Like Gloucester, the audience can neither hear nor see Banquo's
birds, but we credit his description and supply the sight he offers.
When Edgar describes Dover Cliff, we might suppose that the lines
work on similar principles. The reiterations of *Dover* seem to have
been leading to the place as surely as the gentleman's lines in III.i.
describing the almost unimaginable scene of Lear in the raging
storm, cursing and screaming as the storm unleashes its parallel rage,
become the staged fact in III.ii. Kent exits in III.i to seek his master,
and the empty stage then discovers Lear enacting what the words
before had done. This transformation realises the words; but, on the
other hand, the scene works in part because it has first been imagined
and verbalised. What is staged has already been supplemented be-
forehand by the gentleman's lines. Language has been there before
the act, and the scene is all the more potent because of what has come
before it. *Dover* tantalises us with these expectations only to deny
them.

The arrival at Dover in *King Lear* may be less overtly self-conscious about staging than the opening lines of the Chorus in *Henry
V*; it is nonetheless much more incisive about the problems that such
a moment represents. For in *King Lear*, the possibility of the creation
of the illusion of place through language is entangled in the significance of that illusory place in the text.[4] To reach Dover means
something crucial in the careers of Gloucester and Lear, and the
testing of the limitations of representation collapses at one time both
the questions about the stage's capacity to represent as well as the
hopes and desires that have constellated around the cliffs of Dover.
For unlike the imagined scenes that the Chorus of *Henry V* offers, the
scene that Edgar paints is couched in a language of illusionistic
rendering that is virtually unprecedented in Shakespeare. The representation of the real, the realisation of representation, is in question. Edgar's description of Dover recasts a version of illusionistic
representation upon which Renaissance painting depends. The lines
offer a perspective on perspective.[5]

The theory of (Italian) Renaissance painting as presented in a
treatise like Alberti's *Della pittura* depends on a few elements.[6] The
viewer is imagined as stationary. The surface of the painting is

considered as a framed window, and the distance of the viewer's eye from the surface of the painting determines the distance into space of the painting, which is organised around a vanishing point that represents the horizon of vision, and which is placed exactly correspondent to the fixed eye viewing the scene. All elements beyond the frame diminish proportionally until they reach the limit of vision which organises the pictorial space.

Blind Gloucester is positioned to have this illusionistic experience. Edgar roots him to 'the place' and insists that he 'stand still' (IV.vi.11). Between the spot where they are supposed to stand and the dizzying prospect, a series of midpoints is marked, dividing the space into mathematical segments. Birds appear the size of beetles; a man at this distance 'seems no bigger than his head' (IV.vi.16). Further down, they are even smaller; men become mice. The last objects seen are described in a kind of algebra that expresses a verbal version of a formula of proportion, $a:b::b:c$, 'yond anchoring bark, / Diminished to her cock; her cock, a buoy, / Almost too small for sight' (IV.vi. 18–20). The diminution in scale is insistent. Equally important is the illusionism of this carefully constructed view, the truth of what is apparent: *show, seem, appear* are the operative terms in Edgar's account.

The exactitude of visual placement in Edgar's scene is remarkable. When Banquo draws our eyes to see his nesting birds, he fills every 'jutty, frieze, / Buttress . . . [and] coign of vantage' (I.vi.5–6) with scenes of procreation. These reflect his mind and his host's, and the moral and rhetorical pointing is telling.[7] But the audience to these lines is not asked to imagine an exact sense, but to countenance the meanings read into it. We grant Banquo his sight because we measure his imagination by it. We need not see where the architectural elements are in relation to each other, or where precisely each bird builds. Similarly, the Chorus of *Henry V* instructs: 'Think, when we talk of horses, that you see them / Printing their proud hoofs i' th' receiving earth' (Prologue, 26–7). The scene he asks to be seen derives its realisation from a graphic art, the translation of words heard into the imprinting of an impression. The words stamp themselves on the mind so that what is seen as a picture is something like words as they come to be on a page. The Chorus focuses on a particular action here, just as Banquo does. But unlike Edgar's vision, the emphasis is verbal, on the power of words to work on the imagination. By respecting the limits of representation and not insisting that the stage can go beyond itself, Banquo's birds or the horses of the Chorus can make their imaginary mark. But in Edgar's lines, 'imaginary puissance', as the Chorus called it (Prologue, 25), the power of images, is pushed to its limits. Dover is to be realised, not simply to be imagined.

The moral meanings to be read in Edgar's description derive precisely from the attempt at passing from representation to actual presentation. Like Banquo's, his lines measure the mind of the beholder, too. The lines comment, in their visual form, on the limits of possibility in the real and on the impossibility of the realisation of language and desire. The real rests on an insubstantial basis. One sign of this is that Edgar's vision is fearfully reductive, not only in its mathematics, but also in valuation: the birds metamorphosed into beetles or the fishermen turned mice are diminished on the scale of being; the 'dreadful' trade of the herbgatherer is further horrific in his dismemberment – he has become nothing but a head. Intimated, then, in Edgar's lines is the notion that the creation of illusionistic space and a belief in it depend upon acts of annihilation. To make the scene plausible, it must draw towards the limits of visibility. Illusion-istic representation depends upon reductions. The illusion of continuous space rests upon what cannot be seen, on exhausting the limits of sight and arriving at what is 'too small for sight' (IV.vi.20). Vision depends upon both blindness and invisibility; it rests upon a vanishing point.

These lines, spoken for the benefit of a blind man, establish him as the best audience for a mode of vision. Similarly, this diminishing scene is, like a painting, utterly silent: 'The murmuring surge / That on th' unnumbered idle pebble chafes / Cannot be heard so high' (IV.vi.20–2). And, seeing this way, Edgar feels that he will go blind and be drawn into the scene, and be destroyed by it: 'I'll look no more / Lest my brain turn, and the deficient sight / Topple down headlong' (IV.vi.22–4). Albertian notions of the continuity between the viewer's space and the space of the painting become a prospect of madness in which the conviction of illusion produces the annihila-tion of the viewer. Gloucester embraces this illusion and plunges into it. He has been convinced by the *trompe l'oeil* of representation and his fall shows that he is the perfect audience for it.

Yet the effect of the scene, at least in retrospect, is to call represen-tation into question. If the lines demonstrate that pictorial space is an illusion, they also show that words succeed only in perpetrating illusion. If they show that our eyes cannot be trusted, they do not, therefore, give us confidence that what we see subsequently can be believed. Nor do they restore faith in blindness, for they make blindness and sight coincident. When we return to Gloucester's initial perspective – the stage is flat, there is no roaring sea to be heard – we come back to a bare stage stripped of the possibilities that Edgar's language invoked. Gloucester's life is no 'miracle' (IV.vi.55), but a cheat. And all miracles that we might have supposed to lie at Dover will be equally guilty of the charge of illusion. The scene, employing the language by which a convincing real space is created, shows up the power of the stage.

The perspective from the imagined cliffs of Dover is so unusual in Shakespeare that there is barely the linguistic evidence that such a scene lay within his knowledge.[8] Only in sonnet 24 is the word *perspective* used with some possibility that it means what Alberti meant by it: 'perspective it is best painter's art' (line 4). The sonnet describes how the beloved's picture has been inscribed in the lover's heart; it is a matter of the exchange of eyeglances that transfers what is seen to what is within, this picture displaying the art of the painter and framed by the body of the seer:

> Mine eye hath played the painter and hath stelled
> Thy beauty's form in table of my heart;
> My body is the frame wherein 'tis held,
> And perspective it is best painter's art.
>
> (1–4)

The more usual use of *perspective* can be found in *Richard II*. There, attempting to talk the queen out of her grief, Bushy offers this description of misprision: 'sorrow's eye, glazed with blinding tears, / Divides one thing entire to many objects, / Like perspectives, which rightly gazed upon, / Show nothing but confusion – eyed awry, / Distinguish form' (II.ii.16–20). Bushy's perspective is anamorphosis, the art of placing an object in a picture, which, to be seen correctly, must not be seen head on.[9] In anamorphic art, the spectator must be in two places at once to take in the picture. Only in the mind can the double act of seeing be reconciled. There is some possibility that the 'painter's art' of sonnet 24 is an optical illusion of this sort rather than the illusion of actuality since it is about seeing through others' eyes and the discrepancy between what is seen without and within. 'Now see what good turns eyes for eyes have done' (line 9), the final quatrain opens, and the 'turns' may well be anamorphic metamorphoses. At any rate, the conclusion of the sonnet opens a distance between 'painter's art' and knowing: 'Yet eyes this cunning want to

grace their art; / They draw but what they see, know not the heart'
(lines 13–14).

It is striking to note that Bushy's version of misprision anticipates
the Chorus of *Henry V* asking for what is seen to serve as the basis
for multiplication; by not seeing what is on stage and taking single
things as signs of more, the viewer can provide the false perspective
necessary to the truth of theatrical illusion. The Chorus to *Henry V*
thus implies that Shakespeare's is, regularly, a theatre of perspective,
but of the sort that Bushy describes, a stage where what is seen and
heard invites one to go beyond the evidence of the senses. In this
respect, a quintessential moment occurs at the end of *Twelfth Night*
when the twins Viola and Sebastian are finally on stage together and
in the Duke's sight. Orsino comments, 'A natural perspective that is
and is not' (V.i.209). The stage has made itself at that moment a
multiplying glass; the opposing tendencies in the language and desires of the characters have been realised – as if naturally – when the
twins face each other. This 'natural perspective', however, is not
Albertian. Rather, it issues in an art of multiplicity and not an order
determined by a vanishing point. The Chorus of *Henry V* is intent
upon a mathematics in which a 'wooden O', the theatre-as-nothing,
can contain all. In *King Lear*, nothing comes of nothing, and the very
language which would seem (to us) solidly to locate the world slides
into an abyss, an uncreating, annihilative nothingness.

In the scene that Edgar presents, two perspectives are in question,
the one that can be associated with the optical illusion of anamorphosis
– the theatre, that is, as illusion and multiplicity, and another perspective, associated with representation (or illusionism), theatrical
reality, and one-point mathematics. Ironically, the latter system,
which we might be inclined to say shows the capacities of the mind
and the reality of the material world, seems wanting. And it undermines even the first perspective, which is embedded in the notion that
Edgar's *lines will give us a scene*. What is of further interest here is
the fact that these two modes of perspective are crucial in understanding the history of the stage in Shakespeare's time; theatrical
representation offers another perspective on Edgar's lines.

Two or three years before *King Lear*, English audiences, at least
those privileged to attend court theatricals, had first seen illusionistic
scenery. We know, from some contemporary eyewitness accounts,
that these proved baffling, unconvincing. The distortions that Edgar
enumerates as the enabling conditions of perspective, birds become
beetles, men become heads, were all that Sir Dudley Carleton saw at

a performance of Ben Jonson's *The Masque of Blackness*. Rather than seeing the representational necessity in what Inigo Jones had designed, here is what Carleton saw: an 'Engine . . . which had Motion . . . in it the Images of Sea-Horses . . .', and, he concludes, 'The Indecorum was, that there was all Fish and no water'. Carleton saw the elements, but not the design.[10] Unlike Edgar, he was in no danger of being absorbed in the illusion. He didn't see it. Edgar's lines present the new convention of staging that was to challenge and ultimately supplant representation at the Globe. Gloucester's initial affirmation of the flat stage in which representation depends almost entirely on language is challenged by Edgar's pictorialism. Shakespeare in the scene is not only enacting a version of the familiar trope analogising the arts, *ut pictura poesis*, he is posing one kind of stage against another. And, of course, he was implicated in both. From 1603 on, Shakespeare's company had worn the royal livery, and by the time of *King Lear* they did not only continue to perform at the Globe, but were performing at court as well, where the King's Men took part in the masques that Jones was designing for the royal eye.

Those scenes, in fact, are the best evidence for Shakespeare's knowledge of Albertian perspective. Certainly, English painting until the 1620s conceived of the surface of a painting in terms more akin to anamorphic than to illusionistic perspective. Summarising the qualities of the Elizabethan image, Roy Strong comments on the 'schematic and episodic view of a picture's surface', and concludes: 'Inscriptions, emblems, symbolic objects and whole inset scenes are meant to be read separately as well as together; they are not governed by the single perspective viewpoint as re-created by the artists of Renaissance Italy.'[11] It was Inigo Jones's importation of Italian scene design that changed the conception of the surface of English painting, replacing an organisation of two-dimensional surface co-ordinates with a three-dimensional hierarchy that invited the translation of surface positions into perceptions of depth. Subordination replaced co-ordination.

Edgar's lines cross and recross these pictorial paths. Hearing them, Gloucester kneels, addressing the 'mighty gods', renouncing the world 'in your sights' (IV.vi.34–5). What is *our* sight at that moment? What is our perspective on the scene? Edgar has presented an illusion one must be blind to see, has disabled *at once* Gloucester's stage that depends on language and the stage that depends on pictorial illusion. The scene, summoning up the powers of representation, shows the limits of representation. Gloucester makes something of Edgar's nothing, and Edgar's imagined Dover is a working out of illusion that rests on nothing: silence, invisibility, blindness. Pictorial space is founded on the meeting of the eye and the vanishing point. Acceding to this representation, Gloucester passes through the vanishing point and topples down headlong into double blindness, for he has agreed to see what cannot be seen – as we do when we refer to IV.vi as the Dover Cliff scene, or credit it with working miracles. The scene, however, insists that it is an illusion, and what it offers is an anatomy of the techniques of illusion – verbal and pictorial – upon which Shakespearean theatre depends. The 'eyeless rage' (III.i.8) that beat upon King Lear's head and that would 'make nothing of' him is visited upon Gloucester and upon the audience to the scene. 'Nothing will come of nothing' (I.i.90), Lear had told Cordelia, and the anatomy of representation in IV.vi is spaced between the nothing of the vanishing point and Gloucester's assumption of Lear's 'poor old eyes' (III.vii.57). This is the space of representation. By invoking these nothings as the condition of representation, IV.vi shows just what we accede to in seeing *King Lear*, and implicates the audience in its annihilative vision.

From David M. Bergeron and G. Douglas Atkins (eds), *Shakespeare and Deconstruction* (New York, Bern, Frankfurt and Paris, 1988), pp. 245–56.

NOTES

[The above book in which Jonathan Goldberg's reading of *Lear* appeared was the first collection of essays exclusively concerned with the application of deconstruction to Shakespeare. As Gary Waller points out in the opening essay, 'Decentring the Bard: The Dissemination of the Shakespearean Text':

> There is clearly a radical break between the traditional scholarly insistence on 'order', 'unity' or 'meaning' and the deconstructive emphasis on the disruptiveness of textuality, on the infinite deferral of meaning, on the real emptiness of language and the insistence that textual practices always operate in contradiction to their own intended existence.
>
> (p. 22)

The deconstructive approach is sharply distinguished by Waller from both the old and the new historicism, which pose and resolve quite different kinds of problem. Deconstruction resists reducing the Shakespearean text to a completed theme, however complex its definition. It insists instead on our tackling the text at the level of its language, teasing out the involuntary repressions, opacities and deadlocks generated in its linguistic struggle to attain a meaning which constantly eludes its grasp. And, in Waller's view,

> Therein lies deconstruction's challenge to both orthodox and 'new historicist' Shakespeare criticism: that we approach his works as language, not as vision, meaning or thematisations of universal (or even historically specific) concerns, and that we watch his plays unravel our (and Shakespeare's) attempts to fix meaning in words.
>
> (p. 23)

This is precisely the challenge posed by Goldberg's account of *King Lear*. Ed.]

1. All citations are from Alfred Harbage (ed.), *The Complete Pelican Shakespeare* (Baltimore, 1969).

2. Stephen Orgel, 'Shakespeare Imagines a Theatre', *Poetics Today*, 5 (1984), 549–61, especially 556–7.

3. For a discussion of Shakespearean representation that shares many of the concerns of this essay, see David Marshall, 'Exchanging Visions: Reading *A Midsummer Night's Dream*', *English Literary History*, 49 (1982), 543–75.

4. On linguistic places (*topoi*), see Marion Trousdale, *Shakespeare and the Rhetoricians* (Chapel Hill, Carolina, 1982).

5. Edgar's lines have been seen in the context of perspective by Marshall McLuhan in *The Gutenberg Galaxy* (Toronto, 1962), pp. 15–17, and again in McLuhan and Harley Parker, *Through the Vanishing Point* (New York, 1968), pp. 14, 74–5; the emphasis in both treatments is on the fragmentation of the visual.

6. See Leon Battista Alberti, *On Painting*, trans. John R. Spencer (New Haven, 1956), pp. 45–8, 56, for the summary I offer. For a particularly stimulating discussion, see Harry Berger, Jr, 'L. B. Alberti: Art and Actuality in Humanist Perspective', *Centennial Review*, 10 (1966), 237–77. On the subject in general, see John White, *The Birth and Rebirth of Pictorial Space* (Boston, 1967), and the review essay by Robert Klein, 'Studies on Perspective in the Renaissance', in his *Form and Meaning* (New York, 1979). Svetlana Alpers, *The Art of Describing* (Chicago, 1983) might point to a non-Italian tradition of representation (linking graphic representation, writing and description) which provides an alternative to Albertian perspective within Edgar's speech.

7. For a provocative reading of these lines, see Harry Berger, Jr, 'The Early Scenes of *Macbeth*: Preface to a New Interpretation', *English Literary History*, 47 (1980), 1–31, especially 28–30.

8. On the knowledge of Italian theories in England, and the terminology of sixteenth-century Englishmen, see Lucy Gent, *Picture and Poetry: 1560–1620* (Leamington Spa, 1981), especially pp. 23–5 on perspective. For a reading of sonnet 24 that takes up many of the issues pursued here and places them within the broader context of ideas of vision in the sequence, see Joel Fineman, *Shakespeare's Perjured Eye* (Berkeley, 1986), pp. 135–40. See also Jonathan Goldberg, *Voice Terminal Echo* (New York, 1986), pp. 92–8.

9. On anamorphosis, especially in its literary use, see Claudio Guillén, 'On the Concept and Metaphor of Perspective', in Stephen G. Nichols, Jr and Richard B. Vowles (eds), *Comparatists at Work* (Waltham, Mass., 1968), and Ernest B. Gilman, *The Curious Frame* (New Haven, 1978). For the broader cultural implications, see Stephen Greenblatt, *Renaissance Self-Fashioning: From More to Shakespeare* (Chicago, 1980).

10. My comments depend upon Stephen Orgel and Roy Strong, *Inigo Jones: The Theatre of the Stuart Court*, 2 vols (London and Berkeley, 1973), vol. 1, pp. 6–8, 11–12, 89.

11. Roy Strong, *The Cult of Elizabeth* (London, 1977), p. 111.

11

The Cultivation of Anxiety: King Lear and his Heirs

STEPHEN GREENBLATT

I want to begin this essay far from the Renaissance, with a narrative of social practice first published in the *American Baptist Magazine* of 1831. Its author is the Reverend Francis Wayland, an early president of Brown University and a Baptist minister. The passage concerns his infant son, Heman Lincoln Wayland, who was himself to become a college president and Baptist minister:

> My youngest child is an infant about 15 months old, with about the intelligence common to children of that age. It has for some months been evident, that he was more than usually self willed, but the several attempts to subdue him, had been thus far relinquished, from the fear that he did not fully understand what was said to him. It so happened, however, that I had never been brought into collision with him myself, until the incident occurred which I am about to relate. Still I had seen enough to convince me of the necessity of subduing his temper, and resolved to seize upon the first favourable opportunity which presented, for settling the question of authority between us.
>
> On Friday last before breakfast, on my taking him from his nurse, he began to cry violently. I determined to hold him in my arms until he ceased. As he had a piece of bread in his hand, I took it away, intending to give it to him again after he became quiet. In a few minutes he ceased, but when I offered him the bread he threw it away, although he was very hungry. He had, in fact, taken no nourishment except a cup of milk since 5 o'clock on the preceding afternoon. I considered this a fit opportunity for attempting to subdue his temper, and resolved to embrace it. I thought it necessary to change his disposition, so that he would receive the bread *from me*, and also be

so reconciled to me that he would *voluntarily* come to me. The task I found more difficult than I had expected.

I put him into a room by himself, and desired that no one should speak to him, or give him any food or drink whatever. This was about 8 o'clock in the morning. I visited him every hour or two during the day, and spoke to him in the kindest tones, offering him the bread and putting out my arms to take him. But throughout the whole day he remained inflexibly obstinate. He did not yield a hair's breadth. I put a cup of water to his mouth, and he drank it greedily, but would not touch it with his hand. If a crumb was dropped on the floor he would eat it, but if *I* offered him the piece of bread, he would push it away from him. When I told him to come to me, he would turn away and cry bitterly. He went to bed supperless. It was now twenty-four hours since he had eaten anything.

He woke the next morning in the same state. He would take nothing that I offered him, and shunned all my offers of kindness. He was now truly an object of pity. He had fasted thirty-six hours. His eyes were wan and sunken. His breath hot and feverish, and his voice feeble and wailing. Yet he remained obstinate. He continued thus, till 10 o'clock, A.M. when hunger overcame him, and he took from me a piece of bread, to which I added a cup of milk, and hoped that the labour was at last accomplished.

In this however I had not rightly judged. He ate his bread greedily, but when I offered to take him, he still refused as pertinaciously as ever. I therefore ceased feeding him, and recommenced my course of discipline.

He was again left alone in his crib, and I visited him as before, at intervals. About one o'clock, Saturday, I found that he began to view his condition in its true light. The tones of his voice in weeping were graver and less passionate, and had more the appearance of one bemoaning himself. Yet when I went to him he still remained obstinate. You could clearly see in him the abortive efforts of the will. Frequently he would raise his hands an inch or two, and then suddenly put them down again. He would look at me, and then hiding his face in the bedclothes weep most sorrowfully. During all this time I was addressing him, whenever I came into the room, with invariable kindness. But my kindness met with no suitable return. All I required of him was, that he should come to me. This he would not do, and he began now to see that it had become a serious business. Hence his distress increased. He would not submit, and he found that there was no help without it. It was truly surprising to behold how much agony so young a being could inflict upon himself.

About three o'clock I visited him again. He continued in the state I have described. I was going away, and had opened the door, when I thought that he looked somewhat softened, and returning, put out my hands, again requesting him to come to me. To my joy, and I hope gratitude, he rose up and put forth his hands immediately. The agony

was over. He was completely subdued. He repeatedly kissed me, and
would do so whenever I commanded. He would kiss any one when I
directed him, so full of love was he to all the family. Indeed, so entirely
and instantaneously were his feelings towards me changed, that he
preferred me now to any of the family. As he had never done before,
he moaned after me when he saw that I was going away.

Since this event several slight revivals of his former temper have
occurred, but they have all been easily subdued. His disposition is, as
it never has been before, mild and obedient. He is kind and affectionate, and evidently much happier than he was, when he was determined
to have his own way. I hope and pray that it may prove that an effect
has been produced upon him for life.[1]

The indignation and disgust that this account immediately excited
in the popular press of Jacksonian America, as it does in ourselves,
seem to me appropriate but incomplete responses, for if we say that
tyranny here masquerades as paternal kindness, we must also remember that, as Kafka once remarked of his father, 'love often wears
the face of violence'. Wayland's behaviour reflects the relentless
effort of generations of evangelical fathers to break the child's will,
but it would be a mistake to conceive of this effort as a rejection of
affective familial bonds or as a primitive disciplinary pathology from
which our own unfailing decency toward the young has freed itself.
On the contrary, Wayland's struggle is a strategy of intense familial
love, and it is the sophisticated product of a long historical process
whose roots lie at least partly in early modern England, the England
of Shakespeare's *King Lear*.

Wayland's twin demands – that his son take food directly from
him and come to him voluntarily, as an act of love and not forced
compliance – may in fact be seen, from the perspective of what
French historians call the *longue durée*, as a domesticated, 'realistic',
and, as it were, bourgeoisified version of the love test with which
Shakespeare's play opens. Lear too wishes to be the object – the
preferred and even the sole recipient – of his child's love. He can
endure a portion of that love being turned elsewhere, but only when
he directs that it be so divided, just as Reverend Wayland was in the
end pleased that the child 'would kiss any one when I directed him'.
Such a kiss is not a turning elsewhere but an indirect expression of
love for the father.

Goneril, to be sure, understands that the test she so successfully
passes is focused on compliance: 'you have obedience scanted', she
tells Cordelia, 'And well are worth the want that you have wanted'

(I.i). But Lear's response to his youngest daughter's declaration that she does not love him all suggests that more than outward deference is at stake: 'But goes thy heart with this?' From Cordelia at least he wants something more than formal obedience, something akin to the odd blend of submission to authority and almost erotic longing depicted at the close of Wayland's account: 'He repeatedly kissed me, and would do so whenever I commanded. . . . As he had never done before, he moaned after me when he saw that I was going away.'

To obtain such love, Wayland withholds his child's food, and it is tempting to say that Lear, in disinheriting Cordelia, does the same. But what is a technique for Wayland is for Lear a dire and irreversible punishment: the disinheriting and banishment of Cordelia is not a lesson, even for the elder sisters, let alone for Cordelia herself, but a permanent estrangement, sealed with the most solemn oaths. Wayland's familial strategy uses parental discipline to bring about a desired relationship rather than to punish when the relationship has failed. In his account, the taking away of the child's food *initiates* the love test, whereas in *King Lear* the father's angry cancellation of his daughter's dowry signals the abandonment of the love test and the formal disclaimer of all paternal care. In the contrast between this bitter finality and a more calculating discipline that punishes in order to fashion its object into a desired shape, we glimpse the first of the differences that help to account for the resounding success of Wayland's test and the grotesque and terrifying failure of Lear's.

A second crucial difference is that by the early nineteenth century the age of the child who is tested has been pushed back drastically; Wayland had noticed signs of self-will in his infant son for some months, but had not sought to subdue it until he was certain that the child could 'fully understand what was said to him'. That he expected to find such understanding in a fifteen-month-old reflects a transformation in cultural attitudes toward children, a transformation whose early signs may be glimpsed in Puritan child-rearing manuals and early seventeenth-century religious lyrics and that culminates in the educational philosophy of Rousseau and the poetry of Wordsworth.

King Lear, by contrast, locates the moment of testing, for Cordelia at least, precisely in what was for Shakespeare's England the age that demanded the greatest attention, instruction, and discipline, the years between sexual maturity at about fifteen and social maturity at about twenty-six. This was, in the words of a seventeenth-century clergyman quoted by Keith Thomas, 'a slippery age, full of passion, rashness, wilfulness', upon which adults must impose restraints and exercise shaping power. The Elizabethan and Jacobean theatre returned almost obsessively to the representation of this age group, which, not coincidentally, constituted a significant portion of the play-going population. Civic officials, lawyers, preachers, and moralists joined dramatists in worrying chiefly about what Lawrence Stone in *The Family, Sex and Marriage in England 1500–1800* calls 'potentially the most unruly element in any society, the floating mass of young unmarried males', and it was to curb their spirits, fashion their wills, and delay their full entry into the adult world that the educational system and the laws governing apprenticeship addressed themselves. But girls were also the objects of a sustained cultural scrutiny that focused on the critical passage from the authority of the father or guardian to the authority of the husband. This transition was of the highest structural significance, entailing complex transactions of love, power, and material substance, all of which, we may note, are simultaneously at issue when Lear demands of his youngest daughter a declaration she is unwilling or unable to give.

Love, power, and material substance are likewise at issue in the struggle between Reverend Wayland and his toddler, but all reduced to the proportions of the nursery: a kiss, an infantile gesture of refusal, a piece of bread. In the nineteenth-century confrontation, punishment is justified as exemplary technique, and the temporal frame has shifted from adolescence to infancy. Equally significant, the spatial frame has shifted as well, from the public to the private. Lear is of course a king, for whom there would, in any case, be no privacy, but generally Renaissance writers do not assume that the family is set off from public life. On the contrary, public life is itself most frequently conceived in familial terms, as an interlocking, hierarchical system of patriarchal authorities, while conversely the family is conceived as a little commonwealth. Indeed the family is widely understood in the sixteenth and early seventeenth centuries as both the historical source and the ideological justification of society: 'for I admit', writes Bacon, 'the law to be that if the son kill his father or mother it is petty treason, and that there remaineth in our laws so much of the ancient footsteps of *potestas patria* and natural obedience, which by the law of God is the very instance itself, and all other government and obedience is taken but by equity.' In other words, the Fifth Commandment – 'Honour thy father and mother' – is the original letter of the law which equity 'enlarges', as the Elizabethan jurist Edmund Plowden puts it, to include all political authority.

This general understanding of the enlargement by which the state is derived from the family is given virtually emblematic form in representations of the ruling family; hence the supremely public nature of Lear's interrogations of his daughters' feelings toward him does not mark him off, as other elements in the play do, from the world of Shakespeare's audience, but rather registers a central ideological principle of middle- and upper-class families in the early modern period. Affairs of family shade into affairs of state, as Gloucester's anxious broodings on the late eclipses of the sun and moon make clear: 'Love cools, friendship falls off, brothers divide: in cities mutinies; in countries, discord; in palaces, treason; and the bond crack'd twixt son and father' (I.ii). The very order of the phrases here, in their failure to move decisively from private to public, their reversion at the close to the familial bond, signals the interinvolvement of household and society. By the time of Jacksonian America, the family has moved indoors, separated from civil society, which in turn has been separated from the state. Reverend Wayland's account of his domestic crisis is also, of course, intended for public consumption, but it was published anonymously, as if to respect the protective boundaries of the family, and more important still, it makes public a private event in order to assist the private lives of others, that is, to strengthen the resolve of loving parents to subdue the temper of their own infants.

We will return later to the temporal and spatial problems touched upon here – the cultural evaluation of differing age groups and the status of privacy – but we should first note several of the significant continuities between Renaissance child-rearing techniques and those of nineteenth-century American evangelicals. The first, and ground of all the others, is the not-so-simple fact of observation: these parents pay attention to their children, testing the young to gauge the precise cast of their emotion and will. This is more obviously the case with Reverend Wayland, who when his child was scarcely a year old was already scrutinising him for signs of self-will. The fathers in Shakespeare's play seem purblind by comparison: Lear apparently cannot perceive the difference between his eldest daughters' blatant hypocrisy and his youngest daughter's truth, while Gloucester evidently does not know what his eldest (and sole legitimate) son's handwriting – his 'character' – looks like and is easily persuaded that this son (with whom he had talked for two hours the night before) wishes to kill him. This seeming obliviousness, however, signifies not indifference but error: Lear and Gloucester are hopelessly inept at reading their children's 'characters', but the effort to do so is of the utmost importance in the play, which, after all, represents the fatal consequences of an incorrect 'reading'. We may say, with the Fool, that Lear was 'a pretty fellow' when he had 'no need to care' for his daughter's frowns (I.iv), but this indifference only exists outside the play itself, or perhaps in its initial moments; thereafter (and irreversibly) parents must scrutinise their children with what Lear, in a moment of uncharacteristic self-criticism, calls a 'jealous curiosity' (I.iv). In initiating the plot against Edgar, Edmund gauges perfectly his father's blend of credulity and inquisitorial curiosity: 'Edmund, how now! what news? . . . Why so earnestly seek you to put up that letter? . . . What paper were you reading? . . . What needed then that terrible dispatch of it into your pocket? . . . Let's see: come; if it be nothing, I shall not need spectacles' (I. ii). Children in the play, we might add, similarly scrutinise their fathers: 'You see how full of changes his age is', Goneril remarks to Regan in their first moment alone together; 'the observation we have made of it hath not been little' (I. i). The whole family comes to exist *sub specie semioticae*; everyone is intent on reading the signs in everyone else.

This mode of observation is common to Shakespeare's play and Wayland's account, but not because it is intrinsic to all family life: intense paternal observation of the young is by no means a universal practice. It is, rather, learned by certain social groups in particular cultures and ages. Thus there is virtually no evidence of the practice in late medieval England, while for the seventeenth century there is (given the general paucity of materials for intimate family history) quite impressive evidence, especially for the substantial segment of the population touched by Puritanism. For example, the Essex vicar Ralph Josselin (1617–83) has left in his diary a remarkably full record of his troubled relationship with his son, particularly during the latter's adolescence. 'My soule yearned over John', notes one characteristic entry, 'oh lord overcome his heart.' The conflict between them reached a crisis in 1674, when, in a family discussion held in the presence of his wife and four daughters, Josselin put the following proposition before his twenty-three-year-old heir:

> John set your selfe to fear God, & bee industrious in my business, refrain your evill courses, and I will passe by all past offences, setle all my estate on you after your mothers death, and leave you with some stocke on the ground and within doores to the value of an £100 and desire of you, out of your marriage portion but £400 to provide for my

daughters or otherwise to charge my land with so much for their porcions; but if you continue your ill courses I shall dispose of my land otherwise, and make only a provision for your life to put bread in your hand.

The father's strategy was at least temporarily successful, as John prudently accepted the offer and 'ownd his debauchery'.

Josselin's insistence upon the economic consequences of disobedience provides an immediate link to *King Lear*, where the father's power to alter portions and to disinherit is of crucial importance. We should note that primogeniture was never so inflexibly established in England, even among the aristocracy, as to preclude the exercise of paternal discretion, the power to bribe, threaten, reward, and punish. Lear's division of the kingdom, his attempt both to set his daughters in competition with each other and to dispose of his property equitably among them, seems less a wanton violation of the normative practice than a daring attempt to use the paternal power always inherent in it. This power is exhibited in more conventional form in the subplot: 'And of my land, / Loyal and natural boy', the deceived Gloucester tells his conniving bastard son, 'I'll work the means / To make thee capable' (II. i). This economic pressure is not, of course, immediately apparent in Reverend Wayland's dealings with his infant, but Josselin's threat to 'make only a provision . . . to put bread in your hand' curiously anticipates the symbolic object of contention in the Wayland nursery and suggests that there too the paternal power to withhold or manipulate the means of sustenance is at issue.

This power should not be regarded as exclusively disciplinary. It is instead an aspect of a general familial concern with planning for the future, a concern that extends from attempts to shape the careers of individual children to an overarching interest in the prosperity of the 'house'. Francis Wayland's struggle with his son is not a flaring-up of paternal anger but a calculated effort to fashion his child's future: 'I hope and pray, that it may prove that an effect has been produced upon him for life.' Similarly, Lear's disastrous division of the kingdom is undertaken, he claims, so that 'future strife / May be prevented now' (I. i), and the love test marked the formal entry into his planned retirement.

These efforts to shape the future of the family seem to reflect a conviction that there are certain critical moments upon which a whole train of subsequent events depends, moments whose enabling conditions may be irrecoverable and whose consequences may be irreversible. Such a conviction is formally expressed most often in relation to great public events, but its influence is more widespread, extending, for example, to rhetorical training, religious belief, and, I would suggest, child rearing. Parents must be careful to watch for what we may call, to adapt the rhetorical term, kairotic moments and to grasp the occasion for action. Hence Francis Wayland, wishing to alter his son's nature for life, 'resolved to seize upon the first favourable opportunity which presented, for settling the question of authority between us'. Had the father not done so, he would not only have diminished his own position but risked the destruction of his child's spiritual and physical being. Moreover, Wayland adds, had he received his stubborn child on any other terms than 'the unconditional surrender of his will', he would have permitted the formation of a topsy-turvey world in which his entire family would have submitted to the caprices of an infant: 'He must have been made the centre of a whole system. A whole family under the control of a child 15 months old!' This carnivalesque reversal of roles would then have invited further insurrections, for 'my other children and every member of my family would have been entitled to the same privilege'. 'Hence', Wayland concludes, 'there would have been as many supreme authorities as there were individuals, and contention to the uttermost must have ensued.'

King Lear depicts something very much like such a world turned upside down: Lear, as the Fool says, has made his daughters his mothers, and they employ on him, as in a nightmare, those disciplinary techniques deemed appropriate for 'a slippery age, full of passion, rashness, wilfulness'. 'Old fools are babes again', says Goneril, 'and must be us'd / With checks as flatteries, when they are seen abus'd' (I. iii). In the carnival tradition, tolerated – if uneasily – by the medieval church and state, such reversals of role, provided they were temporary, could be seen as restorative, renewing the proper order of society by releasing pent-up frustrations and potentially disruptive energies. As we know from a family account, even Francis Wayland could allow his children occasional bursts of festive inversion, always returning in the end to the supreme paternal authority that his early discipline had secured. But in *Lear* the role reversal is permanent, and its effect is the disintegration of the entire kingdom. Wayland similarly links permanent disorder in the family to chaos in the political, moral, and theological realms; indeed his loving struggle with his son offers, he suggests, a precise and resonant analogy to

God's struggle with the sinner: it is infinitely kind in God to resist the sinner's will, 'for if he were not resisted, he would destroy the happiness of the universe and himself together'.

Here again, in Wayland's conviction that the fate of the universe may be linked to the power struggle in his nursery, we may hear an echo of *Lear*:

> O Heavens,
> If you do love old men, if your sweet sway
> Allow obedience, if you yourselves are old,
> Make it your cause; send down and take my part.
> (II. iv)

Of course, as these very lines suggest, what is assumed in Wayland is deeply problematical in *Lear*: the fictive nature of the play, reinforced by its specifically pagan setting, seems to have licensed Shakespeare to anatomise the status and the underlying motives of virtually all of the elements that we have noted as common to the two texts. This difference is crucial, and it comes as no surprise that *King Lear* is more profound than Francis Wayland's account of his paternal authority: celebration of Shakespeare's profundity is an institutionalised rite of civility in our culture. We tend to assume, however, that Shakespearean self-consciousness and irony lead to a radical transcendence of the network of social conditions, paradigms, and practices in the plays. I would argue, by contrast, that Renaissance theatrical representation itself is fully implicated in this network and that Shakespeare's self-consciousness is in significant ways bound up with the institutions and the symbology of power it anatomises.

But if its local ideological situation, its historical embeddedness, is so crucial to Shakespeare's play, what accounts for the similarities I have sketched between *King Lear* and Wayland's family narrative? The explanation lies first in the fact that nineteenth-century evangelical child-rearing techniques are the heirs of more widely diffused child-rearing techniques in the late sixteenth and early seventeenth centuries – Wayland's practices may be seen almost fully articulated in a work like John Robinson's *Of Children and Their Education*, published in 1628 though written some years earlier – and second in the fact that the Renaissance English drama was one of the cultural institutions that expressed and fashioned just those qualities that we have identified as enabling the familial love test in the first place. That is, the mode of the drama, quite apart from any specific content, depended upon and fostered in its audience *observation*, the close reading of gesture and speech as manifestations of character and intention; *planning*, a sensitivity to the consequences of action (i.e. plot) and to kairotic moments (i.e. rhetoric); and a sense of *resonance*, the conviction, rooted in the drama's medieval inheritance, that cosmic meanings were bound up with local and particular circumstances.

I am not, of course, suggesting that the nineteenth-century American minister was fashioned by the Renaissance theatre (a theatre his seventeenth-century religious forebears detested and sought to close) nor that without the theatre Renaissance child-rearing techniques would have been far different. But the theatre was not merely the passive reflector of social forces that lay entirely outside of it; rather, like all forms of art, indeed like all utterances, the theatre was itself a *social event*. Artistic expression is never perfectly self-contained and abstract, nor can it be derived satisfactorily from the subjective consciousness of an isolated creator. Collective actions, ritual gestures, paradigms of relationship, and shared images of authority penetrate the work of art and shape it from within, while conversely the socially overdetermined work of art, along with a multitude of other institutions and utterances, contributes to the formation, re-alignment, and transmission of social practices.

Works of art are, to be sure, marked off in our culture from ordinary utterances, but this demarcation is itself a communal event and signals not the effacement of the social but rather its successful absorption into the work by implication or articulation. This absorption – the presence within the work of its social being – makes it possible, as Bakhtin has argued, for art to survive the disappearance of its enabling social conditions, where ordinary utterance, more dependent upon the extraverbal pragmatic situation, drifts rapidly toward insignificance or incomprehensibility. Hence art's genius for survival, its delighted reception by audiences for whom it was never intended, does not signal its freedom from all other domains of life, nor does its inward articulation of the social confer upon it a formal coherence independent of the world outside its boundaries. On the contrary, artistic form itself both expresses and fashions social evaluations and practices.

Thus the Renaissance theatre does not by virtue of the content of a particular play reach across a void to touch the Renaissance family; rather the theatre is itself already saturated with social significance and hence with the family as the period's central social institution.

Conversely, the theatre contributes, in a small but by no means entirely negligible way, to the formal condensation and expression of patterns of observation, planning, and a sense of resonance. Hence it is fitting that when Cordelia resists Lear's paternal demand, she does so in an anti-theatrical gesture, a refusal to perform: the theatre and the family are simultaneously at stake.

To these shared patterns that link the quasi-mythical family of King Lear to the prosaic and amply documented family of Francis Wayland, we may now add four further interlocking features of Wayland's account that are more closely tied not to the mode of the theatre as a whole but to the specific form and content of Shakespeare's tragedy: these are the absence or displacement of the mother, an affirmation of absolute paternal authority, an overriding interest in the will and hence in differentiating voluntary from merely forced compliance, and a belief in salutary anxiety.

Francis Wayland's wife was alive in 1831, but she is entirely, even eerily, missing from his account. Where was she during the long ordeal? In part her absence must depend upon her husband's understanding of the theological significance of the incident: in Francis Wayland's Christianity, there is no female intercessor, no Mother of Mankind to appeal to the stern Father for mercy upon a wayward child. Even if Mrs Wayland did in fact try to temper (or reinforce) her husband's actions, he might well have regarded such intervention as irrelevant. Moreover, we may speculate that the timing of the incident – what we have called the perception of the kairotic moment – is designed precisely to avoid such irrelevant interventions. We do not know when any of the Wayland children were weaned, but fifteen months would seem about the earliest age at which the disciplinary withdrawal of food – the piece of bread and the cup of milk – could be undertaken without involving the mother or the nurse.

Thus the father is able entirely to displace the nurturing female body and with this displacement make manifest his 'supreme authority' in the family, a micropolitics that, as we have seen, has its analogue both in the human world outside the home and in the divine realm. Between the law of the father and the law of God there is a perfect fit; between the father's authority and worldly authorities there is a more complicated relation, since Wayland, though an absolutist within his family, could not invoke in Jacksonian America a specific model of absolute power. The most he can do is to invoke, in effect, a generalised image of the social world and of the child as misfit: had his son been left unchecked, he 'would soon have entered a *world where other and more powerful beings than he* would have opposed his will, and his disposition which I had cherished must have made him miserable as long as he lived'.

This social vision does not mean that Wayland's primary interest is in outward compliance; on the contrary, a 'forced yielding', as he terms it, is worthless. 'Our voluntary service he requires', says Milton's Raphael of the Divine Father in *Paradise Lost*,

> Not our necessitated, such with him
> Finds no acceptance, nor *can* find, for how
> Can hearts, not free, be tri'd whether they serve
> Willing or no . . .
> . . . freely we serve.
> Because we freely love.

The proper goal is conversion, and to achieve this the father cannot rely on physical compulsion. He employs instead a technique of disciplinary kindness designed to show the child that his misery is entirely self-inflicted and can only be relieved by a similarly voluntary and inward surrender. In short, Wayland attempts to generate in his son a salutary anxiety that will lead to a transformation of the will.

With salutary anxiety we return powerfully to the mode and the content of *King Lear*. The very practice of tragedy depends upon a communal conviction that anxiety may be profitably and even pleasurably cultivated. That is, tragedy goes beyond the usual philosophical and religious *consolations* for affliction, and both exemplifies and perfects techniques for the creation or intensification of affliction. To justify such techniques, Renaissance artists could appeal to the theoretical account of tragedy that originated with Aristotle and was substantially elaborated in the sixteenth century, especially in Italy. But like most such theories, this one was inert until it intersected with a set of powerful social practices in the period.

From the perspective of Wayland's account, we may say that the most enduring of these practices is the Protestant cultivation of a sense of sin, the deliberate heightening of an anxiety that can only be relieved by a divine grace whose effect can only be felt by one who has experienced the anxiety. (I should emphasise that I am speaking here not simply of a set of theological propositions but of a programme, prescribed in great detail and carried out by English Protestants from Tyndale onward.) To this religious practice, we may add the child-rearing techniques that also appear in Wayland's account, techniques that once again made a self-conscious and programmatic attempt to arouse anxiety for the child's ultimate good. But what is lost by early nineteenth-century America is the practice of salutary anxiety at the symbolic centre of society, that is, in the characteristic operations of royal power. That power, concentrated and personalised, aroused anxiety not only as the negative limit but as the positive condition of its functioning. The monarchy, let us remind ourselves, did not conceive its purpose as the furthering of the subject's pursuit of happiness, nor was the political centre of society a point at which all tensions and contradictions disappeared. On the contrary, Elizabethan and Jacobean charismatic absolutism battened on as well as suffered from the anxiety that arose from the instability of favour, the unresolved tensions in the religious settlement, the constantly proclaimed threats of subversion, invasion, and civil war, the spectacular public maimings and executions, and even the conspicuous gap between the monarch's ideological claim to perfect wisdom, beauty, and power and the all-too-visible limitations of the actual Elizabeth and James. The obedience required of the subject consisted not so much in preserving a genuine ignorance of this gap but in behaving as if the gap, though fully recognised, did not exist. The pressure of such a performance, demanded by the monarch's paradoxical yoking of the language of love and the language of coercion and registered in the subject's endless effusions of strained but not entirely hypocritical admiration, was itself an enhancement of royal power.

Throughout his career Shakespeare displays the deepest sensitivity to this production of salutary anxiety, a production he simultaneously questions and assimilates to his own authorial power. The fullest metatheatrical explorations of the phenomenon are in *Measure for Measure* and *The Tempest*, where both Dukes systematically awaken anxiety in others and become, for this reason, images of the dramatist himself. But Shakespeare's fullest embodiment of the practice is *King Lear*, and the vast critical literature that has grown up around the play, since the restoration of the text in the early nineteenth century, bears eloquent witness to the power of this anxiety to generate tireless expressions of love. *King Lear* characteristically incorporates several powerful and complex representations of salutary anxiety, the most notable of which, for our purposes, is the love test itself, a ritual whose intended function seems to have been to allay the retiring monarch's anxiety by arousing it in others. As the opening words of the play make clear, the division of the kingdom has in effect already taken place, with the shares carefully weighed. Lear's pretence that this prearranged legal agreement is a contest – 'which of you shall we say doth love us most?' – infuses symbolic uncertainty into a situation where apparently no real uncertainty exists. This is confirmed by his persistence in the test even when its declared occasion has been rendered wholly absurd by the disposition of the first two-thirds of the kingdom, complete with declarations that possession is 'perpetual', 'hereditary ever'. Lear wants his children to experience the anxiety of a competition for his bounty without having to endure any of the actual consequences of such a competition; he wants, that is, to produce in them something like the effect of a work of art, where emotions run high and practical effects seem negligible.

Why should Lear want his children, even his 'joy' Cordelia, to experience such anxiety? Shakespeare's sources, going back to the distant folk tale with its salt motif, suggest that Lear wishes his full value to be recognised and that he stages the love test to enforce this recognition, which is crucially important to him because he is about to abdicate and hence lose the power to compel the deference of his children. Marks of deference such as kneeling for blessings, removing the hat, and sitting only when granted leave to do so, were of great significance in medieval and early modern families, though John Aubrey testifies that by the mid-seventeenth century they seemed strained and arbitrary. They figured as part of a complex, interlocking system of public signs of respect for wealth, caste, and, at virtually every level of society, age. The period had a deep gerontological bias. It told itself constantly that by the will of God and the natural order of things authority belonged to the old, and it contrived, through such practices as deferral of marriage, prolonged apprenticeships, and systematic exclusion of the young from office, to ensure that this proper arrangement of society be observed. At stake, it was thought, was not only a societal arrangement – the protection, in an economy of scarcity, of the material interests of gerontological hierarchy against the counterclaims of the young – but the structure and meaning of a world where the old in each generation formed a link with the old of the preceding generation and so, by contiguity, reached back to the ideal, sanctified order at the origin of time.

But paradoxically the late Middle Ages and the early modern period also kept telling itself that without the control of property and the means of production, age's claim to authority was pathetically vulnerable to the ruthless ambitions of the young. Sermons and, more generally, the writings of moralists over several centuries provide numerous monitory tales of parents who turn their wealth over to their children and are, in consequence, treated brutally. 'Your father were a fool', Gremio, echoing the moral of these tales, tells Tranio in *The Taming of the Shrew*, 'To give thee all, and in his waning age / Set foot under thy table' (II. i).

The story of King Lear in its numerous retellings from at least the twelfth century on seems to have served precisely as one of these admonitions, and Shakespeare's Edmund, in the forged letter he passes off as Edgar's, gives full voice to the fears of the old, that is, to their fantasy of what the young, beneath the superficial marks of deference, are really thinking:

> This policy and reverence of age makes the world bitter to the best of our times; keeps our fortunes from us till our oldness cannot relish them. I begin to find an idle and fond bondage in the oppression of aged tyranny, who sways, not as it hath power, but as it is suffr'd.
>
> (I. ii)

This recurrent nightmare of the old seems to challenge not only the material well-being of fathers but the conception of the natural order of things to which the old appeal in justification of their prerogatives. 'Fathers fear', writes Pascal, 'that the natural love of their children can be erased. What kind of nature is this, that can thus be erased? Custom is a second nature that destroys the first. But what is nature? Why isn't custom natural? I am very much afraid that this nature is only a first custom, as custom is a second nature.' Shakespeare's *King Lear* is haunted by this fear, voiced not in the relative privacy of the *Pensées* but in the public agony of family and state relations: ' . . . let them anatomise Regan, see what breeds about her heart. Is there any cause in nature that makes these hard hearts?' (III. vi).

But it would be misleading simply to associate Shakespeare's play with this uneasiness without specifying the practical measures that medieval and early modern fathers undertook to protect themselves when retirement, always frowned upon, could not be avoided. Such situations arose most frequently in Shakespeare's own class of origin, that is, among artisans and small landowners whose income depended upon continual personal productivity. Faced with a precipitous decline in such productivity, the old frequently did have to transfer a farm or workshop to the young, but for all the talk of the natural privileges and supernatural protection of the aged, there was, as we have seen, remarkably little confidence in either the inherent or customary rights of parents. On the contrary, as Alan Macfarlane has noted in *The Origins of English Individualism*, 'contemporaries seem to have been well aware that without legal guarantees, parents had no rights whatsoever'. There could even be a ritual acknowledgement of this fact, as testimony in a thirteenth-century lawsuit suggests: having agreed to give his daughter in marriage to Hugh, with half of his land, the widower Anseline and the married couple were to live together in one house. 'And the same Anseline went out of the house and handed over to them the door by the hasp, and at once begged lodging out of charity.'

Once a father had given up his land, he became, even in the house that had once been his own, what was called a 'sojourner'. The connotations of the word are suggested by its use in the Authorised Version of the Old Testament: 'We are strangers before Thee, and sojourners, as were all our fathers. Our days on the earth are as a shadow, and there is none abiding' (1 *Chron.* 29).

Threatened with such a drastic loss of their status and authority, parents facing retirement turned, not surprisingly, to the law, obtaining contracts or maintenance agreements by which, in return for the transfer of family property, children undertook to provide food, clothing, and shelter. The extent of parental anxiety may be gauged by the great specificity of many of these requirements – so many yards of woollen cloth, pounds of coal, or bushels of grain – and by the pervasive fear of being turned out of the house in the wake of a quarrel. The father, who has been, in Sir Edward Coke's phrase, 'the guardian by nature' of his children, now has these children for his legal guardians. The maintenance agreement is essentially a medieval device, linked to feudal contractualism, to temper the power of this new guardianship by stipulating that the children are only 'depositaries' of the paternal property, so that, in the words of William West's early seventeenth-century legal manual *Simboleography*, 'the self same thing [may] be restored whensoeuer it shall please him that so leaueth it.' Thus the maintenance agreement can 'reserve' to the father some right or interest in the property that he has conveyed to his children.

We are, of course, very far from the social world of *King Lear*, which does not represent the milieu of yeomen and artisans, but I would argue that Shakespeare's play is powerfully situated in the midst of precisely the concerns of the makers of these maintenance agreements: the terror of being turned out of doors or of becoming a stranger even in one's own house; the fear of losing the food, clothing, and shelter necessary for survival, let alone dignity; the humiliating loss of parental authority; the dread, particularly powerful in a society that adhered to the principle of gerontological hierarchy, of being supplanted by the young. Lear's royal status does not cancel but rather intensifies these concerns: he will 'invest' in Goneril and Regan, along with their husbands, his 'power, / Pre-eminence, and all the large effects / That troop with majesty', but he wants to retain the hundred knights and 'The name and all th'addition to a king' (I. i). He wishes, that is, to avoid at all costs the drastic loss of status that inevitably attended retirement in the early modern period, and his maddened rage, later in the play, is a response not only to his daughters' vicious ingratitude but to the horror of being reduced to the position of an Anseline:

> Ask her forgiveness?
> Do you but mark how this becomes the house:
> 'Dear daughter, I confess that I am old;
> Age is unnecessary: on my knees I beg
> That you'll vouchsafe me raiment, bed, and food.'
>
> (II. iv)

His daughter, in response, unbendingly proposes that he 'return and sojourn' – a word whose special force in this context we have now recovered – 'with my sister'.

Near the climax of this terrible scene in which Goneril and Regan, by relentlessly diminishing his retinue, in effect strip away his social identity, Lear speaks as if he had actually drawn up a maintenance agreement with his daughters:

> **Lear** I gave you all –
> **Regan** And in good time you gave it.
> **Lear** Made you my guardians, my depositaries,
>   But kept a reservation to be follow'd
>   With such a number.
>
> (II. iv)

But there is no maintenance agreement between Lear and his daughters; there could be none, since as Lear makes clear in the first scene, he will not as absolute monarch allow anything 'To come betwixt our sentence and our power' (I. i), and an autonomous system of laws would have constituted just such an intervention. For a contract in English law implied bargain consideration, that is, the reciprocity inherent in a set of shared obligations and limits, and this understanding that a gift could only be given with the expectation of receiving something in return is incompatible with Lear's sense of his royal prerogative, just as it is incompatible with the period's absolutist conception of paternal power and divine power.

Lear's power draws upon the network of rights and obligations that is sketched by the play's pervasive language of service, but as Kent's experience in the first scene makes clear, royal absolutism is at the same time at war with this feudal legacy. Shakespeare's play emphasises Lear's claim to unbounded power, even at the moment of his abdication, since his 'darker purpose' sets itself above all constraints upon the royal will and pleasure. What enables him to lay aside his claim to rule, the scene suggests, is the transformation of power into a demand for unbounded love, a love that then takes the place of the older contractual bond between parents and children. Goneril and Regan understand Lear's demand as an aspect of absolutist theatre; hence in their flattering speeches they discursively *perform* the impossibility of ever adequately expressing their love: 'Sir, I love you more than word can wield the matter / . . . A love that makes breath poor and speech unable; / Beyond all manner of so much I love you' (I. i). This cunning representation of the impossibility of representation contaminates Cordelia's inability to speak by speaking it; that is, Goneril's words occupy the discursive space that Cordelia would have to claim for herself if she were truly to satisfy her father's demand. Consequently, any attempt to represent her silent love is already tainted: representation is theatricalisation is hypocrisy and hence is misrepresentation. Even Cordelia's initial aside seems to long for the avoidance of language altogether and thus for an escape from the theatre. Her words have an odd internal distance, as if they were spoken by another, and more precisely as if the author outside the play were asking himself what he should have his character say and deciding that she should say nothing: 'What shall Cordelia speak? Love, and be silent' (I. i). But this attempt to remain silent – to surpass her sisters and satisfy her father by refusing to represent her love – is rejected, as is her subsequent attempt to say nothing, that is, literally to speak the word 'nothing'. Driven into discourse by her father's anger, Cordelia then appeals not like her sisters to an utter dependence upon paternal love but to a 'bond' that is both reciprocal and limited. Against paternal and monarchical absolutism, Cordelia opposes in effect the ethos of the maintenance agreement, and this opposition has for Lear the quality of treason.

Lear, who has, as he thinks, given all to his children, demands all from them. In place of a contract, he has substituted the love test. He wants, that is, not only the formal marks of deference that publicly acknowledge his value, but also the inward and absolute tribute of the heart. It is in the spirit of this demand that he absorbs into himself the figure of the mother; there can be no division for Lear between authority and love. But as the play's tragic logic reveals, Lear cannot have both the public deference and the inward love of his children. The public deference is only as good as the legal constraints that Lear's absolute power paradoxically deprives him of, and the inward love cannot be adequately represented in social discourse, licensed by authority and performed in the public sphere, enacted as in a court or theatre. Lear had thought to set his rest – the phrase means both to stake everything and to find response – on Cordelia's 'kind nursery', but only in his fantasy of perpetual imprisonment with his daughter does he glimpse, desperately and pathetically, what he sought. That is, only when he has been decisively separated from his public authority and locked away from the world, only when the direct link between family and state power has been broken, can Lear hope, in the dream of the prison as nursery, for his daughter's sustaining and boundless love.

With this image of the prison as nursery we return for the last time to Francis Wayland, who, to gain the love of his child, used the nursery as a prison. We return, then, to the crucial differences, as we sketched them, between the early seventeenth- and early nineteenth-century versions of salutary anxiety, differences between a culture in which the theatre was a centrally significant and emblematic artistic practice, profoundly linked with family and power, and a culture in which the theatre had shrivelled to marginal entertainment. The love test for Wayland takes place in the privacy of the nursery where he shuts up his fifteen-month-old infant. In consequence, what is sought by the father is not the representation of love in public discourse, but things prior to and separate from language: the embrace, the kiss, the taking of food, the inarticulate moaning after the father when he leaves the room. It is only here, *before* verbal representation, that the love test could be wholly successful, here that the conditional, reciprocal, social world of the maintenance agreement could be decisively replaced by the child's absolute and lifelong love. And, we might add, the father did not in this case have to renounce the public tribute entirely; he had only to wait until he ceased to exist. For upon the death of Francis Wayland, Heman Lincoln Wayland collaborated in writing a reverential two-volume biography of his father, a son's final monument to familial love. Lear, by contrast, dies still looking on his daughter's lips for the words that she never speaks.

From Stephen Greenblatt, *Learning to Curse: Essays in Early Modern Culture* (New York and London, 1990), pp. 80–98.

NOTES

[Stephen Greenblatt has described his work movingly as driven by the urge to speak with the dead by restoring lost life to the textual traces they have left us to decipher. (See *Shakespearean Negotiations* [Oxford, 1988], pp. 1–4.) Greenblatt's strategy for releasing the 'resonance and wonder' stored in the literature of the past deliberately diverts critical attention away from its customary absorption in the language and form of the text. His brand of new historicism, or 'cultural poetics' as he also calls it, proposes 'to look less at the presumed centre of the literary domain than at its borders, to try to track what can only be glimpsed, as it were, at the margins of the text' (ibid., p. 4). Greenblatt recognises the charges to which neglect of the work's distinctively literary qualities lays him open, but hopes 'to offer a compensatory satisfaction: insight into the half-hidden cultural transactions through which great works of art are empowered' (ibid., p. 4). As in the essay on *Lear* reprinted here, that rush of insight is triggered invariably for Greenblatt by a telling anecdote, whose seeming remoteness from, or incongruity with, the literary work in question rapidly dissolves under the pressure of Greenblatt's ingenuity. In the Introduction to *Learning to Curse* [New York and London, 1990] Greenblatt is at pains to stress, however, that for him

> The historical anecdote functions less as explanatory illustration than as disturbance, that which requires explanation, contextualisation, interpretation. . . . The historical evidence – 'mere anecdotes' – conventionally invoked in literary criticism to assist in the explication of a text seemed to me dead precisely because it was the enemy of wonder: it was brought in to lay contingency and disturbance to rest. I do not want history to enable me to escape the effect of the literary but to deepen it by making it touch the effect of the real, a touch that would reciprocally deepen and complicate history. (pp. 5–6)

The present essay is vibrant with Greenblatt's unrivalled feel for the quiddity and sheer strangeness of both the literature and the life of the past. Ed.]

1. Wayland's letter is reprinted in full in William G. McLoughlin, 'Evangelical Childrearing in the Age of Jackson: Francis Wayland's Views on When and How to Subdue the Wilfulness of Children', *Journal of Social*

History, 9 (1975), 20–43; it was first brought to my attention by Philip Greven, *The Protestant Temperament: Patterns of Child-Rearing, Religious Experience and the Self in Early America* (New York, 1977).

Further Reading

EDITIONS

The standard modern texts are:

G. Blakemore Evans (ed.), *The Riverside Shakespeare* (Boston: Houghton Mifflin, 1974).

Russell Fraser (ed.), *King Lear*, The Signet Shakespeare (New York: New American Library, 1963).

Alfred Harbage (ed.), *The Complete Pelican Shakespeare* (Baltimore: Penguin, 1969).

G. K. Hunter (ed.), *King Lear*, New Penguin Shakespeare (Harmondsworth: Penguin, 1972).

Kenneth Muir (ed.), *King Lear*, The Arden Shakespeare (London: Methuen, revised edn, 1985).

Stanley Wells and Gary Taylor (eds), *William Shakespeare: The Complete Works* (Oxford: Oxford University Press, 1986).

THE EDITORIAL CONTROVERSY

Most current editions of *King Lear* conflate in varying proportions the two original texts of the play: the individual quarto text (the so-called Pied Bull quarto) published in 1608 and the more carefully printed and presented version published as part of the folio edition of Shakespeare's plays in 1623. Until recently the common presupposition of editorial practice was that the folio text was the more reliable overall, but that a number of local readings, more substantial passages and sometimes entire scenes from the quarto were to be preferred or incorporated in the final composite edition. Since the 1980s, however, conventional editorial assumptions have been fundamentally challenged by scholars who contend that the quarto and folio texts mark separate, successive phases in the evolving composition of *King Lear*. The folio should be regarded, it is argued, as Shakespeare's own deliberate artistic revision of his earlier quarto version. If this is true, modern editions that splice the folio and quarto together have created mongrel texts which violate the integrity of both versions and scramble Shakespeare's verbal and theatrical development of the play's vision. In order to avoid this, and to do justice to the new theory of the relationship between quarto and folio, the Oxford edition by Stanley Wells and Gary Taylor (see above) prints both texts of the play instead of a single amalgamated version. It must be stressed that textual scholars are far from universally persuaded by this case, and that even where Shakespeare's responsibility for the cuts and emendations is accepted, the question of whether they were artistically motivated rather than simply practical or in response to censorship remains open to debate. Nevertheless, the debate has obliged all critics seriously engaged with *King Lear* henceforth to recognise the hypothetical, disputed status of whatever edition they use, and thus the questionable authority of the textual evidence on which their accounts of the tragedy may rely.

The controversy can be pursued through the following studies:

Peter W. M. Blayney, *The Texts of King Lear and their Origins* (Cambridge: Cambridge University Press, 1982).

P. W. K. Stone, *The Textual History of King Lear* (London: Scholar Press, 1980).

Annabel Patterson, *Censorship and Interpretation* (Madison, Wisc.: University of Wisconsin Press, 1984), pp. 61–71.

Gary Taylor and Michael Warren (eds), *The Division of the Kingdoms: Shakespeare's Two Versions of King Lear* (Oxford: Clarendon Press, 1983).

Steven Urkowitz, *Shakespeare's Revision of King Lear* (Princeton, NJ: Princeton University Press, 1980).

Stanley Wells and Gary Taylor (eds), *William Shakespeare: A Textual Companion* (Oxford: Clarendon Press, 1987).

CRITICISM ON 'KING LEAR'

A lively, short and up-to-date review of the issues animating twentieth-century critics is furnished by:

Ann Thompson, *King Lear: The Critics Debate* (London: Macmillan, 1988).

For an invaluable annotated list of criticism on *Lear* up to the end of the 1970s, see:

Larry S. Champion, *King Lear: An Annotated Bibliography*, 2 vols (New York and London: Garland Publishing, 1980).

Two useful collections of essays ranging from the earliest commentators through to the major critics of the 1960s are:

Frank Kermode (ed.), *Shakespeare: King Lear: A Casebook* (London: Macmillan, 1969; revised edn, 1992).

Kenneth Muir (ed.), *King Lear: Critical Essays* (New York and London: Garland, 1984).

Critical preoccupations of the 1970s can be sampled in:

Rosalie L. Colie and F. T. Flahiff (eds), *Some Facets of King Lear: Essays in Prismatic Criticism* (Toronto and London: 1974).

Lawrence Danson (ed.), *On King Lear* (Princeton, NJ: Princeton University Press, 1981).

S. L. Goldberg, *An Essay on King Lear* (Cambridge: Cambridge University Press, 1974).

Michael Long, *The Unnatural Scene* (London: Methuen, 1976), ch. 7.

Of the accounts, or books containing accounts, of *King Lear* published since around 1980 the following offer further stimulating points of departure from previous approaches to the play:

David Aers and Gunther Kress, 'The Language of Social Order: Individual, Society and Historical Process in *King Lear*', in David Aers, Bob Hodge and Gunther Kress, *Literature, Language and Society in England 1580–1680* (Dublin: Gill and Macmillan, 1981), pp. 75–99.

Stephen Booth, *King Lear, Macbeth, Indefinition and Tragedy* (New Haven and London: Yale University Press, 1983), pp. 1–57.

Graham Bradshaw, *Shakespeare's Scepticism* (Brighton, Sussex: Harvester Press, 1987), pp. 85–94.

Jackson I. Cope, 'Shakespeare, Derrida and the End of Language', in G. Douglas Atkins and David M. Bergeron (eds), *Shakespeare and Deconstruction* (New York, Bern, Frankfurt and Paris: Peter Lang, 1988), pp. 267–83.

Peter Erickson, *Patriarchal Structures in Shakespeare's Drama* (Berkeley, Los Angeles and London: University of California Press, 1985), pp. 103–15.

Malcolm Evans, *Signifying Nothing: Truth's True Contents in Shakespeare's Text* (Brighton, Sussex: Harvester Press, 1986), pp. 224–34.

Stephen Greenblatt, *Shakespearean Negotiations: The Circulation of Social Energy in Renaissance England* (Oxford: Clarendon Press, 1988), ch.4: 'Shakespeare and the Exorcists', pp. 94–128.

David Simpson, 'Great Things of Us Forgot: Seeing *Lear* Better', in Colin MacCabe (ed.), *Futures for English* (Manchester: Manchester University Press, 1988), pp. 15–31.

John Turner, '*King Lear*', in Graham Holderness, Nick Potter and John Turner, *Shakespeare: The Play of History* (London: Macmillan, 1988), pp. 89–118.

NEW HORIZONS IN SHAKESPEARE STUDIES

This section divides into broadly defined critical approaches a range of innovative and challenging books published on Shakespeare since 1980.

For feminist criticism see:

Peter Erickson, *Patriarchal Structures in Shakespeare's Drama* (Berkeley, Los Angeles and London: University of California Press, 1985).

Coppélia Kahn, *Man's Estate: Masculine Identity in Shakespeare* (Berkeley: University of California Press, 1981).

Carolyn Lenz, Ruth Swift, Gayle Greene and Carol Thomas Neely (eds), *The Woman's Part: Feminist Criticism of Shakespeare* (Urbana, Illinois: University of Illinois Press, 1980).

Marianne Novy, *Love's Argument: Gender Relations in Shakespeare* (Chapel Hill, Carolina: University of Carolina Press, 1984).

Poststructuralist perspectives and deconstructive readings are developed in:

G. Douglas Atkins and David M. Bergeron (eds), *Shakespeare and Deconstruction* (New York, Bern, Frankfurt and Paris: Peter Lang, 1988).

Terry Eagleton, *William Shakespeare* (Oxford: Basil Blackwell, 1986).

Malcolm Evans, *Signifying Nothing: Truth's True Contents in Shakespeare's Text* (Brighton, Sussex: Harvester Press, 1986).

The following are seminal collections of cultural materialist criticism:

Jonathan Dollimore and Alan Sinfield (eds), *Political Shakespeare: New Essays in Cultural Materialism* (Manchester: Manchester University Press, 1985).

Graham Holderness (ed.), *The Shakespeare Myth* (Manchester: Manchester University Press, 1988).

Different kinds of radical humanist approach are available in:

Graham Bradshaw, *Shakespeare's Scepticism* (Brighton, Sussex: Harvester Press, 1987).
Graham Holderness, Nick Potter and John Turner, *Shakespeare: The Play of History* (London: Macmillan, 1988).
Kiernan Ryan, *Shakespeare* (Hemel Hempstead and Atlantic Highlands, NJ: Harvester-Wheatsheaf and Humanities Press, 1989).

The following illustrate the diversity of new-historicist criticism:

Stephen Greenblatt, *Shakespearean Negotiations: The Circulation of Social Energy in Renaissance England* (Oxford: Clarendon Press, 1988).
Leah Marcus, *Puzzling Shakespeare* (Berkeley, Los Angeles and London: University of California Press, 1988).
Annabel Patterson, *Shakespeare and the Popular Voice* (Oxford: Basil Blackwell, 1989).
Leonard Tennenhouse, *Power on Display: The Politics of Shakespeare's Genres* (New York and London: Methuen, 1986).

Three excellent collections of essays shuffle together exercises in all the above modes of criticism:

John Drakakis (ed.), *Alternative Shakespeares* (London and New York: Methuen, 1985).
Jean E. Howard and Marion F. O'Connor (eds), *Shakespeare Reproduced: The Text in History and Ideology* (New York and London: Methuen, 1987).
Patricia Parker and Geoffrey Hartman (eds), *Shakespeare and the Question of Theory* (New York and London: Methuen, 1985).

For surveys and discussions of the new wave of Shakespeare criticism, see:

Walter Cohen, 'Political Criticism of Shakespeare', in Jean E. Howard and Marion F. O'Connor (eds), *Shakespeare Reproduced: The Text in History and Ideology* (New York and London: Methuen, 1987), p. 18–46. This contains a helpful bibliography of books and essays in this vein published between 1980 and 1987.
Don E. Wayne, 'Power, Politics and the Shakespearean Text: Recent Criticism in England and the United States', ibid., pp. 47–67.
Hugh Grady, *The Modernist Shakespeare* (Oxford: Clarendon Press, 1991), ch. 5.

Notes on Contributors

Terry Eagleton is Warton Professor of English Literature at the University of Oxford. His most recent books include *Walter Benjamin* (London, 1981), *The Rape of Clarissa* (Oxford, 1982), *Literary Theory: An Introduction* (Oxford, 1983), *The Function of Criticism* (London, 1984), *William Shakespeare* (Oxford, 1985), *The Ideology of the Aesthetic* (Oxford, 1990) and *Ideology: An Introduction* (London, 1991).

Howard Felperin is Professor of English at Macquarie University, Sydney. He is the author of *Shakespearean Romance* (Princeton, 1972), *Shakespearean Representation* (Princeton, 1977), *Beyond Deconstruction: The Uses and Abuses of Literary Theory* (Oxford, 1985) and *The Uses of the Canon: Elizabethan Literature and Contemporary Theory* (Oxford, 1990).

Jonathan Goldberg is Sir William Osler Professor of English at the Johns Hopkins University. His publications include *Endlesse Worke: Spenser and the Structures of Discourse* (Baltimore and London, 1981), *James I and the Politics of Literature: Jonson, Shakespeare, Donne, and Their Contemporaries* (Baltimore, 1983), *Voice, Terminal, Echo: Postmodernism and English Renaissance Texts* (New York and London, 1986) and *Writing Matter: From the Hands of the English Renaissance* (Stanford, 1990).

Stephen Greenblatt is the Class of 1932 Professor of English at the University of California at Berkeley. He is the author of *Renaissance Self-Fashioning: From More to Shakespeare* (Chicago and London, 1980), *Shakespearean Negotiations: The Circulation of Social Energy in Renaissance England* (Oxford, 1988), *Learning to Curse: Essays in Early Modern Culture* (New York and London, 1990) and *Marvelous Possessions: The Wonder of the New World* (Oxford, 1991).

Coppélia Kahn is Professor of English at Brown University. She is the author of *Man's Estate: Masculine Identity in Shakespeare* (Berkeley and London, 1981) and has co-edited three anthologies: *Representing Shakespeare: New Psychoanalytic Essays* (Baltimore and London, 1980), *Shakespeare's 'Rough Magic': Renaissance Essays in Honor of C.L. Barber* (Newark, Delaware and London, 1985), and *Making a Difference: Feminist Literary Criticism* (London, 1985). She is currently writing a book on the sexual politics of Shakespeare's Roman works.

Arnold Kettle (1916–86) was Professor of Literature at the Open University. His major publications include *An Introduction to the English Novel*, 2 vols (London, 1951 and 1953) and, as editor, *Shakespeare in a Changing World* (London, 1964) and *The Nineteenth-Century Novel: Critical Essays and Documents* (London, 1972). *Literature and Liberation*, ed. Graham Martin and W. R. Owens (Manchester and New York, 1988) gathers together his most important critical essays.

Leah Marcus is Professor of English at the University of Texas, Austin. She is the author of *Childhood and Cultural Despair* (Pittsburgh, 1978), *The Politics of Mirth: Jonson, Herrick, Milton, Marvell and the Defense of Old Holiday Pastimes* (Chicago and London, 1986) and *Puzzling Shakespeare: Local Reading and Its Discontents* (Berkeley, Los Angeles and London, 1988).

Kathleen McLuskie is a Lecturer in English at the University of Kent. She is the author of *Renaissance Dramatists* (Hemel Hempstead, 1989).

Annabel Patterson is Professor of English at Duke University. Her books include *Marvell and the Civic Crown* (Princeton, 1978), *Censorship and Interpretation: The Conditions of Writing and Reading in Early Modern England* (Madison, Wisc., 1984), *Pastoral and Ideology* (Berkeley, 1988) and *Shakespeare and the Popular Voice* (Oxford, 1989).

Kiernan Ryan is Fellow and Director of Studies in English at New Hall, University of Cambridge. He is the author of *Shakespeare* (Hemel Hempstead and Atlantic Highlands, NJ, 1989).

Leonard Tennenhouse is a Visiting Professor in the Department of Literature at Wesleyan University in Connecticut. He is the author of *Power on Display: The Politics of Shakespeare's Genres* (New York and London, 1986); the editor (with Nancy Armstrong) of *The Ideology of Conduct: Essays on Literature and the History of Sexuality* (New York and London, 1987) and *The Violence of Representation: Literature and the History of Violence* (London, 1989); and the co-author (with Nancy Armstrong) of *The Imaginary Puritan: Literature, Intellectual Labor, and the Origins of Personal Life* (Berkeley, 1992).

Index